The IRM
Imperative

The IRM Imperative

Strategies for Managing Information Resources

James M. Kerr

John Wiley & Sons, Inc.

NEW YORK / CHICHESTER / BRISBANE / TORONTO / SINGAPORE

Library of Congress Cataloging in Publication Data:
Kerr, James M.
   The IRM imperative: strategies for managing information resources
/ James M. Kerr.
      p.   cm.
   Includes bibliographical references and index.
   1. Information technology—Management. 2. Management information
systems—Planning. I. Title.
HC79.I55K47 1990
658.4'038—dc20
ISBN 0–471–52434–4
         90–39806
         CIP

Printed in the United States of America

10 9 8 7 6 5 4 3 2 1

For Irene

Contents

List of Figures

Preface

We're at the dawn of a new era! In years past, Information Systems (IS) departments were viewed as a back-room function that provided companies with the automation capabilities needed to help them manage their data effectively. The scenario has changed.

IS professionals are moving out of the back room and into the boardroom. They are becoming equal partners in the direction setting of their organizations. Many of the applications being built today are more than mere data management mechanisms. Systems are used to make decisions, define opportunities, and run businesses. However, there's still work to be done.

The IRM Imperative discusses the tools, techniques, and infrastructural changes that must be adopted if firms are to make the transition from data management to information leverage. The book challenges many of the assumptions currently made about the Information Systems function and suggests a new set of roles and responsibilities which, if implemented, will ensure that companies will stay competitive in the 1990s.

Each of the twelve chapters is aimed at a different aspect of systems development. Topics range from the role of the Chief Information Officer to CASE (computer-aided systems engineering) implementation. Every concept is fully described and its interrelationships to other IS elements are discussed.

A prognosis for each strategy's future is presented in order to provide a full picture of IRM as it is today and how it will be tomorrow. Chapter summaries are included as a means of providing a quick reference for material presented.

The examples sprinkled throughout the text illustrate how some of the more advanced concepts are being applied in today's global marketplace. Companies were identified whenever possible; some firms are unnamed because of their wish to stay anonymous.

The IRM Imperative presents a vision of the future that includes automation factories, application globalization, IS specialty shops, and other organizational enhancements that will make significant differences in the future services that systems departments provide.

Enjoy the book. It should provide some insight into where IS is heading, while contributing to keeping business professionals abreast of the technologies and approaches that will become the backbone of application development in years to come.

JAMES M. KERR

New York City
October 1990

Acknowledgments

To the people who made a difference:

My family, Denny, Ellie, Lisa,
Myrtice, Jim, Mary, Tom, Adam,
Mark, Joe, Burgi, JoAnn, and Elke
who encouraged me.

My friends, Baird Kaake,
the Speedys, the Whalens,
the Bickleys and the Stones
who never let me take it too seriously.

My "sounding board," Doc Schilke, Ron Oberg,
Ed Wyatt, Larry Jones, and Mike Karfopolous
who listened to my mad ravings.

My teachers, Georges Desrosiers, Gene Ott, and Fred Wadsworth
who always challenged me.

My editors, Diane Cerra, Terri Hudson, and Maryan Malone
who never stopped believing in the project.

My technical team, Linda Tittmann, Jay Edson, Odile and Michel
Delsol, Ralph Gonzalez, and Karen Del Santo
who helped make it happen.

My "creative consultant," Kelly Shea,
who guided me through the struggle.

My wife, Irene,
whose faith kept me going.

Thank you.

J.M.K.

1

Why IRM?

"Well, Mr. Baldwin! This is a pretty kettle of fish!"
Queen Mary, 1936

A management philosophy called Information Resource Management (IRM) is pervading computer departments across America. IRM, simply put, is the belief that information is an asset that should be managed rigorously and can contribute to the success of businesses.

This notion has been around for a long time. Authors like Synott and Gruber wrote about it as early as 1981 (1). However, much has changed since then. It's time that we begin to consider seriously what IRM is all about. The timing couldn't be better.

Changing Times

For the first time since the computer was introduced to the workplace, failure to automate may lead to business failure. We are already seeing some firms collapse because they are unable to match the cost savings and performance advantage of their better automated competitors.

The Baxter Company is a classic example. In the late 1970s, Baxter (then known as American Hospital Supply) used its internal expertise in information systems development to build an automated ordering system that tied Baxter to the hospitals that buy its products. Today, Baxter's competition—companies like A.S. Aloe and Will Ross Inc.—are out of the national hospital supply business. They simply cannot compete with Baxter (2).

To complicate matters further, we are finding that "off-the-shelf" solutions, which we used to enlist when our own development shops couldn't produce applications fast enough to meet business demands, will no longer suffice. They don't integrate well with the applications developed in-house.

The Information Systems (IS) department is another matter. In some organizations, IS professionals rarely even speak to the business leaders

1

whom they are supposed to support through automation; IS stays in the precarious situation of building applications from sketchy requirements.

Look at what happened at American Airlines in 1988. AA's flight ticketing system, SABRE, was to be enhanced. One of the programs aimed at optimizing the product mix (i.e., discount seats and full-price fares) was introduced to SABRE untested. The program indicated "sell-outs" prematurely and cost AA $50 million in lost revenue. More user involvement during development might have prevented the problem from ever occurring (3).

Something must be done to avoid this kind of scenario from happening at any level.

A New Paradigm

For firms to meet the highly competitive challenges of tomorrow, a fundamental paradigm shift must take place within IS (see Figure 1-1). The new IRM model calls for:

- An aggressive management initiative that recognizes the need to involve IS executives in the direction setting of their organizations;
- A different IS professional with a unique mix of business knowledge and technical expertise;
- Infrastructural changes that dedicate IS personnel to the growth, nurturing, and control of corporate data;
- Enhanced training and development programs that prepare staffs to work effectively within this new age of information management.

Old Model	New Model
IS is a back room function	IS is a business partner
IS staff is comprised of technology wizards, who lack business knowledge	IS staff is comprised of well informed business professionals, who are technically proficient
Business areas own the data they manipulate	Data is a corporate asset managed by the Data Administrator
Users must be trained in new applications	Users must be trained to use technology to its fullest

Figure 1-1. *A fundamental paradigm shift within IS*

Through IRM, systems professionals will begin to improve their ability to support businesses by developing strategic applications.

Strategic Application Development

Historically, IS has done a good job of automating the operational levels of U.S. companies. Accounts payable, billing, and general ledger systems, for example, are abundant across corporate America. However, the tactical and strategic layers of most companies lack the level of automation that the operational levels enjoy.

The time has come to change that. Firms must begin to dedicate resources to providing middle and top managers with the information they need to make better decisions. Figure 1–2 suggests a framework for information systems that qualifies applications by strategic significance and user type.

In most companies, transaction-driven systems far outnumber any others, but the strategic and tactical applications provide the greatest long-term advantages. Executive information systems (EIS) provide senior management with unique insights into their organizations. Simple front-ends and graphical displays deliver summary information to executives in timely and easy-to-read formats (i.e., tables, pie charts, bar charts, and so on).

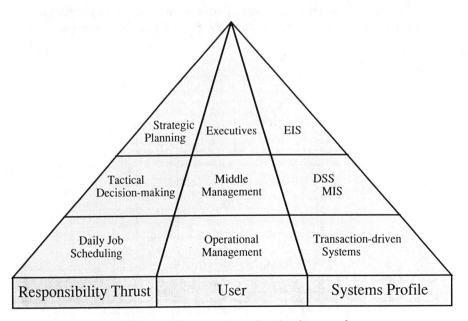

Figure 1–2. *A systems planning framework*

Decision support systems (DSS) and management information systems (MIS) help middle managers make better decisions by providing historical information and details about past decisions that can be applied to today's decision making. Like EIS, these applications will take advantage of the simple front-ends that make technology more accessible to business users and will help managers become accustomed to using technology to make decisions. As more middle and senior managers become familiar with what information processing technology can do, more firms will begin to use technology as a differentiator in the marketplace.

Differentiation

Firms that use technology or systems in creative ways can achieve many advantages. As Figure 1–3 suggests, companies can use their technology platforms to lock in customers, to integrate suppliers, and to create new distribution channels.

Examples of firms that have done this well include:

- Sears, Roebuck & Co., which markets products to particular customers by maintaining a system called the Sears Household File. This repository contains huge sums of data about the buying patterns of every Sears client (4).
- The Buick Division of General Motors, which transfers product information to its dealers worldwide through its Epic system—an

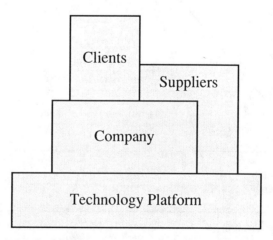

Figure 1-3. *Locking-in customers and suppliers through technology*

application that not only helps salespeople track inventory and locate cars on order but also lets customers choose options and calculate payment schedules (5).

- IBM, which formed a relationship with Federal Express in which time-sensitive parts can be sent to clients in need through FedEx's next-day service. FedEx's Federal Parts Bank system is at the heart of the venture (6). (See below for more details.)

These firms have gained competitive advantages by striving to couple their internal resources (the ones they control) with external ones (those they influence directly or indirectly through business relationships) to create strategic opportunities. Their ability to overcome inherent business and technical problems is the root of their success.

A STEP BEYOND NEXT DAY

What makes an IRM strategy effective? Usually simple things, like applying existing technology in innovative ways or redefining a current business relationship. Take the venture that IBM and Federal Express embarked on in the spring of 1988. It allows IBM to use FedEx as its distribution channel for the delivery of crucial mainframe parts to IBM clients.

The dynamics of the arrangement are quite simple. A client calls IBM for a part. IBM invokes delivery by placing an order through FedEx's Federal Parts Bank system (an inventory/parts management application located at FedEx's hub in Memphis, Tennessee). FedEx personnel pull the parts ordered, package them, and ship them directly to the customer (see Figure 1–4).

The relationships that are forged through this deal are astounding. FedEx becomes a warehouse for IBM. IBM offers clients unprecedented support. Clients quickly get the parts they need to repair an ailing CPU (central processing unit). Everybody wins.

Although the financial details of the agreement are not public, many speculate that FedEx is offering IBM substantial discounts in return for the prestige associated with being the sole provider of time-sensitive parts distribution for Big Blue.

The venture works for both companies. Already leaders in their respective industries, this arrangement locks in customers while locking out the competition. How much more strategic can you get?

Source: Charles von Simpson, "FedEx: America's Warehouse," *Information Week,* May 16, 1988, pp. 28–32.

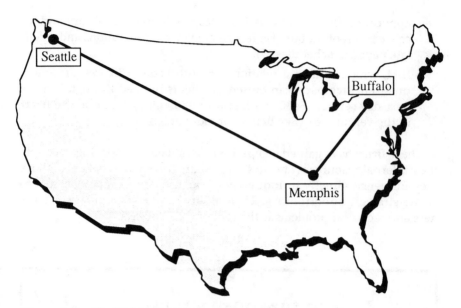

Figure 1-4.   *The IBM/Federal Express partnership to service clients across America*

Business Issues

Before they will be able to take advantage of technology, companies must address many issues. They include managing false expectations, technology sharing, and data sharing.

Managing False Expectations

Perhaps the biggest problem companies face when folding technology into strategic plans involves a false expectation on the part of upper management that technology investments must make money *today*. The fact is that many technology investments *don't make money*, period. But, the investments should still be made, to create a platform on which to build the systems needed for the 1990s and beyond.

For example, can we really say that the acquisition of a relational database management system is going to save our firms $X million this year? Probably not. Does that mean relational technology is a poor investment? No! In fact, the firms that embrace it now may be able to build a database environment in the future that will differentiate them in the marketplace.

Once we come to grips with the fact that some technology investments won't make money or cut costs, we'll be in a much better position to determine how technology can be used to achieve business goals and objectives. In many cases, the burden of proof can be removed from the equation. Technology investments become capital investments in support of IRM.

Technology Sharing

The next challenge arises after the technology is acquired: How do we leverage the investment? We have to be able to get the biggest "bang for the buck," while reducing the costs associated with managing and using the resource.

Computer-aided design and manufacturing (CAD/CAM) systems are a good example of a technology that has been misapplied. Many firms have acquired more than one such system and the disparity among the systems creates an interesting logistics problem.

A leading aerospace company, for example, had more than a dozen CAD/CAM systems in operation throughout its shop. Shop floor managers were faced with a real dilemma. They were accustomed to moving workers to different areas of the plant as needed to meet production schedules, but they couldn't move the CAD/CAM workers because these workers knew how to operate only one system. The company formed a task force to look into the problem. Eleven CAD/CAM vendors lost the company as an account.

Data Sharing

Besides technology-sharing problems, companies have data-sharing problems. The organizational boundaries that act to inhibit the creation of integrated systems must be broken down. Systems that support the business must be built independently of how the firm is organized. Firms must recognize that a single application that meets a multitude of requirements is better than many smaller applications that promote redundancies and introduce data quality problems to the business environment.

We can start to lay the foundation for this kind of development by attempting to change the corporate culture. Many business data users today suffer from "data ego." Data ego underlies the belief that a user owns all the data he or she uses. Many business professions believe that since they own the data, they don't have to share it with anyone.

This has to change or we will continue to build stand-alone applications that are difficult to maintain and impossible to integrate. We must begin to promote the idea that all data assets are owned by the corporation and that users are merely custodians who keep them current.

Education and training are essential. An MIS director from a leading bank in New York City believed so strongly in the importance of data sharing that he made his whole staff internal consultants. After spreading them across the company, he charged them with teaching users that "data is a corporate asset." We should all follow suit.

Expectation management, technology sharing, and data sharing are the most pressing business issues that IS must address. Of course, there are some IS issues that need attention before companies can achieve the benefits of IRM.

IS Issues

Building systems in this world of global competition is quite a challenge. IS must wrestle with systems prioritization, infrastructural improvements, and personnel turnover.

Systems Prioritization

Not every business activity can be automated. How do we decide which needs should be supported through a system and which should be done manually? A planning process involving IS and business professionals will lead to a prioritization of systems development efforts that is aligned with business direction.

Infrastructural Improvements

Systems planning isn't all we need; we must also carefully plan methodology, tools, and organizational designs. For instance, we need development approaches that build the necessary flexibility into our systems so that applications can be changed quickly and easily to accommodate business shifts. We need tools that will automate automation. We need new systems groups dedicated to end-user support. These changes must be made. IS must oversee them.

Personnel Turnover

The recruitment and retention of qualified systems professionals is another challenge that requires thought and planning. We must be sure that we establish an environment in which we can keep the right people doing the right things. We have to develop strategies that motivate and satisfy our technical staffs so that they'll be around for the long haul.

Obviously, these issues won't be resolved overnight. However, we can begin to address them by recognizing their existence and dedicating time to their resolution through planning and hard work.

Planning for IRM

IS professionals aren't known for their planning ability. They tend to be constantly "putting out fires" rather than defining their own destinies. As Synott and Gruber pointed out, companies have to adopt a "fire prevention cycle" (see Figure 1–5).

A fire prevention cycle begins with making time to plan, which leads to fewer problems to solve, which provides more time for planning. Better planning leads to better strategies and the identification of hidden opportunities.

If we don't adopt a fire prevention program soon, we're sure to fall prey to the bad planning practices Synott and Gruber described. Our planning environments will become like the ones depicted in Figure 1–6:

- "Squeaky wheels" determine the amount of resources dedicated to a particular area of the business, regardless of the strategic significance of the projects within those areas.
- IS leaders use straight-edged rulers at planning meetings, to draw lines through the projects that don't add up to the budget dollars allocated to systems development that year.
- Centralized planning groups spend years documenting strategies behind closed doors while operational groups continue to do business their way, believing the "ivory tower" just doesn't understand their problems.

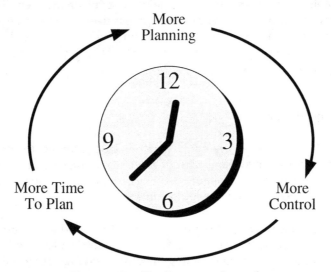

Figure 1-5. *The fire prevention cycle*

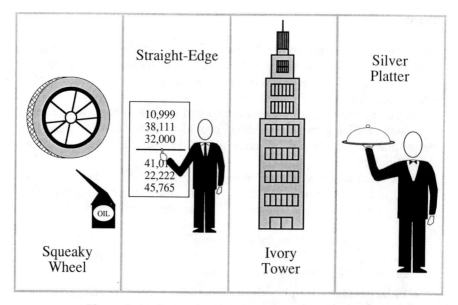

Figure 1-6. *Some examples of bad planning techniques*

- External consultants are paid to deliver plans on a silver platter, even though senior managers know that the plans they are buying from the consultants are the same ones the competition bought.

These poor planning practices lead to a bifurcated environment where incompatible systems isolate business users from each other (see the description of problems at NASA, on page 12). The only way to avoid poor planning practices is to make a serious commitment to change them.

Improving the Process

Chapter 11 focuses on the steps that must be adopted to effectively perform information systems planning; we'll save discussion of them for that chapter. However, as Figure 1–7 suggests, there are some possibilities for improvement that IS should consider:

- Shifting away from short-term prerogatives and adopting a long-term perspective that allows for investment in baseline technologies, regardless of their money-making or savings potential.

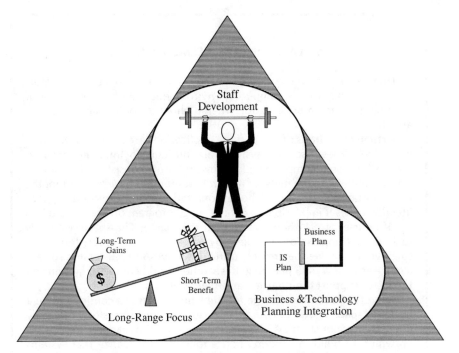

Figure 1-7. *Avoiding the pitfalls of bad planning*

- Dedicating resources to the development of IS personnel who create, use, and manage technology. Technology can do very little without the people to exploit it.

- Committing to the integration of business and technology planning practices. We can't properly invest IS resources until we understand the business goals and objectives of our organizations. In turn, those goals and objectives can't be defined until we reach an understanding of our technological capabilities.

Although not a panacea for all the ills of IS, we should keep these ideals in mind as we move toward the establishment of IRM practices.

Summary

Information management has never been more important to companies than it is today. IRM is the practice of managing information as a corporate asset. A new paradigm is upon us, and IS professionals are expected

▼

IS PLANNING PROBLEMS AT NASA

They put a man on the moon, but they can't build an integrated information system. NASA's computing environment is a classic example of what happens to an organization when it chooses not to plan its systems architecture.

Virtually hundreds of stand-alone applications are sprinkled throughout NASA. These isolated systems are difficult to integrate because they're built on incompatible platforms and use inconsistent data definitions. Scientists, in the midst of research, sometimes have to wait months for important information to be reformatted for their use—a delay that literally makes it impossible to get the space program off the ground.

Of course, NASA shouldn't take all the blame. The space agency is funded by Congress on a project-by-project basis—a short-term perspective that makes it extrémely difficult for NASA to muster and sustain a long-term view of IS planning. Researchers build computer systems on the fly, to support their particular project's efforts.

Some things have to change for the United States to continue to be a leader in space research. NASA can no longer run successful projects by doing the "paper shuffle." The agency needs a solid planning framework on which to build integrated applications. It must realize that systems support is essential to designing missiles and launching shuttles.

Perhaps the privatization of the space program (Congress wants NASA to oversee the launch of a commercial space station as early as 1991) will drive the institutionalization of systems planning. Obviously, an integrated design and project management application must be built to tie NASA to its vendors. It remains to be seen whether the agency has the discipline to do it.

Source: Lisa Stapleton and Michael Puttre, "NASA's MIS Crashes," *Information Week,* March 21, 1988, pp. 8–10.

to take a more active role in the direction setting of their organizations. Better planning procedures will give firms a better position for IRM.

Key Points

1. Information resource management (IRM) is a practice by which information is managed like any other corporate asset.
2. Today's IRM practices must be improved because of the errors and redundancies that are rampant across businesses today.

3. Transaction processing systems have traditionally been an IS department's forte, but they will not suffice in the 1990s. Other systems aimed at helping middle and top managers must be built to allow companies to stay competitive.

4. Systems that lock in customers and suppliers will be the focus of future development.

5. Organizations must come to grips with the fact that not every technology investment will make money.

6. Data ego, the belief that users own data, must be replaced by a corporate ownership concept that makes the user the custodian of data, responsible for keeping it current and accurate, for the company's benefit.

7. Business realities like limited resources, rapid changes in technology and the marketplace, and a shortage of qualified people point to the need to improve IS planning.

8. A fire prevention cycle that forces firms to set time aside to plan should be adopted.

9. Some accepted planning practices lack the precision needed in the 1990s. Commitment to adopting a long-range view of IS, coupled with a dedication of resources aimed at managing information as an asset, will be needed to keep firms competitive in years to come.

References

1. William R. Synott and William H. Gruber, *Information Resource Management,* New York: John Wiley & Sons, 1981.

2. James Martin, "The Revolution in IS Tools and Techniques," seminar presented at Park Plaza Hotel, New York, NY, November 30, 1987.

3. Nina Andrews, "Software Bug Cost Millions at Airline," *New York Times,* September 12, 1988, p. D3.

4. Steve Weiner, "They Buy Their Stocks Where They Buy Their Socks," *Forbes,* March 7, 1988, p. 60.

5. Stephen Sabatini, "Buick Sales Move into the Information Age," *Information Week,* August 1, 1988, p. 25.

6. Charles von Simpson, "FedEx: America's Warehouse," *Information Week,* May 16, 1988, pp. 28–32.

2

The New IRM

Fools rush in where angels fear to tread!
Alexander Pope, 1720

There is no longer any doubt: IS *is* gaining influence in corporate America. If for no other reason, IS is getting business management's attention because of the significant dollar investment that is currently being dedicated to application systems development.

Major strides in the use of technology have been made over the past 20 years. In the 1970s, computers were used strictly to automate clerical activities, like billing and collections. By 1985, things had changed: IS was asked to build systems for managers. Trend analysis and spreadsheet applications became very popular. By 1995, IS will "kick-up" another notch in significance by providing chief executive officers (CEOs) with the technology they need to keep a watchful eye on their companies' future.

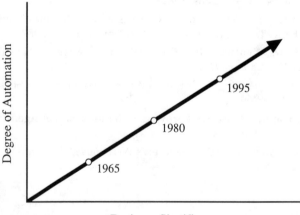

Figure 2-1. *The significance of IS as automation increases*

Figure 2–1 reminds us that IRM's importance to a business increases with the degree of automation within a firm. By 1995, every business activity will be supported (at least partially) by automation. Consequently, IS professionals must become stronger, fine-tuning their business knowledge along with their analytical skills.

IRM in the 1990s

The 1990s will bring about fundamental changes in IS management:

- *Team decisions* will replace "seat-of-the-pants" planning. Resources will be dedicated to the projects and technologies that make the most sense.
- IS managers will become *more accountable* for their technology dollars. To grow and be profitable, companies must be able to track return on all investments. IS investments will be no exception.
- *Alternative techniques* for application development will be adopted. Advanced technology will be used to generate systems. Users will be asked to play a stronger role in defining business requirements.

This means that IS personnel of tomorrow will need a different skill-set: strong communication skills to be effective in team play, better budgeting and financial planning expertise, and the ability to manage dissimilar technologies, as fast-paced changes in IS tools continue to bring about heterogeneous environments.

As IRM becomes more sophisticated, IS managers will have to play a stronger role in the leadership of their companies. Executive-level positions like chief information officer (CIO) are beginning to spring up, leading the way to a new kind of IS management.

The Improved IS Manager

It's no longer acceptable for IS departments to be inhabited by nerdy, barefoot stereotypes once called *computer wizards*. It's time that the wizards became worldly—the type of person we can complain with about the weather, without getting a cosmic explanation of cloud masses.

Today's IS professionals need to learn the businesses that they're servicing. They need to get involved in corporate planning. Managing the information resources gives IS personnel a different perspective on their companies than, say, the accountants who manage financial assets or the operations officers who manage personnel. IS managers can show their firms how to apply technology to gain a competitive advantage.

Chase Manhattan Bank believes so much in this concept that it sends dozens of its IS managers to a "mini MBA" every year (1). In a three-day course, its managers are given an opportunity to learn basic business principles so they can better support their users.

But getting the chance to participate in business planning requires more than a three-day course. Some IRM evangelists are proclaiming that IS managers must take charge and demand participation. It's difficult to imagine that determination alone will get them a piece of the planning pie.

A redefinition of IS roles is needed so that business leaders will begin to view the IS professional as an equal rather than some "techie wizard" who sits in a back room playing with a computer. Tomorrow's IS leaders should strive to become:

Proactivists who seek opportunities to serve the business through the application of technological solutions.

Futurists who look over the horizon and identify the technologies and approaches that, when applied, will give the firm a competitive advantage for years to come.

Strategists who help to define the company's goals and objectives by identifying opportunities to use technology in achieving the corporate mission.

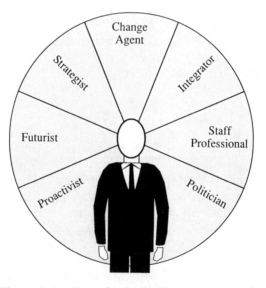

Figure 2-2. *New roles for the IS manager to ponder*

Change agents who introduce new tools, techniques, and organizational designs that will help achieve stated goals and objectives.

Integrators who meld existing application systems and technologies into solid platforms from which to run the business.

Staff professionals who oversee the management of special projects and develop one-time solutions that help pull the firm through a challenging stretch.

Politicians who are sensitive to the corporate culture and know how to get the job done by working within the system.

As Figure 2–2 suggests, the adoption of these simultaneous roles will be quite a challenge for most IS personnel to ponder. It's difficult to imagine that IS environments will evolve into a climate that facilitates the nurturing and development of these kinds of skills. This is where the Chief Information Officer comes in.

Chief Information Officer

A quick scan of the environment shows the evolution of a new executive position in many U.S. firms—the chief information officer (CIO). The CIO is the senior manager in charge of Information Systems, a peer of the CFO (chief financial officer) and the COO (chief operations officer). The difference between the CIO and the traditional MIS director is the scope of the CIO's influence.

The CIO is a businessperson first and a "technocrat" second. A full member of the management team, the CIO is on an even par with other chief executives who report directly to the board or the CEO. The CIO's charge is simple: to develop and promote IS planning and to tie it to the strategic plan of the business.

By being part of the planning team, the CIO gains a first-hand insight into the organization's current direction. He or she not only translates business goals and objectives into system development efforts but, by keeping an eye on technical trends, helps to identify opportunities to exploit technology and gain competitive advantage.

A Rocky Road Lies Ahead

Experience has shown that the CIO faces many challenges. For instance, the CIO is likely to meet some resistance from the current management team. Most CEOs are not noted for relinquishing much authority.

▼

THE STATS BEHIND THE TITLE

A 1988 survey conducted by the international accounting firm of Coopers & Lybrand and *Datamation* magazine showed that 35 percent of the 400 IS executives polled were in firms where IS reported to the CFO. Firms with IS reporting to the CEO were not far behind, with 27 percent working in that environment.

Why do so many IS departments work under the CFO? As mentioned in Chapter 1, IS has done a fine job of automating the clerical functions within the company—and most of the clerical functions reside in Accounting and Finance. With so many accounting systems in operation today, it's not surprising that most IS executives still report to CFOs.

There are problems inherent with that organizational design. It's difficult for the CFO to objectively manage the IS resource when his or her own department may have need for system support. Thus, more and more companies are reorganizing and placing IS under the CEO's control (as evidenced by the findings of the survey).

This shift will continue to evolve as CIOs begin to deliver their message to their superiors: "We need to be involved in business planning." The CIO position is sure to grow in popularity, until all leading firms have one.

As always, change is slow. But look at how far IS has come. Ten years ago no one knew what a CIO was. Figure 2–3 has some interesting facts and opinions about the CIO position.

Source: Ralph Emmitt Carlyle, "CIO: Misfit or Misnomer," *Datamation,* August 1, 1988, pp. 50–56.

Decentralized environments can be extremely difficult to manage, as well. How do a CIO's arms wrap around a management problem when his or her staff is spread halfway across the world? More importantly, how will the staffs that ran autonomously for so long react to a new manager?

As if these issues were not enough, the CIO position is still evolving. Many uncertainties surround the roles a CIO should play. With few role models to reference, many CIOs are making it up as they go along.

The road for most CIOs will be rocky. However, as more and more business leaders become aware of the opportunities that technology offers, and some CIOs move on to other executive positions, tomorrow's CIOs will get the support they need to succeed.

Until then, IS executives must stick with the basics and continue to do a fine job at what they've been assigned to do.

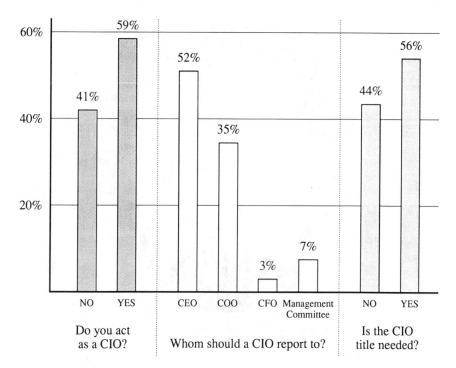

Figure 2–3. *Some results of the Coopers & Lybrand/Datamation poll*

Management Aspects of Information Systems

What does it take to be an effective IS chief? As Figure 2–4 suggests, managing an IS department can truly be a juggling act. Some IS personnel may consider these roles rudimentary, but they should not take them for granted. They're what IS managers are judged by.

Quality Assurance

If an IS shop does nothing else, it must absolutely deliver service to its user base. Quality assurance is a major responsibility of all IS managers. Quality must be folded into everything they do! Otherwise, systems professionals will never outlive their reputation for providing poor support to struggling business areas. Better quality can be assured by:

- Implementing a project development procedure (or project life cycle) that contains the proper "checks and balances," like logical design reviews and program walk-throughs (refer to Chapter 9 for further information on project development life cycles).

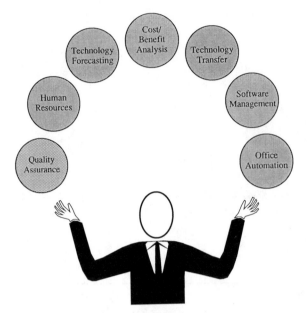

Figure 2-4. *An IS manager's juggling act*

- Defining service level measurement programs that measure machine performance and "stress-test" all new applications before promoting them to the production environment.
- Establishing management reporting practices that inform IS and business managers of project status and help them define contingencies as needed.

It's amazing how easy these are to implement; yet few firms have put such practices in place.

The Human Resources Game

We're in the midst of a demographic revolution. There will be an estimated 23 percent fewer people entering the job market by the turn of the century. Astonishingly, only 2 to 3 percent of the college-educated entrants will be computer science majors (2). This means firms will suffer a tremendous human resources "crunch" as they enter the 21st century. There are some things that can be done to soften the blow:

- *Reexamination of hiring and assignment practices.* IS managers may need to become more creative in the ways they attract and retain

▼

WHAT HAPPENS WHEN YOU
CHANGE THE "I" TO "E" IN CIO?

Some IS executives have done such an outstanding job at managing information resources that their firms are asking them to manage part of the business. Look at what Boeing's Robert Dryden and John Hancock's Ed Boudreau have done.

Robert Dryden, an ex-IBM salesman, was the CIO of Boeing Computer Services for eight years, before accepting the presidency at Boeing Military. He is the first CIO to make the transition from head of IS to head of the company (3).

John Hancock's Ed Boudreau left his position as MIS Chief at Hancock to become the president and COO of John Hancock Advisors, a $3.5 billion retail financial services subsidiary. Boudreau, with years of financial management experience, will run the mutual funds business and oversee the retail bank (4).

While at the helm of IS, Dryden and Boudreau won over their colleagues with shining performances. Both have forged solid relationships with the business units that they supported through information systems. They helped to make their IS organizations equal partners in the success of their companies.

It will be interesting to watch the changes that each man will make. Will IS personnel be part of the executive planning team? Will resources be dedicated to the management of information assets? Time will tell.

In any event, they are living testament that IS professionals are gaining status within their organizations. The time will come when moves like Dryden's and Boudreau's will be more the rule than the exception. After all, if IS's influence spans the entire company, who other than a well rounded IS exec is better equipped to run the business?

---

good help. Flexible work hours, work-at-home programs, signing bonuses, and rotational training need to be considered. Many of the insurance companies in Hartford, Connecticut, for example, offer employees flex-time programs as a way to compete with United Technologies, a major employer in the Hartford area, which tends to offer higher salaries.

- *Career pathing.* Job candidates want to see a future in every career move. Companies owe potential employees a glimpse of what the future will hold in store for them if they join the firm. Documenting the career path for every IS position is important.

- *Dual career options.* High-level technical positions must be created to accommodate technically oriented people who would rather not be bothered with management responsibilities. IBM institutionalized this practice in 1986, as a way to reward the individual contributor.

- *Mentoring.* Another way to develop and retain good talent is through the creation of mentor programs that match each new hire with a seasoned professional (other than a direct supervisor) within the firm. Mentors should help the new hires get acquainted with the organization. The relationship can expedite the individual's understanding of company culture, policies, and challenges. In 1984, Digital Equipment Corporation (DEC) implemented this approach in its IS management training program.

- *Performance evaluation improvements.* Many companies evaluate their IS staffs on the basis of systems developed. This is often an unfair assessment, since many systems are never delivered because of a change in business plans. New ways to measure performance are needed. Staff members' ability to converse with users or their willingness to apply new tools or techniques in a systems development effort are good measurement criteria; they are needed to make IRM successful.

Technology Forecasting

The technology forecasting function is one that many managers attempt but few master. If done well, forecasting can save companies millions; if done poorly, it can be very expensive. Steps for improving the process include:

- Identifying emerging trends and estimating their potential impact on an organization.
- Defining resources required to implement and manage the new tool or technique.
- Performing cost/benefit analysis, to help firms determine the investment viability of a new technology.
- Determining a strategy for further investigation, acquisition, and institutionalization of the tool or technique, if desired.

Decisions on technological directions made today will impact company destinies tomorrow. At Chrysler's Belvidere, Illinois plant, a 14.3-mile assembly line is manned by 244 robots and 1432 camera-guided lasers. This $367 million investment is sure to shape the destiny of Chrysler (5). It would never have happened without quality technology forecasting.

Cost/Benefit Analysis

A good cost/benefit analysis begins with an honest assessment of the present environment and concludes with a reliable estimate of the benefit that the proposed system will bring. Models like the one in Figure 2–5 are used to determine the point where a systems investment will begin to make money for an organization.

With these benefits determined, the IS manager can then go off and define the financial components of the analysis. Personnel costs, cash flow, future investment projections, and return on investment are just some of the variables that must be estimated.

Since few IS professionals today have experience with these techniques, many firms are hiring staff professionals who have accounting or financial management background, to oversee the cost/benefit analysis process.

Software Development

Once a project is justified and ready to be built, IS must manage the process. Several components of software development are worth discussing:

- *Contracting.* Hiring consultants to build state-of-the-art systems is an attractive option as long as the hired hands possess the proper

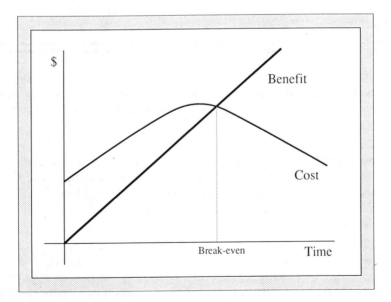

Figure 2-5. *Determining the costs and benefits of new development*

▼

RUNAWAY TRAIN SYSTEM

San Francisco's Bay Area Rapid Transit (BART) is in trouble. It lacks the routing and scheduling system it will need to accommodate the increased capacity expected in the years to come. As of late 1989, the project was $27 million over budget and considered a dismal failure by BART officials (6).

BART had used two different consulting groups during the project development effort and neither was able to deliver. The original contractor, Lawrence Berkeley Laboratories, pulled out in 1982 amid staff conflicts. The Laboratories' replacement, Logica Systems, has done little but pare down the original requirement.

The fact that the consultants:

- Underestimated the cost of equipment,
- Forgot to include site preparation costs, and
- Incorrectly stated the cost of training and documentation

contributed greatly to the project's demise.

However, BART's IS management team is truly to blame. They put BART in jeopardy by relinquishing control of the project to outsiders. Their blunders serve as a startling example of what can happen when an organization allows a project to get away from it: IS managers must assume full responsibility for everything that goes on in their shop, including contract programming. BART's didn't, and Bay Area commuters may suffer.

Source: Paul E. Schindler, Jr., "A Train System Derails," *Information Week,* February 22, 1988, pp. 29–30.

skillset and can be properly managed. IS shops shouldn't be training grounds for contractors, nor should contractors be allowed to take over the IS department.

- *CASE (computer-aided systems engineering).* CASE tools improve productivity by automating systems design and programming. However, firms should do a thorough investigation of the CASE arena before embracing a particular product. All too often, hasty decisions lead to dust-ridden shelfware (see Chapter 8 for more details).

- *Canned packages.* The acquisition of preprogrammed applications can be an IS manager's dream or a maintenance programmer's nightmare. It's true that packaged programs help companies meet tough deadlines, but a firm is in trouble if it thinks it can easily change a

▼

A MODEL FOR PACKAGE SELECTION

Selecting application packages has become so commonplace that we often trivialize the task. Trivialization at the expense of quality selection isn't prudent because we must live with these packages for years to come. Figure 2–6 outlines an eight-step approach for software acquisition.

1. *Determine business requirements.* Define the boundaries of the application. Evaluate a needed function versus "nice to have" requirements. Define reporting and query needs. Think about response time and the application's interfaces to existing systems.

2. *Develop evaluation criteria.* Prioritize the needed features. Don't forget items such as cost (up-front and maintenance), vendor support and reputation, and training requirements.

3. *Seek packages that meet requirements.* With requirements defined, identify the applications available in the marketplace that might meet the firm's needs. There are several ways to get started— colleague recommendations, advertisements, and research publications, for example.

4. *Call vendors for information.* Once the packages are identified, contact vendors. Ask for the marketing material and current customer list. You won't want to schedule a demonstration right away, but it's good to have more information.

5. *Perform paper evaluation.* Analyze the marketing material that was sent. Chances are you can eliminate a package or two by just reviewing the marketing blurbs.

6. *Ask for a demonstration.* The packages that haven't been eliminated through the paper evaluation process deserve further consideration. Ask the vendor for a demo—in-house, if possible—or go visit the vendor's site. But see the product!

7. *Perform final evaluation.* Call or visit some clients who have already acquired the packages that are still in the running. Generally, by then, the choice is obvious. If not, consider weighted averaging selection criteria.

8. *Negotiate the deal.* Work on price and service. Consider being a showcase account in exchange for local support in the coming year. If applicable, inquire about volume discounts. Insist on a software trial. Don't pay a cent until you've taken the software on a test run. Have a pilot project in mind.

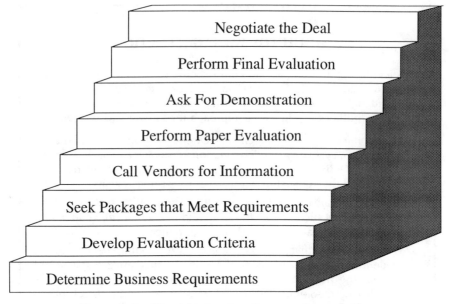

Negotiate the Deal

Perform Final Evaluation

Ask For Demonstration

Perform Paper Evaluation

Call Vendors for Information

Seek Packages that Meet Requirements

Develop Evaluation Criteria

Determine Business Requirements

Figure 2-6.   *The eight steps to software package selection*

store-bought solution. Many of today's packaged systems are ill-documented and pieced together with spagetti code. To avoid the problem, don't bypass the steps recommended for package selection in "A Model for Package Selection" (page 25).

Technology Transfer

Another important aspect of IS management responsibility is technology transfer—the act of exposing IS personnel to the latest tools and techniques shaping the systems development business.

IS personnel should be encouraged to seek out:

- *User groups.* Organizations that sponsor information sharing among current users of a particular technology. For example, SHARE is a user group for IBM customers. This group meets once a year to share insights into the use of IBM's products and future directions. User groups are recommended for gaining tips on how to do things better.

- *Industry groups.* Another good place to bounce around ideas. These groups tend to focus on how an emerging technology or IS trend may be used effectively by members of a specific industry. Examples are LOMA (Life Office Management Association), an insurance industry group, and the Automotive Industry Action Group, for the automobile industry.

- *Technical seminars.* Perhaps the quickest way to gain insight into the latest technology shaping the course of businesses today. The topics covered in public seminars vary from: "How to Manage Information as an Asset" to "Tuning Tips for DB2." Participants generally walk away from these seminars with some innovative insights on how to tackle new technology.

- *Public training.* The most obvious way to impart knowledge to IS staffs. Training is available publicly through technology vendors, consultants, and third-party players. Public training should be considered when devising IS training plans.

- *Subscriptions.* An inexpensive yet effective way to keep abreast of the latest developments in technology. The cost of putting quality magazines on the desk of every IS professional is small compared to the benefits gained from a forward-thinking IS staff.

Technology transfer is important but is often forgotten. Many firms have cultures that view participation in industry seminars and user groups as unimportant, or threatening to competitive advantage (i.e., employees might drop a trade secret while fraternizing with their colleagues).

These firms are guaranteeing their future demise. Not only are they contributing to the obsolescence of their systems base by cutting themselves off from information sources, but they are promoting employee turnover in the process. Who wants to work for a laggard?

Office Automation

There are many current and emerging office automation (OA) technologies to consider:

- Word processing
- E-Mail
- Laser printing
- Calendaring packages
- Scanning
- Imaging
- CD-ROM

Firms must determine where they are in the implementation of these tools. A model, adapted from the work of Richard L. Nolan of Nolan,

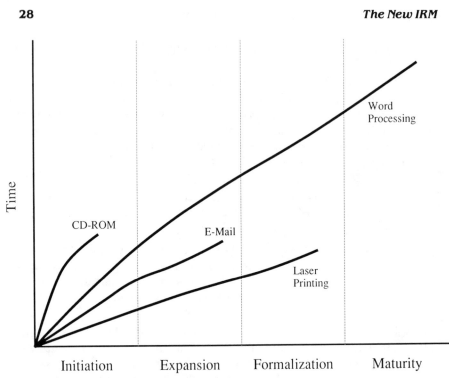

Figure 2-7. *Charting OA technology within a firm*

Norton & Company (7), appears in Figure 2–7. It can be used to help firms plot the course of their OA implementations.

Knowing where tools sit on the chart will help determine the plans needed to institutionalize them. The strategies used in the initiation stage in Figure 2–7 are different from the ones that are used when a technology is expanding, formalizing, or maturing within a company.

Summary

The systems management game is changing. IS personnel will be asked to learn the business. New IS leaders will emerge and take their place in the chief executive ranks. However, the fundamental job of managing the automation of the company must still be done, no matter how hectic the new game becomes.

As our "view from 50,000 feet" of the changing roles of IS comes to an end, consider the effects that application modeling tools and user-driven program design will have on IS managers of tomorrow.

Key Points

1. IS departments are gaining influence in companies because technology is playing a larger role in supporting business.

2. The IS managers of the future will possess a different skillset than their predecessors. They will be business professionals, first, and technically competent, second.

3. The CIO position will guarantee the creation of an IS environment that harvests better professionals.

4. Involving IS in business planning is a major responsibility of the CIO, who must be on an even par with other senior managers within the firm.

5. Few have made the transition from CIO to CEO. However, that trend is changing. More and more IS chiefs will be called upon to run their businesses because they're gaining the technical knowledge and business savvy to do it successfully.

6. There is a need to concentrate on fine-tuning all management aspects of IS. By understanding the "nuts & bolts," IS managers will position themselves to make a difference in their companies.

7. Demographics suggests that companies must become more creative in their hiring and retention practices. The 1990s will be a battle to keep the best.

8. Contract help, CASE, and packaged programs can help IS shops meet the demand for systems. But their use should be carefully monitored.

9. Office automation technology requires a context in order to plan its growth in the future. IS must access its current status and determine its destiny.

References

1. Richard Layne, Bruce Caldwell, and Charles Pelton, "MIS Transformed," *Information Week*, February 13, 1989, pp. 42–48.

2. Leslie D. Ball, "The 1990s Will Bring a Shortage of IS Talent," *Information Week*, April 10, 1989, p. 44.

3. Paul E. Schindler, Jr., "CIO To CEO: Dryden's First Ninety Days," *Information Week*, March 7, 1988, p. 15.

4. Charles von Simpson with Richard Layne, 'MIS Boss Becomes Chief Exec," *Information Week*, September 26, 1988, p. 16.

5. Mort Schultz, "Customer Satisfaction Drives Chrysler's IS," *Information Week*, February 1, 1988, pp. 23–27.

6. "Executive Summary," *Information Week*, November 27, 1989, p. 8.

7. Richard L. Nolan, "Managing the Crisis of Data Processing," *Harvard Business Review*, March–April, 1979, pp. 115–126.

3

Better Ways to Build Systems

When a user is abused, he says: Thank God they didn't beat me.
When he is beaten, he thanks God they didn't kill him.

Adapted from Lenin, 1906

The era of the two-year project development life cycle has come and gone. Competitive pressures are forcing firms to discard old modes of business and adopt new ones. For IS to be positioned to meet the challenges that a new business environment will bring, systems professionals must be equipped with a suite of productivity approaches that can enhance systems quality while shortening project life cycles.

Systems development techniques—prototyping, joint application development (JAD), and rapid application development (RAD)—are coming of age. Their use will improve the ability of IS to meet the demand for new systems. The time has come for IS professionals to proactively seek ways to better meet user needs.

Prototyping

Prototyping is an approach used by systems developers to speed up the development of a proposed system by building a working model. The intent of the prototype (working model) is to show the end user how the system will look and "feel." Panel layouts, keying patterns, and screen flows are depicted in the prototype but the logic that underpins the screen flow (i.e., calculations, editing, file manipulation) is not developed.

A prototype helps the user understand the required interaction with the system. If the interface is clumsy or difficult to use, the prototype is enhanced to meet user expectations. Once an agreeable design is reached, the prototype is used to drive the implementation of the system.

The ease with which prototypes are created and enhanced makes them an extremely effective communications vehicle. Because users and IS developers can literally "etch-a-sketch" a system model in days, IS can derive a quick understanding of the functionality that must be built into the final application.

How It Works

Prototyping begins by defining a full-time team comprised of a handful of developers (one to four persons) and two or three users. A prototype facilitator (a member of the team or a consultant) is appointed. The facilitator runs the meetings and drives the development of the prototype.

When a major component of the proposed system is completed, it is presented to other users who are not on the team. This peer review lets the users discuss their system needs with each other. Modifications and enhancements are evaluated and folded into the design. Once the total system design is prototyped, it is reviewed with senior business managers. Systems implementation begins when they give their approval.

Implementation can take one of two forms. The first uses the prototype as a requirements document (also known as a "throwaway prototype" because it's discarded during implementation). The second technique, called "two-phased prototyping," uses the prototype as a foundation stone. It's not discarded; the system is built upon it during implementation.

The implementation approach that is selected and adopted depends on the prototyping philosophy of the firm. Some firms like "throwaway" prototypes because they encourage team members to be free-thinking during system definition. The team is not limited by the capabilities of the development tools.

A leading financial services company prototyped its Common Front-End application (a system that integrates all existing systems under one set of program menus) on a Macintosh computer, even though the system was targeted for an IBM platform. Project leaders wanted the users to freely articulate their requirements without being encumbered by the limitations of the target environment.

Throwaways aren't for everyone. Some firms like to parlay their prototyping work into a production system, as a cost-effective way to build better applications. Either approach is fine as long as the users get a sense of how the system will work when it's finished.

Demonstrating Functionality

As shown in Figure 3–1, a well-designed prototype can demonstrate all aspects of an application, including:

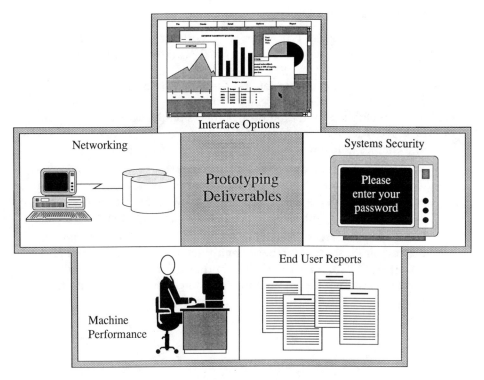

Figure 3-1. *The products of a quality prototype*

- Machine performance, which demonstrates how the system will perform when it is introduced to the production environment,
- Networking, which shows how information will be passed among users of the application,
- Interface options, which address the use of color, reverse video, and cursor selection in the application,
- Systems security, which walks users through logon and backup and recovery procedures, and
- End user reports, which give business professionals a taste of what the system will provide.

The quality of the application simulation is dependent on the prototyping tools employed. Paper and pencil can be used, but automated toolsets make prototypes much easier to modify and manipulate.

Prototyping Tools

Defining a prototype can be challenging, without the right tools. From the myriad of tools to choose from, Figure 3–2 shows what to look for:

- Screen painters. Analysts can use these tools to define the composition of on-line screens. Screen painters have built-in logic that allows for easy manipulation of the objects on the screen. A field can be moved, deleted, or replaced with a keystroke or two. This technology enables IS to quickly develop application front-ends.

- Report generators. This technology is to reports as screen painters are to screens. An easy-to-use report generator is invaluable when it comes to customizing the reports that users would like from the application. It helps IS define the report layouts expected from the system.

- Database simulators. These tools help IS to build an environment that mimics a shared database environment, regardless of the platform (e.g., PC, mini, or mainframe) that the prototype is built on. They help users understand how the application will perform in the

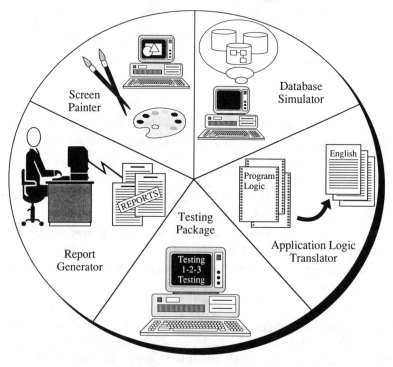

Figure 3–2. *A myriad of prototyping tools*

production environment. Poorly designed applications can be identified and improved prior to production turnover.

- Application logic translators. These tools help IS and users review the application logic, before it is converted into true code, by translating prototyped programs into their English equivalents.

- Testing packages. The two basic varieties are: packages that populate database files with data, and packages that verify application flow by tracing the steps invoked during systems execution. Both kinds are valuable. The "data populator" helps users relate to prototypes by putting copies of user data right on the prototyped screens. Trace packages are used to identify inconsistencies between the actual system flow and the one envisioned by the prototypers.

Individually, these technologies represent immense productivity potential and a single tool that would combine several of them would pack a wallop in the marketplace. Several products are listed in Figure 3–3, but, to date, no single vendor has been able to deliver a comprehensive, integrated, prototyping tool. Even when one emerges, IS should not be lulled into a false sense of security; prototyping has its share of booby traps.

Prototyping Booby Traps

There are several areas where prototyping efforts can go awry. Ego involvement, on the part of prototypers and their users, can be a major obstacle when it's time to retire a prototype and begin using conventional tools to deliver the system. Sometimes prototyping teams fall in love with their masterpieces. The trick to avoiding this problem is to clearly state the intended use of the prototype at its inception. Team members who understand that their work is to be thrown away as soon as it's completed are less likely to become attached to their designs.

Artificially high expectations form a second trap that is commonly confronted. The tools that are used in prototyping make system development appear very simple. Users lose sight of the fact that hard code must be developed to deliver true functionality. It's in IS's interest to help users understand the process and to constantly remind business leaders that prototypes are built only to better define requirements and that the real systems development will take additional time.

Incompletely tested prototypes constitute a third problem area. Some teams don't find out about a system's shortcomings until the project is in production. Correcting an application that is fully coded is much more expensive than changing a prototype. Prototype testing programs must be put into place, to avoid this pitfall.

Product	Vendor	Description	Price
CICS/Replay	Interactive Solutions Bogota, NJ	IBM CICS stress testing and regression testing	$13,000-18,000
COBOL Debug	IBM Armonk, NY	Temporarily alter logic flow for program experimentation	$375/mo lease
Freedom	Dimension Software Systems Las Colinas, TX	Screen builder and report writer for Briton Lee machine	$14,500
GPSS/PC	Minuteman Software Stow, MA	Creates, analyzes and manages system simulation models	$995
Imagine	Computer Corp. of America Cambridge, MA	Menu driven query and report writer	$20,000-67,500
PAWS	Information Research Assoc. Austin, TX	Multiplatform hardware and software simulator	$19,900
PPSF	Certified Software Specialists Androssan, Alberta, CA	CICS and IMS/DC environment screen painter	$4000-15,000
VC Screen	Creative Programmers Consultants Carrollton,TX	Allows users to draw input screens for IBM/DOS	$100

Figure 3–3. *Sample list of prototyping tools*
Source: *Data Sources*, Vol. II. New York: Ziff-Davis Publishing Co., 1989.

Aetna Insurance of Hartford, Connecticut, believed so strongly in thoroughly testing prototypes that they established a People/Technology Services Usability Lab to monitor users as they test prototyped applications. Observers watch through a mirrored wall, as users plug away at the machines. TV cameras capture live footage as the prototyping team looks for areas of improvement. In this way, Aetna nips problems in the bud, and avoids having to rethink applications while in production (1).

Systems integrability is another area of concern. IS often builds the perfect prototype—one that truly meets user needs and demonstrates a wide assortment of features; yet the finished system can't be integrated with those in production.

There are many reasons for this pitfall. The most common is that existing databases and data files are recreated to meet the systems requirement without examining the existing applications for data definitions that could be shared and the incompatibility of implementation platforms. For example, the programming languages and database management systems (DBMSs) of the prototyped system are incompatible with those of the other applications.

A large pay-TV company ran into this problem during the development of a descrambler box activation system. The company was able to build a nice looking system with pop-up screens and plenty of color. However, the new application could not be reconciled with the other databases currently used at the company. The activation system required several months of tweaking before it worked with the other applications.

Such problems can be eliminated with a little discipline. The prototypers need to adopt a methodology that insists on a current data cross-check and current technology review. These techniques help to identify overlaps and discrepancies before they become expensive maintenance chores.

Prototyping and the tools that support it continue to evolve. They help IS deliver systems more quickly and easily than classical requirements gathering ever did. However, the more structured joint application development approach promises to harness user involvement even more.

Joint Application Development

Joint application development (JAD) is a technique used in systems design. Its goal is to improve the quality of project specifications by engaging users in the requirements definition process (see Figure 3–4). JADs are performed in structured workshops driven by a JAD leader and documented by a scribe. Over time, a quality system specification evolves and becomes a blueprint for project development.

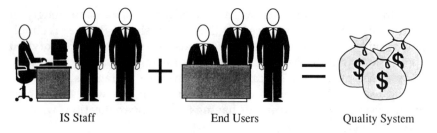

IS Staff   End Users   Quality System

Figure 3-4. *JAD combines the talents of IS and end user personnel to develop quality systems*

The concept has been around a long time—IBM began selling JAD consulting and training services in 1977—but JAD use is not widespread. IS professionals have been reluctant to give it a try because they believed that traditional information gathering techniques would suffice. However, IRM's emphasis on meeting users' needs changes the equation. It's time for JAD, and there's a six-step approach for getting started (2).

Step 1.   Find a Sponsor

User sponsorship is the first ingredient of success. Without it, JAD can be stopped dead in its tracks. Users must be committed to JAD participation or all the benefits are gone. Here are some strategies to engage users' involvement:

Find a friendly user. This approach targets a user area that is reasonably satisfied with the current level of IS support. These users are open to new ideas and would be willing to be pilots for the JAD technique.

Find a hostile user. The antithesis of the first approach, this user involvement strategy targets users who are not pleased with the current level of IS support. A user area that has recently been "burned" by a development effort is a good one to try first. If IS can promise to redeem itself by developing a system through strong user participation (users probably weren't involved as much in the past as they will be with JAD), then how can a sincere business professional resist?

Send a user on the seminar circuit. It's amazing to see the positive response that is generated when users attend technical conferences. They get excited when they hear about other companies that have used JAD and were successful with trying it. Unfortunately, there aren't many seminars that are dedicated to JAD. However, a conference that focuses on end user computing or strategic data planning will tend to discuss the need for user involvement in systems development.

Bring in an expert. Like the seminar circuit approach, this technique attempts to raise users' awareness of their role in systems development by exposing them to a third-party perspective. A consultant who has a flair for presenting ideas can make an audience come alive and is an excellent choice to deliver the message to end-users.

Take a heavy handed approach. Some IS shops wield a lot of influence over the company; a heavy handed approach works well for them. This approach centers on the establishment of a company policy which states: "All systems development will be conducted using JAD. Any users refusing to participate in JAD will not get IS support." Not the best way to impart change, but it can work.

Texaco, Inc. has legislated the use of JAD in its systems development area. Walter Viali, an IS manager at the petroleum giant, and his team of facilitation experts conducted over 100 JADs in 1989. (One hundred more are planned in 1990.) The impetus for such a wide application of JAD has been IS management's commitment to the process.

Step 2. Take Aim at a Project

With the users interested, the next step is to find the "right" project to test JAD. This is not always as simple as it seems. IS needs to embark on a development effort that can be implemented quickly and adequately, while demonstrating the feasibility of the JAD approach.

Find a pilot project that is not critical to the firm's mission and can be completed in three to six months. Transaction-based systems like general ledger and accounts payable are recommended over strategic systems like expert underwriting and advanced sales forecasting.

Selecting a non-mission critical application is essential to JAD's survival. If IS tests JAD on an important project and fails, IS risks losing credibility within the firm. Therefore, it's in IS's best interest to find a simpler, less glamorous project to pilot—just in case.

Step 3: Agree on a Methodology

Agreeing on which analysis methodology to use in JAD is a necessary next step. The methodology selected will determine the target deliverables for the JAD process. The success a firm enjoys is dependent on its ability to "churn out" the required (methodology) documentation.

Many firms have already selected an approach for analyzing require-ments, but most have not. The companies that have a standard approach should use it in JAD. The others need to find one.

There are many methodologies to choose from in the marketplace. FAST (MG Rush Systems), Consensus (Boeing Computer Services), and JAD (IBM) are just a few of the approaches available. Deciding which one to choose isn't easy. Here are some things to consider when evaluat-ing the options:

- Current staff experience. Some members of the IS department may have experience in a given methodology. That methodology should be considered, to ease the learning curve.

- Learning curve. Along with the staff's experience, the learning curve associated with a methodology must be taken into account. An approach that requires six months to master should be disre-garded, especially if the firm wants to embark on JAD today.

- Diagram simplicity. The focus of most methodologies is to offer their practitioners the option of representing user requirements diagrammatically. However, the quality and simplicity vary from approach to approach. Companies should seek a methodology that uses simple diagrams so that JAD teams can get up to speed quickly.

- Availability of consulting support. A consultant may be needed, to help the company make the transition into the methodology. The availability of talent in a given approach should be considered.

- Availability of software support. The 1990s will be the CASE (see Chapter 8) generation. CASE technology can be used to automate JAD. Firms should peruse the marketplace for CASE tools that sup-port their favorite JAD approach, before making a decision on a methodology.

Step 4.   Establish a Team

A JAD team should be established as soon as the pilot project is deter-mined and a methodology defined. There are several key players:

Executive sponsor
Project manager
JAD facilitator
JAD scribe
IS developers
End-users

The *executive sponsor* is a senior business manager who is willing to commit the resources needed to build the system. He or she will make the opening remarks at the first JAD meeting, to ensure user participation in the process. The sponsor will be called upon throughout the development effort to review results and lend guidance.

The *project manager* is the IS professional responsible for delivering the project to the user. Specific charges include estimating resource requirements, scheduling deliverables, and managing the project's budget. A good amount of time is spent with the executive sponsor, establishing project priorities and direction.

The *JAD facilitator* is responsible for driving the JAD discussions. Typically a senior systems analyst who possesses a proven track record in the IS community, this individual has the technical and interpersonal skills needed to build user-driven systems.

The *JAD scribe* is responsible for documenting the JAD meetings. A scribe uses diagramming techniques to represent user requirements, is well versed in the approach, and can use CASE tools to automate the JAD methodology.

IS developers are the technical representatives on the team. They will convert the JAD findings into a true information system. These programmers and database specialists bring a unique perspective to JAD because they tend to offer programming solutions to business problems.

End-users from the business area are responsible for bringing a business perspective to the JAD team. Their duties include defining the business activities they perform as well as identifying their function's business problems.

Step 5. Let 'em Roll!

The typical JAD project spans several months (a project log is presented in Figure 3–5). A series of half-day morning sessions are spent with the user. Afternoons are set aside for the IS members of the team to synthesize results in preparation for the next morning's meeting.

Because user participation is critical to the success of JAD, most companies insist that team members attend every meeting. Others establish ground rules like these:

- No phone calls can be made or accepted while the team is in session.
- No JAD meeting will be interrupted by external business "emergencies."
- All meetings will begin promptly. Tardiness will not be tolerated.
- A member who misses two meetings will be replaced.
- Vacations should be scheduled after projected JAD completion.

In this way, firms ensure the integrity of their JAD results.

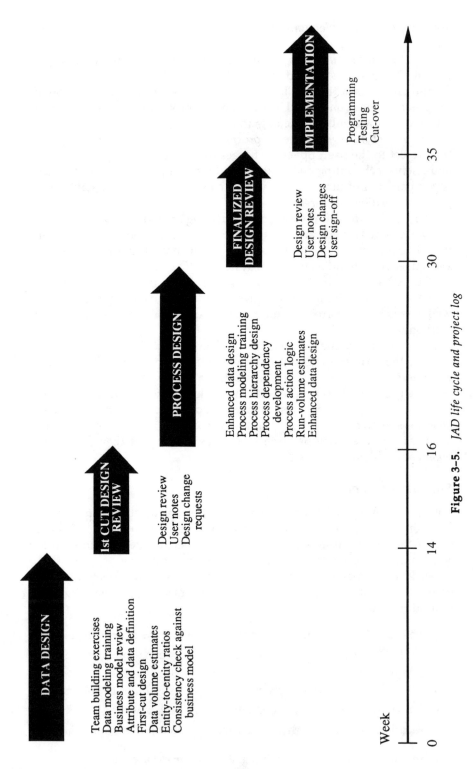

Figure 3-5. *JAD life cycle and project log*

Step 6: Automate It!

As mentioned above, CASE technology can be used to automate JAD. Automated-JAD (AJAD) projects can cut development time in half because systems specifications are maintained by machine instead of by hand. Time-consuming activities, like cutting and pasting systems designs, are replaced by the rigor of an integrated toolset.

The AJAD meeting depicted in Figure 3–6 shows the ease with which system designs can be created and modified using CASE. The challenge for the future will be getting facilitators and scribes up to speed with the new tools. Consultants who are learned in both CASE and JAD can be used while firms "beef up" their talent.

Texas Instruments (TI), for example, offers AJAD services as a way to get clients off to a strong start with their CASE tool, called the IEF. For a set fee, customers can send a JAD team to TI headquarters in Plano, Texas, to work with TI's AJAD facilitators and scribes. After a week, the team comes home with a functioning portion of a design.

Once firms make the transition into AJAD, they will be positioned to begin to develop applications rapidly. Rapid application development (RAD) is the name given a new body of development approaches that uses CASE, prototyping, and JAD to build systems quickly.

Figure 3–6. *The facilitator, at the lecture board, drives the discussion; the scribe, at the terminal, uses CASE technology to document the systems design*

Rapid Application Development

Rapid application development (RAD), an aggressive new systems design approach, is currently gaining acceptance in the IS community. As depicted in Figure 3–7, elements of AJAD and prototyping are combined with a stringent project time limit to create an exciting system construction environment that will help firms build applications faster than ever before.

Like other high productivity techniques, RADs employ small teams with specialized skills; unlike other development approaches, RADs have no interim deliverables. Each RAD team simply builds a piece of a larger prototype and refines it until it becomes a working system.

RADs typically run 60 to 120 days. Careful planning is needed to implement the RAD methodology presented in Figure 3–8. While this exceedingly aggressive deadline becomes a terrific motivator, it can also become the single greatest reason for employee dissatisfaction and turnover.

Here are some ideas for making RAD work within an organization.

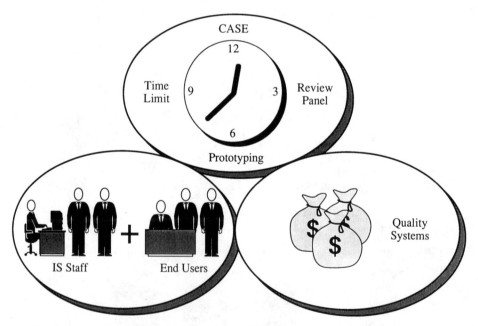

Figure 3–7. *The RAD methodology uses AJAD techniques and stringent time limits to produce quality systems*

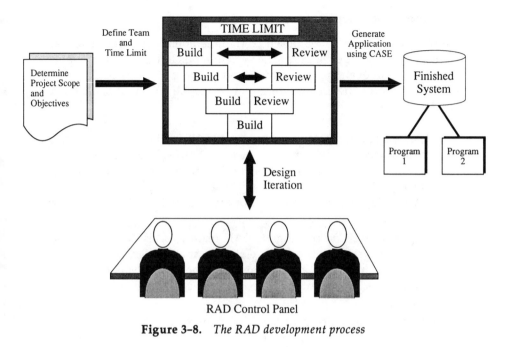

Figure 3–8. *The RAD development process*

Narrow the Scope

Because the RAD team has a limited amount of time to deliver an application, it's essential that the scope of the effort be kept narrow and focused. RAD projects should target a specialized application, like expert underwriting or a component of a larger system. For example, an integrated accounting system would be too large for a single RAD. However, each component piece—accounts receivable, accounts payable, and general ledger—could be handled through successive RAD projects.

Keep in mind that there's no magic in the RAD methodology. An 18-month project still requires 18 months to complete. The essential difference between RAD and conventional development approaches is that a working component of the target system is delivered every 90 to 120 days.

A firm's greatest challenge will be to develop a way to consistently define the implementable "chunks" that will comprise a RAD effort. Some firms are likely to try to bite off more than they can chew. Remembering to keep scopes narrow will help.

Limit the Team Size

The ideal RAD team is composed of five members: one project leader, two users, and two developers. The system tends to be of higher quality when there's an even mix of business and technical expertise. Company politics may force the creation of larger teams, but IS should still try to limit team size, to:

1. Use technical expertise optimally. It's difficult to keep more than two or three developers busy in a RAD project because the scope is so narrow. If too many developers are assigned to the project, they get in each other's way. In this age of extensive backlogs it's best to "free up" as many developers as possible to work on other projects.

2. Expedite decision making. A RAD team is often forced to make design decisions without complete information. Smaller teams expedite the process because they can reach consensus faster than larger ones. When put to a vote, the project leader can act as the tie breaker.

3. Reduce personality conflicts. Companies often overlook the human element when comprising teams, yet IS knows that dissension within a team can sabotage its performance. Keeping teams small will help project leaders address human interaction problems while reducing the potential for conflict.

For all these reasons, small teams make sense. They're easier to lead, they can quickly focus on a common vision, and they facilitate a free exchange of ideas. All these are ingredients of rapid systems development success.

Establish a Reward Incentive

"What's in it for me?" is a question that crosses everyone's mind when asked to perform a difficult task. Firms must answer that question for the people assigned to a RAD project. IS won't get the best performance out of their people until they clearly define a reward.

Surprisingly, rewards don't have to be extravagant to be motivational. Managers might think about mentioning the team in a company newsletter or drafting a memo to the CEO that spells out their accomplishment. The simple recognition of accomplishing a great feat is often enough to excite teams into action.

Passing on some of the savings in the form of tickets to sporting events, dining certificates, or even cash bonuses is a way for firms to say thanks for a job well done. Companies should think about establishing a budget to reward RAD participants.

Money aside, the most important step a company can take to motivate a RAD team is to make them believe they are members of an elite group of individuals within the company. Teams should be told that they were hand-picked to do the impossible because they demonstrated the ability to get the job done.

Create a RAD Control Panel

A RAD control panel (RCP) is the group responsible for receiving and validating the RAD team's design. The RCP is made up exclusively of users of the application. They have final approval of the system. If the RCP questions a design assumption or requests a change, the system is sent back to the RAD team for redesign.

Following system acceptance, members of the RCP will work with their colleagues on the RAD team to train other users. RCP members tend to do a more thorough job of evaluating the system when they know that, down the road, they'll be responsible for training.

As mentioned above, larger systems are broken into smaller RAD projects. A RCP will be named for each project. Each team should be made up of different members. This facilitates user involvement while allowing previous RCP members to go back to their regular work or spend time training their colleagues in the use of the "new" system.

Don't Forget Documentation

System documentation should be recognized as a key deliverable of the RAD team. Progress in a RAD is so fast that the users may not be prepared to implement and use the finished product without good documentation.

Time should be taken to prepare help screens and user guides that will assist users in understanding system intricacies. Such documentation is used in training by the RAD control panel to expedite user acceptance of the delivered system. It also helps in performing maintenance.

Because time is limited, finding CASE and prototyping tools that are self-documenting is very important. The use of these tools is the only way that RAD teams can deliver a system and its documentation within RAD's stringent time limit.

Accept Group Dynamics

A RAD team goes through some very distinct phases of human interaction as the project progresses. These phases are natural and common and companies shouldn't become alarmed as the team moves from one to the next.

Phase 1:   Bewilderment. The first thought that goes through a RAD team member's mind is: "What in the world do we do?" The team will (and should) spend some time discussing how they see the project progressing and the roles each member will play in the process.

Phase 2:   Anger. As the bewilderment fades, anger sets in. The second thought that passes through a RAD team's collective mind is: "How can management do this to me?" Most people can't believe that somebody really expects them to deliver a working system in such a short timeframe. The anger makes for a difficult work environment, but a good RAD leader will channel that anger into the next phase.

Phase 3:   Determination. It's not long before a team realizes that its anger won't deliver the system. Teams will buckle down and do some work. They become determined to show they can do the impossible.

Phase 4:   Bonding. Once the team becomes determined to prove how good they actually are, the members will bond. The stages of bewilderment and anger have created a sense of "us vs. them." The "us" in that equation has to pull together, like a family, in order to beat "them." This carries into the last phase.

Phase 5:   Excitement. At about the midpoint in the project, the team realizes they will beat the odds: They *will* deliver a system on time. This excitement will pull them through the challenges that they'll face through project duration.

Fulfill the Management Challenge

The RAD methodology will be a radical change from anything a firm has done in the past. It requires management disciplines that are rare in today's corporate bureaucracies. It calls for a manager who is forward-thinking enough to set direction and strong enough to empower personnel with the authority to do what's needed to get the job done.

For example, a RAD team should be allowed to establish their own work schedule. Why should a manager care if they start the work day at noon, as long as the project is completed on time? Another team may need a large-screen PC to facilitate a free exchange of ideas during a design session. Get one, even if it's rented! Management's first allegiance must be to the folks on the team with the deadline.

Some staff members working outside of the RAD may come to resent the "prima donnas" on the team. Those individuals should be reminded that the RAD team is working 70 to 80 hours a week, is giving up weekends, and even has lunches brought in each day, just to make the deadline. Any animosity toward the team is usually quelled with this understanding.

▼

DUPONT'S RAD EXPERIENCE

In 1984, the corporate IS department at E.I. du Pont de Nemours & Company formed a task force to investigate the connection between CASE tools and software development techniques. Their objective was to increase productivity and quality simultaneously.

The task force created a RAD approach called RIPP (rapid iterative production prototyping). It fit perfectly with Cortex Company's CASE tool called Application Factory, which DuPont had acquired a year before. Within months, the chemicals giant was enjoying unprecedented productivity gains. (See Figure 3–9 for examples.)

DuPont believed so strongly in their approach that, by 1987, they had formed Information Engineering Associates (IEA), a division charged with selling RAD services to DEC VAX users. IEA generated over $20 million in revenue for DuPont in 1989 under the direction of IEA's general manager Scott Schultz.

IEA has developed over 60 projects, including accounting, environmental, and trust management systems without a hitch. That's impressive, given the diversity of the clients, who range from the FBI to the Christian Science Church.

Dupont's RAD experience is testament to the fact that rapid application development can work, with the proper level of commitment. What started as a small task force in 1984 is now a division of over 100 strong that offers clients a 100 percent money-back guarantee on every project.

Doesn't every IS shop want to offer that kind of guarantee?

Source: Marketing information provided by Du Pont Information Engineering Associates, 1989–1990.

Summary

Three high-productivity approaches aimed at quickening the systems development process were discussed. Prototyping uses the definition of a system's interfaces and screen flow, to determine application requirements. JAD and AJAD look to teams comprised of business and IS

System	Objective	Screens	Reports	Completion Time Est.	Completion Time Act.	Productivity
Personnel Management	To maintain personnel history and assist in employee transfer	12	11	25MM	4MM	6.25/1
Quality Tracking	To ensure continuity of rigid quality controls	152	49	56MM	16MM	3.5/1
Packing System	To maintain historical records and shipping documents	250	27	22MM	10MM	2.2/1

Figure 3–9. *DuPont's RAD experience*

professionals, to create data and process specifications. The RAD method folds prototyping and AJAD practices together with a stringent time limit to motivate personnel to perform.

Each of these approaches has its merits in helping IS meet the demand for user-driven applications.

Key Points

1. Prototyping is an iterative process of defining the user interface to the system. It is used to gather an understanding of the user's information needs.

2. Some prototypes are "throwaways," that is, the outcome of the prototyping is discarded prior to system implementation. This kind of prototype is used primarily to encourage free thinking among the user community.

3. A quality prototype should demonstrate: machine performance, networking, security, system functionality, and end user reporting capabilities.

4. Screen painters, database simulators, report generators, testing packages, and logic translators are popular prototyping tools.

5. Joint application development (JAD) brings business experts and systems developers together to define application requirements. It can be automated through the use of CASE tools. AJAD is the name given to Automated-JAD.

6. The JAD team is comprised of an executive sponsor, a project manager, a JAD facilitator, a JAD scribe, IS representatives, and end users.

7. Consultants can be used as JAD facilitators and JAD scribes. Texas Instruments now offers JAD services to its CASE tool customers.

8. The RAD approach couples prototyping and JAD methods with a stringent time limit to form an aggressive development environment that can motivate even the most complacent of IS staffs.

9. The RAD control panel (RCP) is comprised of end users who will review and accept the system developed during the RAD. Following implementation, RCP members will be responsible to train their colleagues.

10. Dupont's experience with the RAD approach was so positive that a separate division was formed to sell RAD consulting services to other companies.

References

1. Fred Schott and Margrethe Olson, "Driving for Normalcy," *Datamation*, May 15, 1988, pp. 68–76.

2. James M. Kerr, "Systems Design: User's in the Hot Seat," *Computerworld*, February 27, 1989, pp. 87–96.

4

Decision Support and Executive Information Systems

New inventions don't usually improve our lives much;
the most we can hope is that they'll help us stay even.

Andy Rooney, 1982

In Chapter 3 we discussed ways to better meet end users' needs. This chapter focuses on using systems technology, in the form of decision support (DSS) and executive information systems (EIS), to meet management's information requirements. In Chapter 3 we examined methodologies; here we'll examine technologies. Let's begin with decision support systems.

Decision Support Systems

Decision support systems (DSSs) are applications that support and assist managers in the decision-making process. They enhance the decision maker's ability to make an effective decision by offering rule-based intelligence in the form of heuristic and simulation models.

A DSS is comprised of several components, as pictured in Figure 4–1. The two information bases—the problems database and the solutions database—are the heart of a DSS. The former contains information about the nature of the problems that require judgment. Statistical facts—the standard deviation of quarterly sales figures, for example, or historical data such as annual interest rate fluctuations—are included to help the decision maker understand the problem.

The solutions database is a different beast. It keeps track of past decisions made in particular problem areas. The heuristics (general rules of thumb) and simulations used in the solution are maintained, creating

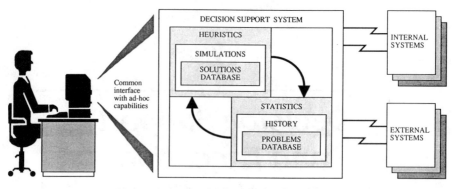

Figure 4-1. *Decision support environment*

a historical decision-tracking capability that is very helpful in forming new decisions.

The third component of the DSS is the user interface. A quality DSS will possess a common interface that allows the user to access either problem information or solution information from the same screen. The ability to conceive ad-hoc queries against either information base fits readily into most users' approach to problem solving.

Figure 4–2 shows the type of graphical, mouse-driven interface that is popular in today's DSS. Notice the overlaid panel feature of the screen.

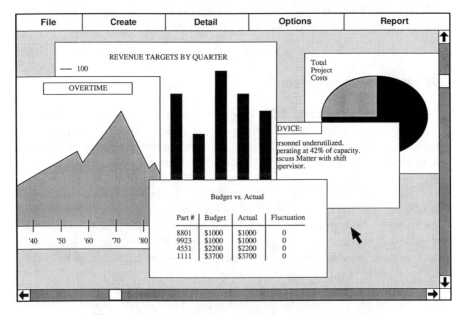

Figure 4-2. *Graphical, mouse-driven interface of DSS*

The user can view the "Total Project Costs" pie chart on the right or explore the budget figures in the middle of the screen, with just a "click" of a mouse.

The ease with which the user can switch among the different facets of the DSS, and the DSS's ability to depict information in a graphical format, makes the tool an easy one to learn and use. Even a manager who is afraid of a computer can be coaxed into using an application that requires only the "point and click" of a mouse.

These three components—problems database, solutions database, and common user interface—make a DSS a flexible management tool.

What can a DSS do? Consider the following example. The accounting department of a small manufacturing company (a job shop) must perform a labor utilization analysis on every job that the company participates in, to ensure that the company's price bidding is accurate. If a labor utilization problem is detected, the manager of the department would like to define the problem area (from a myriad of possibilities), investigate it, and resolve the problem.

Figure 4–3 depicts the type of dialogue that would go on between a DSS and its user, in support of such a process. The system would prompt the user for job numbers and project information (hours worked and revenue generated). Once the information was input, the system would consult its history database to review pertinent facts and then query its solution databases for reasons for any detected fluctuations. The facts it found would be displayed on the screen, for use by the decision maker.

In this example, the DSS prompted for information regarding Job 99999 and performed some calculations to determine cost of labor, target revenue, and labor utilization (Facts 1–5). It then looked to its solutions database for possible reasons for the underutilization detected (Fact 6). A scan of its history database uncovered a budget for Job 99999. A review of the budget showed no fluctuation. The DSS concluded that the "low labor utilization" was "due to a workforce problem" (Facts 7–8).

With the reason for the underutilization determined, the user can begin to investigate the facts behind the workforce's inability to work to capacity.

Who knows? With the right interface, a click of the mouse may uncover other related facts. Another click could display the job foreman's telephone number. Click again, and the number is dialed!

Where Did DSS Begin?

The DSS revolution began in the mid-1970s, when it became apparent that middle and senior management weren't getting the same type of automated support that their operation-level subordinates were enjoying. This

DSS System Prompt	User Keyed Response
Enter Job Number:	**99999**
Enter Revenue generated:	**$10,000**
How many workers assigned to Job?	**3**
How many hours did worker #1 work?	**300**
@ what hourly rate?	**$10**
How many hours did worker #2 work?	**200**
@ what hourly rate?	**$10**
How many hours did worker #3 work?	**150**
@ what hourly rate?	**$10**

DSS System returns the following set of facts:

Fact 1 - 650 hours were dedicated to Job #99999 at $12.30/hour
Fact 2 - $8000 was the cost of labor for Job #99999
Fact 3 - $24,000 should have been generated to justify an $8000 Labor Cost
(3 * Labor Cost =Target Revenue)
Fact 4 - Labor utilization for Job #99999 was 42%
Fact 5 - Labor utilization of less than 90% requires investigation
Fact 6 - Reasons for low labor utilization include:
a. workforce problem (not working to capacity)
b. underbid job
c. unforeseen rework requirement
Fact 7 - Review of bid material budget showed no fluctuation
between budgeted and actual material costs
Fact 8 - Low labor utilization due to workforce problem

Figure 4-3. *Managerial accounting scenario using a DSS*

dissatisfaction, coupled with the popularization of the minicomputer, led to the development of the first decision support systems.

The minicomputer meant that each department within a company could have its own computer. Further, each department manager could build systems that met his or her particular decision-making needs. The question that remained was: "Who will build it?"

IS's inability to react to the need for a localized management system forced many firms to hire consultants or to staff each business area with its own systems personnel. These consultants and business systems analysts were the first DSS architects.

It soon became obvious that these "end user computing groups" were in direct competition with the existing IS department. By the beginning of the 1980s, many firms decided to reconcile the situation by adopting a centralization strategy that placed all computing resources (hardware, software, and personnel) under the IS department. Interestingly, the late 1980s showed a shift back to a decentralized strategy as powerful 386 and 486 workstations became popular.

This cycle of centralization/decentralization forces organizations to constantly rethink their positions on DSS. Organizing for proper DSS deployment is a major concern in many organizations today. The creation of a DSS Center can help.

The DSS Center

Regardless of which processing mode is currently in fashion, a DSS strategy can be defined that will work effectively in both centralized and decentralized environments. The creation of a DSS Center is the heart of the strategy.

The DSS Center oversees the development of all DSS applications within the firm and is charged with establishing DSS standards and guidelines. It's a governing body that develops DSS applications, decides which tools to use, and determines the priority of the systems developed.

The DSS Center is staffed by systems professionals who lead the development of these specialized management applications. The DSS staff is well versed in the latest DSS technology and will manage additional external consulting support as needed.

The manager of the DSS Center reports directly to the firm's senior management. He or she is a peer (not a subordinate) of the IS department head. Such a distinction is important because a peer relationship reduces the possibility of the DSS Center's losing its effectiveness.

In one transportation company, the DSS Center head was placed under the Director of MIS. It seemed that every time a DSS application was proposed, the MIS chief would decide to develop the system through traditional means. The DSS Center was left building "quickie" ad-hoc programs to support clerks in the receiving department. In time, the DSS Center was dissolved and the Center's head left the company.

Creating a DSS Center is solid strategy because it eliminates the costly redundancies of talent and technology usually associated with decentralized DSS groups. But, it must be autonomous to be truly effective.

To help clarify the role of a DSS Center, a sample mission statement and organization chart are shown in Figure 4–4. Review them for more ideas regarding DSS organizations and you'll see that the DSS Center is responsible for the development, support, and acquisition of DSS systems and products.

<u>Mission:</u>

> To facilitate the cost effective development and support of efficient and timely decision support systems. The DSS Center will act as a conduit between their customers and senior management. The Center will provide leadership in DSS software acquisition and reapplication.

<u>Responsibilities Include:</u>

1. assisting management in the prioritization of DSS system requests
2. analyzing and developing decision support systems
3. evaluating and acquiring DSS software packages
4. creating general purpose DSS software for use in systems development
5. supporting DSS applications in the field

<u>Organization Chart:</u>

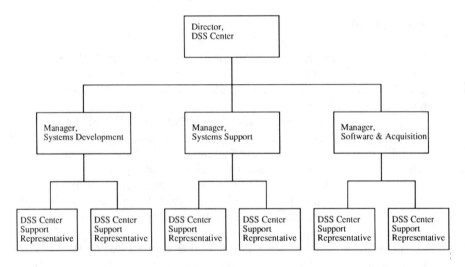

<u>General Areas:</u>

> Systems Development: works with user to analyze and develop DSS applications
> Systems Support: maintains DSS applications in the field
> Software and Acquisitions: Performs software evaluation and develops general purpose DSS tools

Figure 4-4. *DSS Center mission statement and organizational chart*

The Center is organized into three areas that have specific responsibilities:

1. Development—analyzing and implementing new DSS applications,

2. Support—maintaining and evolving production-level DSS applications, and

3. Acquisition—evaluating DSS products and creating development tools for general-purpose use.

Each group is staffed by highly trained support representatives who understand DSS concepts, technologies, and applications. These professionals should be rotated through all areas within the Center, to become well versed in each other's discipline and to allow the director to be flexible in the design of the organization.

Designing Your Own DSS

The thought of designing a DSS may come as a surprise to organizations that are aware of the myriad of DSS software products available in the marketplace (see Figure 4–5). But, the story doesn't end with the acquisition of a DSS tool. Firms need to apply it effectively to meet end users' needs.

The products listed in Figure 4–5 are not solutions unto themselves. They must be rigorously applied to deliver their promised results. It's important, therefore, to understand the steps required to build a system using DSS technology.

DSS Life Cycle

Several steps are involved in designing a DSS. Figure 4–6 shows how the steps for the DSS life cycle differ from the steps taken in traditional systems development.

In a traditional development effort, the scope of the systems design activity is determined in the requirement definition stage. Analysis and design are next, as the application's data and processing specifications are determined. Once the "paper design" is complete, implementation and testing are done. The cycle comes to a close as the application is migrated to the production environment where it's made available to the user.

The DSS life cycle follows a similar progression: the DSS request is scoped, specialized analysis is conducted, and the system is prototyped, tested, and delivered to the user. The differences between this and the traditional methods rest in the nature of the analyses and the prototyping/review activities inherent in the DSS development approach.

Let's examine the DSS development approach in more depth.

DSS Request

Before resources are allocated to the development of a DSS application, a formal request must be submitted to the DSS Center by the end user. The DSS request should contain a brief description of the application (including the nature of the decision process and the general data needed to

Product	Vendor	Description	Price
Control Strategist	Kay Consulting 213-379-4133	Decision support for statistical forecasting and modeling.	$50,000 or $2500/mo
Decision Maker	Ask Computer Systems 415-969-4442	Exception reporting of financial, marketing, and manufacturing information.	$8000-$30,000
Express/MDB	Information Resources 800-528-3546	4th generation database system for business analysis and planning.	$50,000 and up
Foresight DSS	Compro Financial Systems 404-662-8754	Financial planning and modeling decision support tool.	Call vendor for more information
IFPS/DTE	Execucom 512-346-4980	Distributed decision support tool for financial planning and analysis.	$15,000-$130,000
MDSS	MDSS Inc. 216-861-8100	Integrated on-line decision support tool for marketing, operations, and manufacturing.	$36,000-168,000
Metaphor	Metaphor Inc. 415-961-3600	Tailor-made decision support tool that front-ends company databases.	Call vendor for more information
MSA F&M	MSA Advanced Manufacturing 404-239-2000	What-if analysis of financial performance.	Call vendor for more information

Figure 4-5. *Partial list of DSS products*
Source: *Data Sources*, Vol. II. New York: Ziff-Davis Publishing Co., 1989.

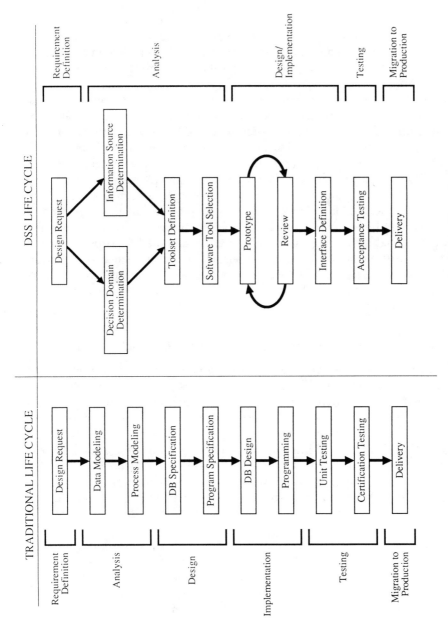

Figure 4-6. *Comparing traditional and DSS life cycles*

61

support the decision) and a brief statement outlining the opportunities, risks, and business impact of the proposed system.

Upon receipt of the request, the DSS Center performs an initial review and files it with other DSS requests received. Once a month, a meeting is scheduled with the DSS Steering Committee (composed of senior business and IS management). All requests received are reviewed and prioritized. Only the highest priority requests are approved for DSS Center support.

As the review process becomes more sophisticated, a request form like the one shown in Figure 4–7 should be developed. Standardization of the form will help the organization make better assessments of the DSS requests. Sorting and evaluating requests received in various formats can be very difficult. A standard form streamlines the process.

Once a request is approved, a DSS development team is formed. The three-member team—a business area manager, a management representative, and a DSS Center support analyst—can begin defining and analyzing the business area's decision domain and information sources.

Note that the management representative and the DSS support analyst work full-time on the development effort. The business manager participates as much as possible but is often pulled away to address more pressing items. The management rep will act as the manager's spokesperson in the manager's absence.

Decision Domain and Information Source Definition

Information sources and decision domains are determined early in the DSS development effort. Information sources provide the business area with the information it needs to make a decision. Decision domains define the context in which decisions are made within the business area.

The DSS development team has several alternatives for defining the decision domains and information sources of a business area. Business modeling as defined in Chapter 6 is the preferred approach because it's a systematic way of determining the actual information received and generated by the business area. Teams can piece together a decision domain by understanding the information sent and received by the function.

However, many business managers and/or their representatives don't understand every facet of the business area's information input or output—when the area is large or they are new to the department, for example. Therefore, an interview approach for defining the decision domains and information sources is often adopted.

Because the interview approach is often free-form and lacks the rigor of the business modeling technique, important information is frequently missed. It's essential that the DSS Center support representative (see

```
┌─────────────────────────────────────────────────────────────────────┐
│                          DSS Request                                  │
│                            Form                                       │
│                                                                       │
│   Date of Request: _____                                   │
│   Requestor Name: _____      Title: _____       │
│   Requestor Phone: _____     Department: _____  │
│   Requestor Mailstop: _____      Target Date: _____   │
│                                                                       │
│   Please complete the following.                                      │
│   1. Proposed System description: _____    │
│      _____      │
│      _____      │
│                                                                       │
│   2. Decision support required: _____    │
│      _____      │
│      _____      │
│                                                                       │
│   3. General data needed to support decision making: _____    │
│      _____      │
│      _____      │
│                                                                       │
│   4. Opportunities created by system: _____    │
│      _____      │
│      _____      │
│                                                                       │
│   5. Risk incurred without system: _____    │
│      _____      │
│      _____      │
│                                                                       │
│   6. Business impact/importance: _____    │
│      _____      │
│      _____      │
│                                                                       │
│      Signature:_____    Date: _____           │
│      Approval:_____    Date: _____           │
│      (If requestor is other than department manager)                  │
│                                                                       │
│      Please submit all requests to Director, DSS Center, floor 12D.   │
└─────────────────────────────────────────────────────────────────────┘
```

Figure 4–7. *Sample DSS Request Form*

Figure 4–4) gain insight into the following factors, to define a decision's domain:

- When a decision is made and under what circumstances (trigger)
- The frequency of such decisions (daily? weekly? monthly?)
- A decision's contingencies (back-up plans)
- The circumstances that allow a decision to be delegated

- The circumstances that force a decision to be made at the next management level

To understand information sources, the DSS representative should find out about:

- The internal sources of information (originating from within the company)
- The external sources of information (clients, government agencies, and so on)
- The frequency and quality of the information provided
- The media through which the information is passed (phone call, memorandum, reports, computer lines, other contacts)

Once these insights are gained, the DSS team can describe the tools needed to support the decision-making process within the business area.

Defining DSS Toolsets

To define the toolset needed to support a decision maker, the DSS team must first understand how that decision maker makes decisions. The team should begin by answering questions like: "What kind of modeling do you use when determining the date to reorder that material?"; "What kind of charts do you create to track sales?"; "How do you seek funding to support a decision?"; and so on. By understanding the answers to questions like these, the team can begin to understand the functionality that will be required of the DSS.

Here's a list of some of the management practices that are often provided in automated form in DSS:

Critical path analysis

Trend curve estimators

Scatter charting

Cluster analysis (affinity determination)

Risk analysis

Linear extrapolations

Contrarian estimations

Statistical analysis (mean, median, mode)

This list is not comprehensive, but it illustrates the type of DSS applications that are being built today. When the team defines its toolset requirements, it can begin to determine which software products (word processing or spreadsheets, for example) must be integrated into its DSS.

Software Selection

Software selection can be the most costly step in the DSS development life cycle. It's the phase in which the team must determine which software programs will be used to automate the management practices discussed above.

For example, Fred Crocker, vice president and controller of Norton Company, in Worcester, Massachusetts, needed a DSS that would improve his ability to access and manipulate the financial data needed to run the fast growing engineering materials manufacturer.

Crocker wanted a system that could calculate P&Ls (profit and loss statements), perform balance sheet analysis, and assist in strategic forecasting. Norton turned to System W, a product sold by Comshare of Ann Arbor, Michigan. Crocker's experience with the DSS package was so positive that Norton intends to extend the system to support e-mail and EIS processing over the next few years (1).

Sometimes the software that is needed to support the decision maker isn't available; that is, the organization has yet to acquire a package that can meet the need. The team has to identify the software requirement and pass it along to the DSS Center, which will formally conduct the make-vs.-buy analysis.

If the decision is to buy the needed software, the DSS Center acquires it and sponsors the training for all support representatives and the members of the DSS development team. If the decision is to "make" the software, then one or more support representatives are assigned to its development.

This approach keeps the creation of DSS software within the DSS Center, which enables the software's reapplication whenever appropriate. When the software is developed, it is made available to the DSS team who submitted the request. In the meantime, the requesting team will begin prototyping.

DSS Prototyping and Review

As mentioned in the previous chapter, prototyping and review comprise an iterative process. Its application in DSS development is no exception. The differences between the use of prototyping for transaction-processing systems and for DSS lie in the size of the development team and the number of reviewers needed for prototype acceptance.

Teams of four or five (i.e., two users, three developers) are typically used to prototype transaction-processing systems. Once developed, these prototypes are reviewed by a panel of users who are not currently on the prototyping team. If the panel approves the prototype, it is said to be accepted and formal implementation begins. If not, the prototype is returned to the team for reworking.

A DSS development effort works basically the same way. However, usually only two people work on the prototype—the senior management representative and the DSS Center support representative. They review their work periodically with the business area manager, who has final review authority over the prototype.

The limited number of participants in the DSS prototyping effort allows the team to be far less formal in its prototype/review iterations than other prototyping teams are. By keeping things simple, the team can build an acceptable prototype rapidly.

▼

KIDDER, PEABODY & CO.
SAVES $100 MILLION THROUGH DSS

One month before "Black Monday" struck Wall Street, Charles Sheehan, CFO of Kidder, Peabody & Co., established these two very important objectives for his department managers:

1. Build a system that will enable all 280 + department managers to control their expenses
2. Ensure that senior management is provided monthly expense reports from each division.

To make things interesting, Sheehan established a year-end delivery date for the system.

Bob Mudry, manager of MIS in Kidder's Finance Division, began to work on the assignment. He knew that a year earlier (September 1986) his staff had built a similar system for the Operations Division and that a DSS tool called Metaphor could handle the throughput of a company-wide application like the one proposed.

In less than two months and with only three people, Mudry's team had built an expense-tracking system that could support all 21 Kidder, Peabody divisions. The ad-hoc capabilities and standard management reports helped controllers and managers keep a watchful eye over departmental and divisional expenses.

Kidder estimated that the system helped to save $100 million in costs. A trade tracking system that combines client and transaction information is the next target for the Metaphor DSS. Kidder hopes the application will be as successful at attracting clients as the expense-tracking system was at reducing costs. The proof will be in the balance sheet.

Source: Marketing material provided by Metaphor Computer Systems, Mountain View, California, August, 1989.

Interface Definition

The team must coordinate the data extraction and file transfers necessary to support their DSS system. The creation of interfaces between the DSS application and the systems that populate its databases (known as feeder systems) can be the most challenging aspect of DSS development. Any system can be a feeder to a DSS. Most feeders are transaction intensive so summary information is used to populate the DSS.

Such coordinations often become logistical nightmares because the custodians of the feeder systems do not have a data extract file established that can meet the DSS requirement. New programs are often needed to create the extract. Many times, these programs are low on the feeder system priority list. The DSS team may have to wait months for the feeder system custodians to provide the data transfer capability that is required.

But it doesn't have to be that way, if firms follow some simple steps:

1. While investigating the information sources of the DSS, list the systems that currently create the data needed by the DSS. In other words, identify the feeder systems.
2. Upon completion of the information sources definition phase, notify the custodians of those systems of the interface needs. Let them know a DSS team will be looking for their support in the future.
3. Schedule a meeting with the custodians during the prototyping phase. Let them begin to understand the *exact* data needs. Ask them to provide the data. Give them some proposed target dates.
4. Revisit the issue in a second meeting, held near the end of the prototyping phase. Check their progress.
5. Keep management aware during each step of the way! Make the interface requirements a management priority.

The last step is easily the most important. When the DSS system becomes a management priority, supporting the development team becomes everyone's priority. That kind of commitment makes interface definition a success.

Acceptance Test and Delivery

The last steps in the DSS life cycle are the acceptance test and delivery of the system. The acceptance test allows the user to give the system a "test drive" in a production-like environment. Any last-minute adjustments can be made during this phase.

It's a good idea to involve the DSS support staff during acceptance testing of the system. They can learn, along with the user, how the system functions and which performance thresholds exist. A performance threshold is a set of circumstances in the production environment that causes performance degradation of the DSS. Acceptance testing is usually a learning experience for user and technician alike.

Delivery of the system involves the establishment of the production jobs needed to support and populate the system. It's important to note that DSSs, unlike traditional transaction-driven systems, are never considered complete. The DSS evolves after it is delivered. The "look and feel" of the system may change as the decision maker gains insight into how the DSS can aid the decision-making process.

Therefore, it's imperative that a DSS Center support person be assigned to the system upon delivery. This person is the user's link to the DSS Center. Be sure each DSS is well supported by a highly skilled technician.

Now that we have a firm grip on what DSS technology is and how a DSS system can be built, let's explore its "kissin' cousin"—executive information systems.

Executive Information Systems

Executive information systems (EISs) are applications that provide senior executives with the information they need to run their companies. EISs facilitate the access and integration of data from a variety of internal and external sources. They monitor particular facts about the business and automatically inform their executive users when those facts require special attention.

Like DSS technology, EIS takes advantage of color graphics and mouse-driven interfaces to make EIS applications easy to use and understand. The primary difference between the two technologies is their end user audiences. DSS seeks to improve the effectiveness of mid-level decision makers. EIS seeks to improve the effectiveness of top-level executives.

This audience difference also shifts the emphasis on the type of data required by each technology. A DSS targets particular functional area data within a company (i.e., marketing, operations, financial data). An EIS targets data from *all* functional areas within the company, as well as data from outside the firm (i.e., competitors, government, economic data).

Figure 4–8 depicts the relationship among the DSS and EIS processing environments. Departmental DSS systems are fed information from various transaction-based systems; the EIS is fed information from those

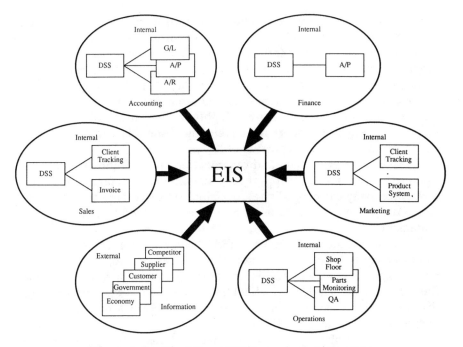

Figure 4-8. *The EIS and DSS processing environments*

systems and from external ones. With this much activity, imagine the significant support infrastructure needed to make EIS successful.

EIS Support Infrastructure

The systems development game changes as soon as IS begins to build end user systems for company executives. Executive users don't have a tolerance for faulty systems. A strong user support mechanism must be in place before an organization embarks on EIS.

Many companies have found that the best way to support the executive user is by assigning an IS support analyst to each executive. In this way, the executive has a direct line to a contact person in IS who can answer questions and help with the procedural elements of the system. For example, if the user is having difficulty maneuvering through the screens, the IS support analyst can be called for advice. In a matter of moments, the support representative has the executive's system up on a workstation and can walk the executive through the screen options. All the support you could ever want, and over the phone!

The risks of this approach come in the form of resource constraints. Does the support analyst have the time to dedicate to the executive user whenever a call comes? More often than not, the support analyst has other responsibilities within IS. These other responsibilities may spread the analyst too thin and jeopardize the quality of the EIS support.

This points to an undeniable need to create a separate EIS support function. EIS applications are too highly visible to afford a support-related problem. EIS support and development should exist in an organizational entity akin to but outside of IS.

The DSS Center mission and organization chart (Figure 4–4) can be extended to include EIS support responsibilities, as depicted in Figure 4–9. A company can centralize all decision and executive support expertise and thereby reduce its learning curves and support personnel requirements.

The new Executive & Decision (E&D) Support Center organization simply expands its scope of control. The Systems Development, Systems Support, and Software & Acquisition areas discussed previously expand their charters to include EIS technology responsibility. The new area, the Executive Help Desk, is charged with providing EIS users with phone support and assistance in EIS use.

An important distinction must be made between the Help Desk area and the Systems Support area within the Center. The Help Desk area consists of troubleshooters who must answer the phone when a panicky executive calls in with a problem. The Systems Support area has a different charge: upgrading and maintaining DSSs and EISs. Help Desk personnel handle ad-hoc problems quickly; Systems Support personnel introduce long-term changes to existing systems.

Does the caliber of the professionals change, as an organization shifts from a DSS Support Center to an E&D Support Center? Not really; the players in the Systems Design and Help Desk roles must be mature professionals who can effectively conduct themselves and communicate with executive staff members. After all, they're the people who must define the EIS requirements. Firms want these personnel to be fine professionals.

Defining EIS Requirements

There's no magic involved in determining EIS requirements—just hard work! Because EIS systems share the same life cycle as DSS applications—iterations of prototyping and review—the initial requirements-gathering interviews are extremely important.

Usually, executives are reluctant to be interviewed. Many fail to understand the importance of their involvement. Others are fearful of the

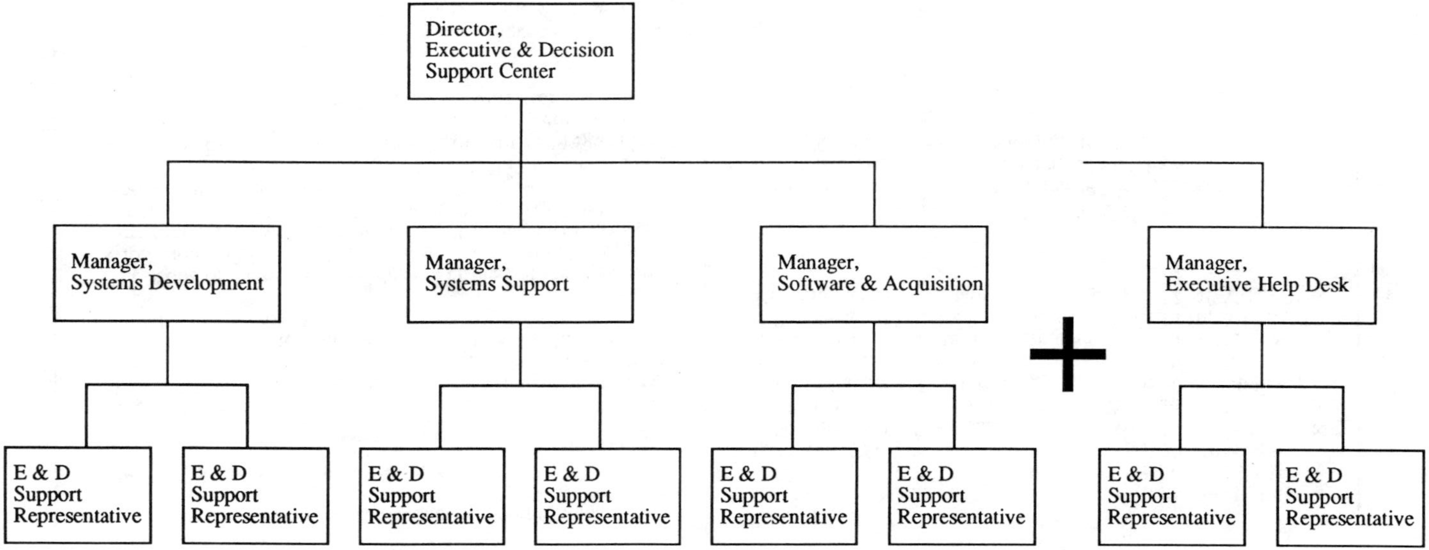

Figure 4-9. *Expanded DSS Center plus Executive Help Desk leg creates an effective Executive & Decision Support Center*

XYZ Publications
"Changing Words To Print"

Date: April 10,1990

To: Executive Distribution List

From: J.D. Smith
Director, Executive & Decision Support Center

Re: EIS Executive Interview Schedule

Attached is the interview shedule for the corporate EIS project that XYZ is about to embark on. The purpose of these executive interviews is to help the Executive & Decision Support Center understand your information needs, so we can build better systems for you.

The scope of the project includes the Offices of the President, CEO and CFO. They, along with their support representatuives, will be interviewed. The interviews will last for two hours and will be held in the Executive Conference Room on the 50th floor of building "B."

Each executive will be asked questions regarding: Responsibilities, Goals, Problems, Current Systems Support, Expected System Support, Planned Organizational Changes and Improvement Opportunities for the 90's.

Upon completion of the interview process, the results will be synthesized and distributed for review. Two weeks will be allowed for enhancements. Systems prototyping will begin May 15.

If you have any questions or concerns, please contact me at x-456.

EIS Executive Interview Schedule

J.B. Norther, President	April 30	3PM-5PM
A.B. Dixon, CEO	April 30	8AM-10AM
I.S. Pruitt, CFO	April 29	3PM-5PM
X.E. Smith, V.P., Distribution	April 27	10AM-NOON
W.W. Treize, V.P.. Finance	April 25	10AM-NOON
D.J. McKenzie, V.P., Marketing	April 20	9AM-11AM
E.M. Iancocci, V.P. Sales	April 19	9AM-11AM
L.A. Schmidt, V.P., Human Resources	April 14	1PM-3PM
D.D. Johnson, Comptroller	April 14	9AM-11AM
M.R. Gold, Staff Assistant	April 12	10AM-NOON

Note: All interviews will be conducted by S.S. Skolowski, EIS Designer and will be held in the Executive Conference Room, building "B", floor 50.

Figure 4-10. *Sample EIS interview schedule memo*

unknown. "Who can be sure what kind of technical jargon will be tossed around?" "How will it look to my subordinates, if I don't understand the issues?" Questions like these bother most executives regarding the interview process. Therefore, it's important for the EIS designer to be well organized and prepared. A haphazard interview will only add to the executive's uneasiness.

An interview schedule should be created and published. It can be written by the EIS designer but, to give it credence, the memo should go out over the signature of the director of the E&D Support Center. The schedule should include a brief explanation of the interview process, sample questions, and a statement of scope and objectives. The designer's ability to eliminate the "mystery" from executive interviews will improve the chances of facilitating a successful interview. A sample memo appears in Figure 4–10.

The memo is simple and to the point. It explains the purpose and scope of the interview process, while pointing to the areas for discussion. An interesting issue concerns the location of the interviews. All should be conducted away from the distractions of the executive's office and in the privacy of a meeting room. This is a good way to keep the executives focused and committed to the subject at hand, rather than distracted by a myriad of everyday interruptions.

Another important factor in executive interviewing is the choice of interviewer. The EIS analyst must be top-notch. There is little time for floundering and nervousness during an executive interview. Remember, the E&D support group has only a couple of hours to ferret-out the basic requirements from each executive. After the interviews, as explained below, the group will be working exclusively with executive intermediaries.

Figure 4–11 contains excerpts from an executive interview. Note the simplicity of the questions and the generality of the responses. The interpretations included with the excerpts show the need for a well-seasoned analyst. A less experienced person may be unable to "read into" the executive's responses; the results will be an ill-understood requirement and a poor system.

Executive Intermediaries

As mentioned in the sample memo (Figure 4–10), interview results are synthesized and distributed for review upon completion of the interview process. At that time, each executive should designate an executive contact person to represent his or her area's interest during prototyping.

This intermediary must be available for daily meetings with the EIS analyst. A system like the one referenced in Figure 4–10 would require

Company: Wilson Electric Products, Inc.

Participants: A.B. Wilson, EVP, Operations (A)
              Q.E. Dudsen, EIS Analyst, EDS Group (Q)

Q: What are your basic goals over the next few years?

A: My goals are very simple (pause). To help Wilson Electric gain 60% market share while improving customer satisfaction.

Q: What will you do to achieve these goals?

A: I plan to focus my attention on the production process. We need less scrap and more finished goods.

Interpretation: The EIS must provide Wilson with production information.

Q: You mentioned earlier that we were being "priced out of the market." How can we avoid that?

A: We have the highest prices, because we have the highest costs in the industry. If we want to lower costs,we must synchronize sales with production. We need to know what orders are coming and when, so we can tool up for production.

Q: You're saying that knowing when orders are coming will reduce costs?

A: That's right! Scrap is expensive. When we rush to make a tight production schedule, we produce lots of scrap. Better coordination with sales would give us the time to build the product right the first time.

Interpretation: The EIS must provide Wilson with sales projections, so he can schedule production accordingly.

Q: What specific information could you use in order to avoid some of those problems we spoke about today?

A: Well, I receive a tremendous amount of paper each month. Most of it is there, I just need more time to review it.

Q: How about scrap reports? Couldn't you use that type of information?

A: I get weekly scrap reports.

Q: How about hourly ones? Would they help?

A: C'mon!

Q: It can be done.

Interpretation: As the interview winds down, it's important that Wilson understands Dudsen is aware of his issues and is thinking about how to help him achieve his goals. This will keep the door open for future discussions.

Figure 4–11. *Excerpts from an executive interview*

three executive contacts (one each for the president, CEO, and CFO). The others on the distribution list (VPs, comptroller, staff assistants) are not primary users of the system and will not participate in the design. However, their input is crucial for understanding the overall scope of the effort.

With the scope understood, the intermediaries and the EIS analysts can begin prototyping the system. As they complete a portion, it is reviewed by the executive users. Appropriate changes are made as the prototype evolves into a production system.

The Production System

EISs, like DSSs, cannot reach production levels until the system interfaces (needed to populate the application) are created and tested. All the IS resistances associated with developing interface files for DSS go away in EIS. IS doesn't want to be the department that impacts senior management's system. A simple request is usually all that's needed for interface development.

The final test for the EIS application comes after the prototyping and system interface testing. The users must be satisfied with the information provided and the features that make the system simple, quick, and easy to read.

At a minimum, the system should provide the executive user with information regarding company performance, economic indicators, governmental actions, competitive intelligence, and progress on current company programs (e.g., new product development). This kind of information gives the executive the comfort needed to make direction-setting decisions with confidence.

A list of ten questions that are most frequently asked by executives appears in Figure 4–12. A firm can "acid test" its EIS by judging the system's ability to answer questions like these. The way in which the information is provided is equally important.

The EIS must deliver summary information, with a flick of a button. The system should also be trigger-driven, that is, it should report certain facts when specific events occur (e.g., indicate when production drops below 80 percent of capacity). Last but not least, the application should report all results in multiple graphical formats. The acceptance of the system is directly proportional to the ease with which the user can maneuver through all its information.

Usually, some adjustments are necessary to make the EIS fully functional. Once those adjustments are made, the organization can begin to enjoy its benefits. The organizational impact can be tremendous.

Important Questions
1. How do our sales look this month?
2. What's our market share?
3. How's the new product development progressing?
4. What are operating expenses this month?
5. What's the prime rate?
6. What's our profit margin?
7. What's the current inventory?
8. Are suppliers meeting our production schedule?
9. Are customers satisfied with our new product?
10. What's the competition doing?

Figure 4–12. *Questions most asked by executives*

Organizational Impact

As EIS use spreads across the firm and the technology is fully institution-alized (e.g., all executive managers are using the tool, middle managers are providing input to the executive databases, the E & D Support Center is staffed with trained professionals), the organization will realize some immediate impacts. These results are typical:

- Operating efficiencies will improve. Redundant activities will be minimized because EIS analysis will uncover their inefficiencies. Value-added processes will be the only ones performed. Departments will eliminate their "post office service" of shuffling paper from one part of the business to another without ever acting upon it. Every process will have its purpose and there will be a purpose for every process.

- The flow of information will change. Information will be delivered directly to the organizational units that need it most. The senior executives in charge of those areas will be able to access the raw data before it gets synthesized by their staff, creating an opportunity for the company to take advantage of executive expertise earlier in the decision-making process.

- Reorganization is likely. Companies can afford to "thin down" once their operations are smooth and their information flow is efficient. EIS offers the company the insight needed to determine how best to organize and, thus, to streamline the business.

The nature of these benefits carries a high risk of political upheaval. The parties responsible for carrying forth the operating efficiencies and information flow changes may resist doing so, for fear of losing their jobs.

To combat a political upheaval, a large food service chain began an all-out education program when it introduced its EIS to its outlets. Middle and lower levels of the company were taught that EIS is necessary to business survival. The message was pure and simple, "If we don't get there first, our competition will."

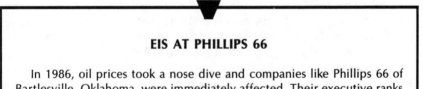

EIS AT PHILLIPS 66

In 1986, oil prices took a nose dive and companies like Phillips 66 of Bartlesville, Oklahoma, were immediately affected. Their executive ranks fell by 40 percent. They had to consider alternatives, to pick up the slack. Phillips 66 immediately turned to executive information systems.

Working with Pilot Software, an EIS vendor, Phillips 66 built a worldwide trading network. Charles Bowerman, vice president of marketing, explained how the EIS integrated electronic pricing with sales data, allowing him to adjust petroleum product prices according to supply and demand. The system saved Phillips 66 a whopping $40 million in crude oil costs.

In light of Phillips 66's success, other industry leaders are beginning to examine the potential of EIS. Phillips 66, on the other hand, has plans to expand its EIS user base from 50 to 500, a feat not often attempted.

It achieved its success through a strong top-down management commitment. Company president Robert G. Wallace thought so much of the technology that he wrote an article in *InformationWeek* about it. He pointed to the elements of EIS success: "An executive manager who's committed to it; middle managers who are involved in it; and EIS technical people who understand . . . the nuts and bolts of the business." With that kind of insight, how can Phillips 66 fail in EIS?

Source: Robert G. Wallace, "An EIS Can Be a Bottom-Line Boon," *Information Week*, January 11, 1988, p. 56.

The Future of EIS Technology

As innovative companies begin to exploit the power of EIS and achieve the benefits that improved managerial insight offers, it won't be long before every firm is exploring executive information technology. What will these firms find?

Executives at Rockwell International's North American Aircraft (NAA) Division, in El Segundo, California, found out that they don't even have to use a keyboard to access corporate information. Touch-screens and mouses are all they need to run the business (2). The next wave of technology promises even more (Refer to Figure 4–13 for a list of current products.)

EISs of the future will incorporate:

- Groupware capabilities that allow the direct sharing of information among EIS users through a local area network. This, of course, will bypass the costly mainframe communications needed to share EIS information today.

- Intercorporate networking capabilities that tie the EIS application directly to the external sources of information (e.g., suppliers' data-bases, service bureaus, and clients' systems), facilitating access to up-to-the-minute information that may be critical to the business.

- Database machine processing that will act as a fast and efficient back-end to the workstation front-end. Copies of production data-bases will be maintained on such systems. They will improve ad-hoc query and reporting performance through enhanced database processing.

- Real-time processing, giving executives the ability to access today's data today, when it counts the most!

- Artificial intelligence that will suggest appropriate action plans based on acquired facts. An EIS will not only provide important in-formation to assist in direction setting but will recommend courses of action.

"Store-bought" EISs may shift the competitive environment so much that firms that *don't* subscribe to the technology will not be able to compete.

Summary

Decision support systems (DSSs) and executive information systems (EISs) improve management's ability to lead the company. The DSS is aimed at middle managers with departmental and operational responsibilities. The

Product	Vendor	Description	Price
CA-Strategem	Computer Associates International 800-645-3003	4th Generation EIS with flexible programming capabilities for report writing and screen painting	Call vendor for more information
Commander EIS	Comshare 800-922-7979	Non-technical user tool for analyzing diverse data through mouse and touch screen interfaces	$59,000-$278,500
EIS	Boeing Computer Services 206-865-5000	Focuses on business planning and control problems, with graphics and reporting support.	$45,000-$115,000
Executive Edge	Execucom Systems 800-531-5038	A senior executive system which facilitates access to company planning and analysis data with a graphical interface.	$60,000-$200,000
Maps/EIS	Ross Systems 415-856-1100	EIS system for DEC VAX users. Graphically reports and manipulates data from PC spreadsheets.	$5000 and up
Pilot	Pilot Executive Software 617-350-7035	Maintains internal and external executive reports. Mouse and touch screen interface for variance and exception reporting	$55,000-$135,000

Figure 4-13. *Partial list of EIS products*
Source: *Data Sources*, Vol. II. New York: Ziff-Davis Publishing Co., 1989.

EIS is aimed at senior managers who set corporate policy and direction. Both are valuable technologies that enable better decision making by providing adequate and timely information to their users.

DSS applications deliver modeling and ad-hoc reporting capabilities unsurpassed by traditional systems. The high-powered graphical interfaces make access to problems and heuristic databases as easy as "point and click," while EIS's friendly front-end makes the use of that technology a true joy.

Senior management can track critical data about the company through the EISs. The systems combine company information with data gathered from outside sources, to give executive users the total picture of a multitude of forces shaping the corporate environment.

The business driver behind an organization's decision to embark on these decision-assistance technologies include a desire for:

Improved market share

Tighter management controls

Reduced operating expenses

New product development

Increased profit margins

Innovative sales planning

While the use of DSS and EIS technology may not guarantee the achievement of these objectives, their implementation will certainly help management position the company for advancement.

Key Points

1. Decision support systems (DSSs) assist mid-level managers in making decisions, by offering rule-based intelligence in the form of heuristic and simulation models.

2. A DSS application is comprised of three major components: a problems database, a solutions database, and a user-friendly graphical front-end.

3. A DSS Center should be formed and dedicated to building, supporting, and investigating DSS applications and technology.

4. The systems development life cycle does not apply to the development of DSS applications. A new life cycle is needed, to emphasize iterations of prototyping and review.

5. Kidder, Peabody & Co. saved $100 million by using DSS technology. They plan to develop a trade tracking system next.

6. Executive information systems (EISs) represent the next wave of DSS applications. EIS provides the same decision support capabilities as its predecessor but targets the executive staff as primary users.

7. A new EIS support infrastructure is needed. The mission of the DSS Center should be extended to include EIS design, support, and investigation. The Executive and Decision (E&D) Support Center will be its new name.

8. An Executive Help Desk function should be added to the DSS Center. It will provide immediate support to executive users of the technology. Only highly skilled analysts will staff the desk.

9. EIS technology, when institutionalized, will bring tremendous change to companies that implement it. Operating efficiencies, improved information flow, and reorganization will be the benefits; political upheaval may be a drawback.

10. In the future, EIS will take advantage of groupware, intercorporate networking, database machine and real-time processing, and artificial intelligence to provide even greater business benefit.

References

1. Arthur J. Tobias, "Today's Executives in a State of Readiness," *Software Magazine,* November 1988, pp. 57–61.

2. David A. Armstrong, "How Rockwell Launched its EIS," *Datamation,* March 1, 1990, pp. 69–72.

5

Management Information Centers

There's one thing stronger than all the armies in
the world and that is an idea whose time has come.

Victor Hugo, c. 1870

Earlier chapters have dealt with the need for stronger and proactive management of information resources and have suggested several ways to improve systems quality while involving business professionals in the development process. Providing better service and support through the establishment of Management Information Centers (MICs) is the focus of this chapter.

The Management Information Center Concept

The Management Information Center (MIC) can be viewed as the next evolutionary step for the mid-1980s Information Center, which focused primarily on managing the selection and acquisition of personal computers. Although it's true that many of the original "Info Centers" offered special training and PC software package demonstration services, most did little (if any) systems development for end users—the function that makes MICs different from their Info Center predecessors.

Figure 5–1 compares the Info Center of old to today's Management Information Center. Chores like maintaining computer inventories and installing packages are augmented by such responsibilities as designing and integrating end user systems. "Augment" is a key word here because the Management Information Center also assumes traditional Information Center roles, making it the "new and improved" Information Center of the 1990s.

Information Center Responsibilities	Management Information Center Responsibilities
Select and acquire PC technology	Investigate user requirements
Demonstrate PC software	Recommend system solutions
Train users in software packages	Design end user computing applications
Maintain end user computing inventory	Leverage end user computing information and technology
Install PC technology and packages	Integrate existing end user applications
Support Install-base	Assume traditional Information Center responsibilities

Figure 5-1. *Comparison of Management Information Center and traditional Information Center responsibilities*

Some History

The Information Center was introduced by IBM Canada in 1982. IBM Canada wanted to improve the level of service that IS was providing the user base. It was believed that the creation of a separate group charged with supporting end user computing would lessen the backlog and help achieve fuller automation across the firm. End users would be, in essence, providing for themselves through PC-based solutions.

It wasn't long before the success at IBM Canada spread. Eighty percent of large firms in a recent American Management Association survey reported staffing an Information Center (1). Many organizations take the Information Center concept seriously. General Motors Corporation (GM), for example, sponsors a cross-corporate user group that allows GM Info Center personnel to compare notes and strategize future undertakings.

The fact that a major corporation is funding information transfer across its member companies is indicative of the importance placed by many executives on Management Information Centers. This kind of support will lead to further growth and to expansion of the Management Information Center Charter.

Management Information Center Charter

The Management Information Center is charged with improving the decision-making potential of end users by providing personalized systems development support. This means that Management Information Center personnel help end users define their systems requirements and then recommend and implement solutions.

The problems that can be solved by gaining access to an existing database, generating a new report, or installing workstation software are addressed by the Management Information Center directly. Problems that are broader in scope and require the creation of new programs and databases are referred to the conventional IS department staff. The Management Information Center doesn't replace the IS department; it simply complements it.

A sample MIC organization chart is presented in Figure 5–2. Four major functions are represented in the MIC organization: training, acquisition and administration, design coordination, and end user support. The first is rather obvious: The training area is responsible for providing instruction in new tools and technologies. Regular classes are scheduled on use of all the hardware and software that the Center supports.

Acquisition and administration assumes the task of investigating and purchasing MIC technology. The MIC analysts assigned to this area will stay abreast of advances in technology, study trends, and make evaluations. Besides arranging the acquisition of hardware and software, the sector also establishes and maintains the end user computing inventory.

Design coordination involves the integration and sharing of end user systems. This area focuses on leveraging MIC solutions across the company. Design coordination analysts consult with the end-user support area to ensure that users take full advantage of the current suite of technology, products, and services available through the MIC.

The end user support area assigns staff members to each business unit. These end user support representatives, as depicted in Figure 5–1, have dotted-line reporting to both the MIC (which pays their salary) and the business areas (which set their priorities).

Paul Schaeffer, manager of information center office systems at the Public Service Indiana (PSI) utility in Plainfield, Indiana, established what he called the "Business Analyst Program." The program places people from his staff within the user community. PSI kills two birds with one stone: A technologist learns the business, and the business gains an Info Center liaison (2).

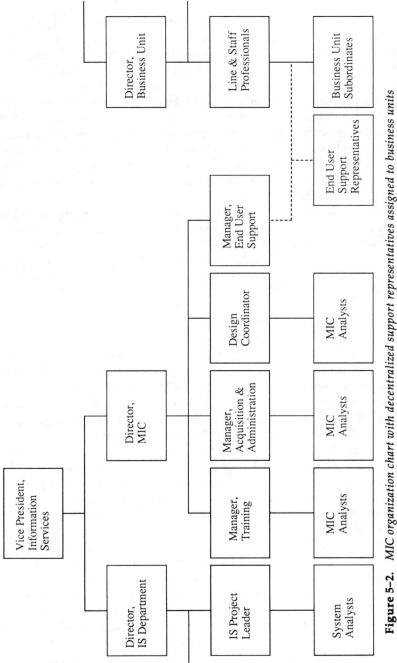

Figure 5-2. *MIC organization chart with decentralized support representatives assigned to business units*

IS's Role in Management Information Centers

A problem often arises if it happens that the Management Information Center is providing better end user service than the IS department. This problem can be avoided by placing the directors of both the MIC and IS under the same manager (see Figure 5–2). Any competition arising over responsibilities can be resolved by the executive in charge.

With the competition issue put to bed, the IS department and the MIC can form a partnership in which each has its place in support of the other. For example, the MIC can recommend IS involvement in certain business issues (like a strategy for supporting tax law changes) because a representative is right in the business unit when the situation arises. Such opportunities are often missed because of a lack of communication between IS and its users.

The establishment of end user access to existing databases and file extracts from IS production systems is the flip side of this partnership. Without such "access rights," the MIC's ability to respond to most user requests is impaired. The Center cannot provide systems development service without IS's full cooperation.

Systems Coordination Meetings

It seems that the MIC needs IS and IS needs the MIC. This relationship can be further enhanced through the scheduling of monthly systems coordination meetings conducted by the MIC. MICs usually initiate and facilitate the meetings, which are sponsored by the MIC's design coordinator. The purpose of the meetings is to encourage the sharing of development ideas between the MIC and the IS department.

Each meeting provides an occasion for the MIC representatives to share project progress with IS project leaders. It gives IS project leaders a chance to discuss major development activities (and their potential role in meeting reported end user needs) with MIC staff. This kind of free exchange is imperative, to avoid redundant activity between the two areas.

Further, these monthly meetings help the design coordinator keep track of the end user applications that each support representative is developing. Opportunities for integration and application reusability are identified. Coordination strategies are discussed among meeting participants.

It's interesting to consider the varied perspectives that each type of systems professional brings to the meeting. Fundamental design approaches can be altered by a well-placed word from either a MIC or IS developer. Each seems to attack the challenge of meeting user requirements quite differently. A MIC professional looks for PC-based solutions or ad-hoc reporting capabilities to solve many problems. An IS professional thinks in terms of building new databases and coding new programs to address user requirements.

Neither tack is absolutely correct and neither is without merit. The challenge is to find the right combination of both and to establish an architecture that allows each to flourish. Systems coordination meetings help companies do this.

Establishing the "Right" Architecture

A MIC processing environment must be developed to effectively meet end user needs. A majority of MIC applications are PC-based, but a strategy should be in place to populate these workstations with information from mainframe systems—and that strategy can present problems.

A solution to those problems lies in the creation of a two-tiered processing architecture that separates the MIC environment from the transaction processing environment. PC, mainframe, and relational tools are used. A target environment is presented in Figure 5–3.

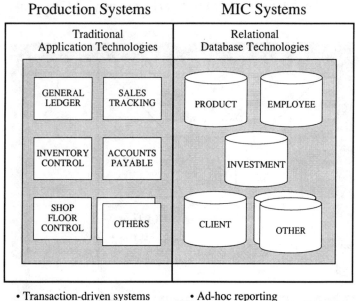

Figure 5–3. *MIC computing environment*

The Mainframe Component

The conventional IS-built systems on the left side of the figure represent the existing base of transaction processing systems. Most firms would have general ledger, sales tracking, and inventory control applications running in this environment, for example. Tools like COBOL, VSAM, and IMS are used to support these applications.

The right side of the figure shows the MIC environment, which has subject area databases at its root. Each subject area (e.g., product, employee, and so on) is populated by summary information from the transaction processing systems on the left. Relational technology like SQL and DB2 is employed to provide MIC users with ad-hoc query capabilities for these databases.

The Workstation Component

Once this environment is established, other end user tools like 4GLs (fourth-generation languages) and PC packages can be used to massage data extracted from the MIC subject area systems. The tools used are determined by the support representative assigned to the user area. The MIC workstation environment would look like the conceptual interface presented in Figure 5–4. Data is at the core of the workstation environment and it can be manipulated in a variety of ways. PC tools like 4GLs

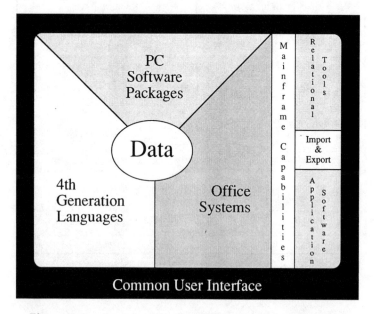

Figure 5–4. *A user's view of an MIC workstation environment*

are used to create reports; software packages (like Lotus 1-2-3) are supplied as necessary. Office systems, like word processing and electronic mail, are used to communicate data to other interested parties across the concern.

Mainframe capabilities are also provided through the workstation environment. Data import/export routines are made available for file transfer across the micro and mainframe platforms. Access to relational query tools and host applications is facilitated as well.

The success of the MIC's two-tiered processing environment is dependent on the data architecture that underpins it.

MIC's Data Architecture

A comprehensive data management strategy must be put into place, to reap the benefits of the MIC environment. At the heart of the strategy is a systematic way of identifying and maintaining the subject area databases needed to support the end users or decision makers.

The best way to define these databases is by interviewing key MIC users across the company. This activity is clearly the role of the data administrator. However, the MIC should coordinate and participate in the process, to gain an understanding of the databases as they're defined.

AJAD techniques (see Chapter 3) are a powerful means of gaining insight into the user's data requirements. In most cases the basic subject areas—product, client, and employee—can be identified in a matter of just a few weeks by a team of users and MIC support representatives (see Figure 5–5).

Once the subject areas are identified, the data that is needed to populate each database must be determined, along with a plan for extracting and moving the data from IS production systems to the MIC databases.

Ford Motor Company, for example, has established an on-line information service that is comprised of 24 separate databases for some 4000 of its users. Vehicle specifications, technical designs, and automotive industry news are just some of the subject areas maintained in the system (3).

With a little discipline, other firms can establish a data architecture like Ford's and can create an opportunity for MICs to concentrate on supporting the business better through the application of advanced technology.

MIC Technologies

As mentioned earlier, the IS transaction processing and MIC environments are logically separate. Physically, though, these systems and databases

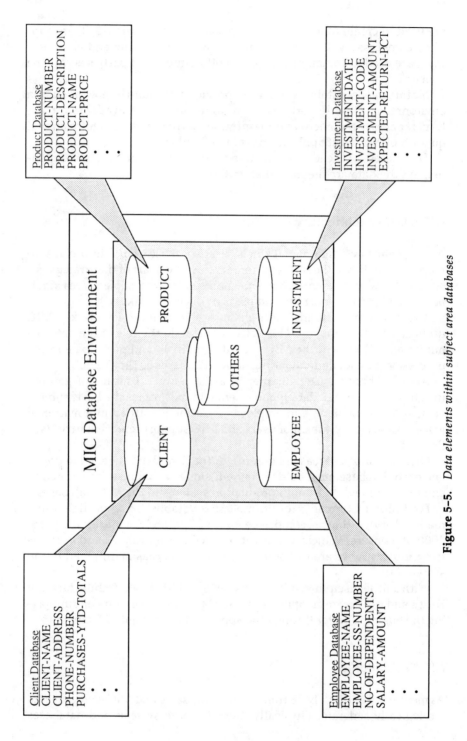

Figure 5-5. *Data elements within subject area databases*

Product Database
PRODUCT-NUMBER
PRODUCT-DESCRIPTION
PRODUCT-NAME
PRODUCT-PRICE
. . .

Investment Database
INVESTMENT-DATE
INVESTMENT-CODE
INVESTMENT-AMOUNT
EXPECTED-RETURN-PCT
. . .

MIC Database Environment

PRODUCT

INVESTMENT

OTHERS

CLIENT

EMPLOYEE

Client Database
CLIENT-NAME
CLIENT-ADDRESS
PHONE-NUMBER
PURCHASES-YTD-TOTALS
. . .

Employee Database
EMPLOYEE-NAME
EMPLOYEE-SS-NUMBER
NO-OF-DEPENDENTS
SALARY-AMOUNT
. . .

INFORMATION CENTER REPORT (1988)

The American Management Association (AMA) began studying Information Centers in 1985. Since then, the AMA has conducted an annual survey on the topic. The 1988 study included 295 companies from various sectors of the economy, including manufacturing, services and non-profit organizations. The respondents ranged from small companies (<$100 million in sales) to multinational conglomerates. The study generated some intriguing results:

1. MIC popularity is on the rise. Only 33 percent of the companies involved in the 1985 survey reported the existence of an information center. In 1988, 60 percent of the companies surveyed had a center for end-user computing.

2. Most firms are dedicating more human resources to MICs than ever before. Average staff size has grown by 50 percent during the past four years. In 1986, the average MIC staff was eight people. The average size was 12 in the 1988 study.

3. The majority of firms still haven't broken the MIC apart from IS departments. Only 25 percent of the respondents had separate IS/MIC organizations.

4. The distribution of MIC personnel into user areas is still not the norm. Only 30 percent of the respondents had MIC specialists reporting directly to business unit managers.

5. MIC budgets are growing. More than 70 percent of the surveyed firms were planning to increase their MIC budgets in 1988 (see Figure 5–6, Part C).

Further insights into the survey are presented in Figure 5–6. Part A shows the top six requested activities of MICs. Part B shows the MIC services performed least often.

It is interesting that PC evaluation, selection, and training were requested most frequently, while application development, computer maintenance and networking were performed least frequently. It seems that most firms still view MIC personnel as resident PC experts and not system developers—a trend that will probably shift as MICs grow and missions expand to include data access and emerging technology management responsibilities.

Source: Eric Rolfe Greenberg, "How Far How Fast," *Information Center,* August 1988, pp. 20–24.

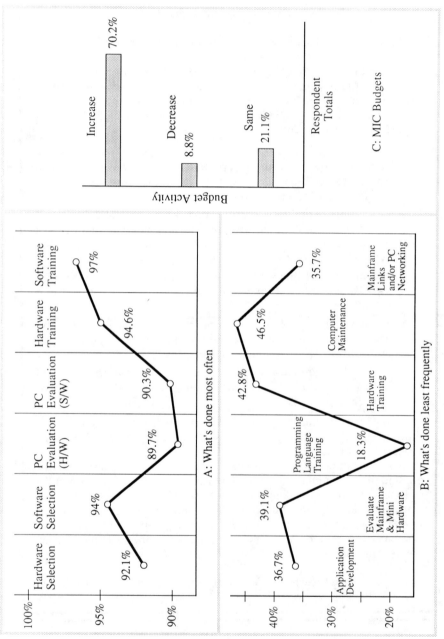

Figure 5-6. *The AMA's MIC survey statistics*

may reside on the same or on different CPUs (central processing units)—anywhere in the world.

The decision regarding processing sites and data distribution schemes is driven strictly by business need. For example, consider a multidivision corporation that performs transaction processing at sites across the country and has a MIC at corporate headquarters. The data distribution scheme, for that company, calls for a decentralized environment of local processors with powerful data communication networks that pass information to the databases at the home office, where MIC users around the country can have access to it (see Figure 5–7).

Centralized processing is another popular scenario. A company may decide that all computing will be done at one location. If that location is running at capacity, then the introduction of MIC processing calls for a new CPU. The additional throughput cannot be supported with the current iron.

These environments can carry some hefty price tags. Costs come in the form of trunk-line expense, network and CPU hardware, and PC communication boards, just to name a few. Therefore, alternative means of processing must be considered. Among the multitude of technologies available to MICs, CD-ROM, database machines, and client-server architectures are the most intriguing.

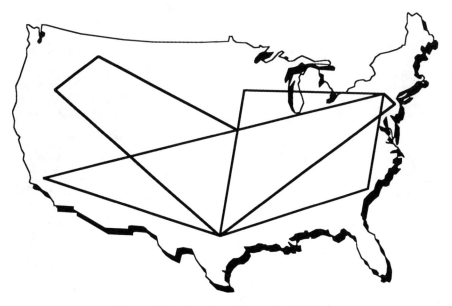

Figure 5–7. *Location-independent MIC sites*

CD-ROM

CD-ROM stands for Compact Disk-Read Only Memory. It is computer memory on a compact disk, equal in size to the music disks (approximately 5 inches in diameter). It has 600 megabytes of capacity, equal to 1500 360K-byte floppy diskettes. This storage capacity makes CD-ROM a stunning data distribution alternative at any price.

Interestingly, CD-ROM is relatively inexpensive if a wide distribution requirement exists. It costs $1500–$2000 to master 100 copies of a CD. Incremental copies are less than $5.00 each. The CD-ROM drives for each workstation cost less than $500 each, when bought in bulk. With prices coming down, CD-ROM is not an expensive undertaking. But, it's wise to be careful.

Because it's "read only," a company that plans to use CD-ROM technology must find a vendor who is willing to master and manufacture the CDs. Once the relationship is defined, all the firm does is create the extract files desired on CD and send them to the vendor. Within two to three days the CDs are ready for distribution.

Some CD-ROM companies, like Discovery Systems in Ohio, will not only master and manufacture the disks but will distribute them according to the client's mailing list specifications—adding convenience to the mass storage appeal of the technology.

Figure 5–8 illustrates the CD-ROM environment. It shows how remote data feeds from processing units around the company are linked to a

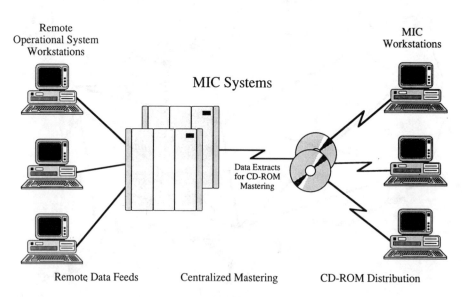

Figure 5-8. *MIC's CD-ROM environment*

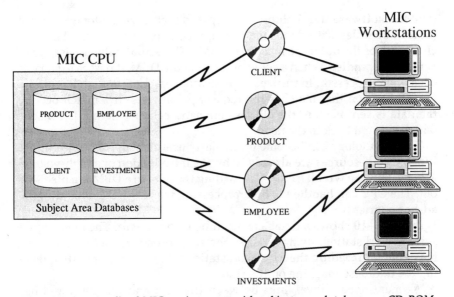

Figure 5-9. *A refined MIC environment with subject area databases on CD-ROM*

centralized CPU at the MIC. The data in the system is then extracted to tape and the tape is mastered to CD-ROM. The CDs are then distributed back to MIC users at various company sites.

Figure 5-9, a variation on the environment presented in Figure 5-8, depicts the various MIC subject area databases that exist in the centralized MIC environment. Each subject area is then extracted and converted to CD-ROM separately. The CDs are then distributed to users who require access.

Each approach has its advantages. The first simplifies the extract/mastering process and allows all users equal access to all MIC databases. The latter has a more complex extract/mastering scheme, but helps to limit data access to those who need to know. For example, the personnel department needs to know employee salaries; the sales department does not. Personnel would receive the employee CD. Sales would not.

CD-ROM technology makes sense in a large, distributed, MIC environment. How do firms handle a full-function, centralized setup?

Database Machines

Database machines are an excellent way to augment the host processing environment. High-volume databases, like MIC systems, can be easily supported by the machines, which can accurately handle more than 100 transactions per second, leaving relational database management system

(DBMS) software far behind. Multiple direct access storage device (DASD) spindles with dedicated microprocessors comprise the basic architecture of the database machine (DBM). The actual database is spread across the spindles. When a command enters the DBM, it passes a query to each microprocessor. In turn, each processor searches through its spindle for information that matches the request parameters. If a match occurs, the data is sent back to the DBM's command center where it is consolidated and sent back to the user.

This technology can become particularly useful in an MIC application. When CPU resources are already tight, the introduction of a high-volume MIC system can wreak havoc. Off-loading the data to a DBM is a nice way out. The CPU can handle the bulk processing while the DBM handles the ad-hoc queries.

Figure 5–10 shows a database machine environment. The operational system workstations bang against the host processor, as they always have, undisturbed by the MIC workstations that are continually querying the database machine on the right.

As mentioned above, links between the host and the DBM and between the host and the MIC workstations are essential. The DBM link keeps the databases stored across the DBM DASD current, while the link to the MIC workstation provides the end user with an ability to access host-based applications as needed.

The cost of establishing a DBM environment varies by configurations. However, many studies show that the cost of the DBM is less than the

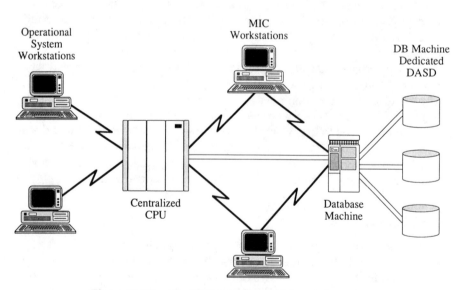

Figure 5–10. *The MIC database machine environment*

cost of installing and maintaining a DBMS. If throughput is a problem area, database machines are a solution.

Client-Server Architecture

Client-server architecture will play a role in MICs as well. Client-server environments divide applications into two portions. One portion resides on the "server" and is available to all "clients" (personal computers). The other portion of the application resides on the client's workstation.

Most of today's client-server architecture implementations use a mainframe as the server and a workstation as the client. However, that picture is changing and minis, LAN drivers, and powerful workstations are playing the role of servers.

As Figure 5–11 suggests, the MIC architecture can be created where operational systems residing on a mainframe will feed less expensive servers the summary information they need to support their clients—who would have ordinarily accessed the mainframe for the information.

In essence, the client-server architecture moves the processing out to the least expensive machines, freeing-up the centralized CPU to do the number crunching that it was meant for.

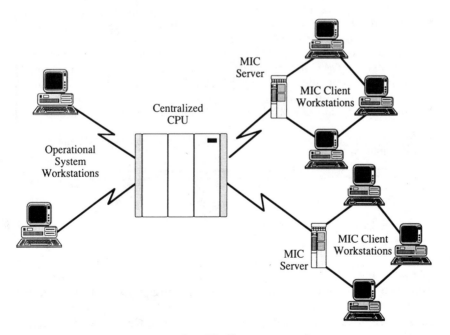

Figure 5–11. *The MIC client-server environment*

▼

KUDOS TO ROCKWELL INTERNATIONAL

What would you think about an IS department that spent $30 million annually on capital expenditures but received an additional $130 million in budget money from the business units it supports? After you revive from the fainting spell, you would probably want to know who did it and how it's done. Rockwell International, a $12 billion aerospace and industrial manufacturer, has created such an environment.

Although the IS area is not formally known as an Management Information Center, it's run like one. Jim Sutter, the vice president in charge, has not only implemented an exemplary chargeback system but has dispersed nearly two-thirds of the IS talent across Rockwell's 14 locations around the country. He has about 1000 employees working for him. There are 1800 computer professionals reporting to various business units.

Decentralization of this magnitude can be very threatening to some IS chiefs, who may be afraid of losing their empire. However, Sutter believes this organizational design is far better positioned to provide quality support to business areas than any other that could be contrived. After all, there are 116,000 employees stretched across 28 divisions of Rockwell. How could a centralized IS department support such a large user base without some decentralization scheme?

Besides orchestrating the firm's financial processing, Sutter's troops coordinate the use of technology and data throughout the company. It's due to their efforts that the firm has lowered mainframe costs and embraced the use of LAN and PC-based solutions so readily.

Packed with all the characteristics of any good MIC—effective chargeback for MIC services, dedicated user support, and a strong cross-company coordination function—Rockwell's IS environment is one of the best in the industry. We should all understand their approach and look for opportunities to apply their techniques in our MIC organizations.

Source: Charles Pelton, "Jim Sutter Pilots Rockwell's MIS Payload," *Information Week,* July 25, 1988, pp. 28–34.

Plotting the Course of MIC Evolution

Like any new IRM tool or technique, the MIC will follow a pattern of evolution from its introduction to a firm through its maturity. Figure 5–12 plots MIC evolutionary activities against the "stages of growth" curve developed by Richard L. Nolan of Norton & Company. (See Figure 2–7.)

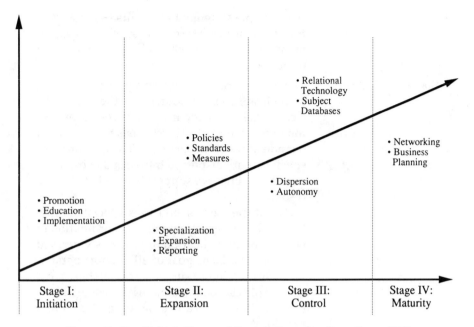

Figure 5–12. *Nolan's "Stages of Growth Curve" as it applies to MICs*

Stage I (Initiation).   The center is created. Its staff and budget are small. The firm wants to pilot the MIC concept before dedicating much resource to it. MIC personnel spend time promoting the new Center to potential business users. Some educational services are provided to first-time users. Implementation of end user tools into work areas is a major deliverable.

Stage II (Expansion).   In time, the Center picks up momentum. It begins to expand its scope to include building larger applications. The implementation of tools shifts toward building solutions for end users. MIC budgets and staff grow and more rigorous management reporting is required of the function. Center support specialists are developed, to tackle particular end user issues.

The new growth experienced in this stage requires a new set of management controls. MIC standards and policies are determined for users and Center personnel alike. Management reporting within the Center changes from simple statement of results to reconciliation against predetermined success measurements (i.e., increase chargeback to 35 percent of operating budget).

Stage III (Control).   The delivery of larger systems prompts the firm to dedicate more resources to the MIC. The Center gains an identity; it becomes an autonomous group of professionals related to but outside of the IS department. The MIC support specialists are dispersed into the business areas as a way to improve support (through dedicated resource).

The dispersion of end user specialists into the field requires a tremendous coordination of effort. The reapplication of previously defined solutions is a basic goal of all support personnel. The creation of subject area databases and the use of relational technology become important first steps toward program and database reusability.

Stage IV (Maturity).   The Center reaches maturity as representatives become involved in business planning with the user areas with which they have become aligned. Expertise within the MIC has matured to the point where sophisticated network solutions can easily be developed. These solutions tie users in one area of the business to users in another area, and tie the company to other companies.

The time required to carry a MIC through these stages will vary from firm to firm. The first two stages can easily be achieved in 18 months or less, given appropriate management commitment. The third and fourth stages are far more difficult to attain.

The third stage assumes that a data architecture exists. If it does not, the MIC must coordinate its creation (a task that spans IS and user territories alike). This effort alone can take years, in organizations that have little or no centralized data management expertise.

The last stage, Maturity, is reached when the MIC assists in business planning and can provide advanced network support. Developing connectivity skills is one thing (it can be hired, if necessary) but being invited to the planning table is quite another. It requires great trust on the part of business managers. The time required to build that trust is difficult to project. Eventually it comes, hand in hand, with success.

Guidelines for Success

There are a few simple rules to follow, in order to make the MIC successful. They range from finding qualified people to work in the MIC to limiting the number of tools supported by MIC personnel. Here is a list of the most important guidelines for success:

1. Staff with quality people. MIC personnel must understand the business areas they support, as well as the technology that's employed to meet user requirements. It takes a special mix of business knowledge, technical talent, and communication skills to be effective in MIC roles. Define ways to hire and train individuals for these positions.

2. Distinguish MIC from IS department responsibilities. Jealousy and competition over end user support will result as soon as the MIC concept is introduced, unless a clear distinction is made between the two by the senior manager in charge. Formal mission statements will help, but management awareness and recognition of the competitive issues will ensure a smooth start for the Center.

3. Distinguish MIC from end user responsibilities. Users should be reminded that they are not MIC professionals and MIC professionals should be reminded that they're not users. Sometimes these roles become blurred when MIC personnel are dedicated to end user areas. Reminders from managers on both sides of the house will avoid problems associated with users' attempting to build systems and support analysts' defining user data needs in a vacuum.

4. Dedicate sufficient resources. MICs are only as good as the people and the support they can provide to end users. Financial and personnel resources must be dedicated to grow and nurture the MIC concept into its maturity.

5. Keep it simple. MIC personnel will be able to provide better service to end users if they're allowed to work from a simple set of standard tools. Support can deteriorate when the suite of technology changes from business area to business area. MIC resources must be dedicated to managing the tools and techniques supported by the Center; otherwise, additional resources will be needed to manage the chaos introduced by dissimilar technology.

These guidelines, as simple as they are, can make or break an MIC as it evolves through its stages of growth. It's amazing how pitfalls can be avoided by finding good people, distinguishing responsibilities, dedicating resources, and keeping it simple.

Summary

MICs are in a state of transition. Traditional roles are giving way to new end user computing responsibilities. No longer will "Info Centers" be only glorified PC management departments. True solutions to business problems will be created through MICs.

The dispersion of end user computing specialists into the business units will provide a service base unequalled by today's centralized IS staff. New technology will introduce new opportunities for meeting user needs more directly.

Adherence to simple guidelines will facilitate MIC transition. Success will be determined by the quality of the support that can be rendered. The future will bring a new era in departmentalized management computing as MICs take their position beside IS and E&D support departments.

Key Points

1. The popularity of MICs is growing; a majority of polled firms in a recent survey report an increase in staff and budgets.

2. PC evaluation, selection, and training are still the most popular activities requested of MICs. Fewer firms look to centers for application development, computer networking, or maintenance.

3. MICs are evolving from a department dedicated to managing PC tools and technology to an end user support group that assists in reducing the application development backlog by building simple user applications.

4. The MIC provides personalized user support through dedicated end user support representatives assigned directly to business units.

5. IS and MIC management should report to the same senior manager. This reporting structure eliminates any competition over end user support that may result.

6. System coordination meetings are effective ways to facilitate the sharing of ideas between IS and MIC personnel.

7. The MIC processing environment contains both mainframe and workstation components. Emerging technologies like CD-ROM and database machines are beginning to be used.

8. Data architecture is an important aspect of the MIC environment. Subject area databases and relational technology are used to support management's ad-hoc reporting requirements.

9. MICs evolve through four distinct stages of growth. Each stage generates new deliverables and requires improved skills. The dedication of resources will determine the time required for a center to reach maturity.

10. Finding good people, distinguishing roles and responsibilities, and keeping MIC technology simple will lead firms to success.

References

1. Eric Rolfe Greenberg, "How Far How Fast," *Information Center*, August, 1988, pp. 20–24.

2. Stan Kolodziej, "End Users Need Not Apply," *Computerworld Focus*, October 7, 1987, pp. 25–26.

3. Esther Dyson, "Why Groupware is Gaining Ground," *Datamation*, March 1, 1990, pp. 52–56.

6

Information Engineering

> Every age has a kind of universal genius, which
> inclines those that live in it to some particular studies.
>
> *John Dryden, 1688*

There are three management layers in every IS department. The top layer is made up of strategic direction setters, who are responsible for defining the long-term direction of the department. The tactical managers, the middle layer, determine the plans for implementing the strategies defined by their seniors. The lower management layer is made up of operational decision makers, who manage the systems development projects on a daily basis. Each management level within IS has a different set of needs.

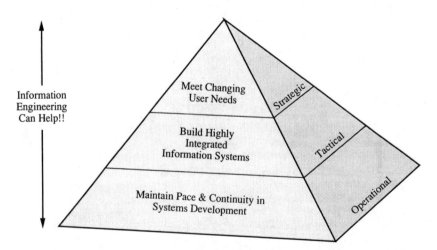

Figure 6-1. *The IRM management pyramid and its focus on major IS objectives*

- Strategic managers, for example, want to build flexible systems that can be quickly modified to reflect changes in business direction.
- Tactical managers want to ensure that all systems being built are integrated. (Integrated systems are easier to maintain than stand-alone systems, which tend to lack the breadth of data needed to satisfy new user requirements.)
- Operational managers face a different dilemma. How do they maintain pace and continuity within a project development effort, given the extensive employee turnover rate within IS?

Each layer of the IS management pyramid (as depicted in Figure 6–1) relies on a systems development methodology to meet its objectives. Deciding on which methodology to use can be a major stumbling block for many firms because every IS professional seems to have a favorite approach for systems building. Reaching consensus on which one to use is nearly impossible.

Information Engineering (IE) is a development methodology that is beginning to attract a lot of fans. Figure 6–2 lists several leading firms

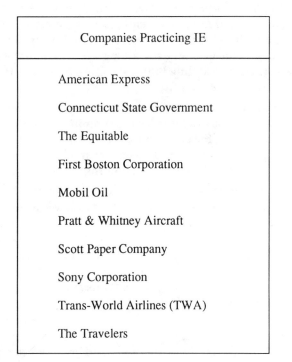

Companies Practicing IE
American Express
Connecticut State Government
The Equitable
First Boston Corporation
Mobil Oil
Pratt & Whitney Aircraft
Scott Paper Company
Sony Corporation
Trans-World Airlines (TWA)
The Travelers

Figure 6–2. *Partial list of Information Engineering users*

that have adopted its use. Since these companies represent major players within their industries, IE is worth a look.

What Is Information Engineering?

Information Engineering is a family of data-driven analysis and design techniques that support the logical design phase of the systems development life cycle. The IE methodology is comprised of business, data, process, and enterprise modeling disciplines, as described below (1):

- *Business modeling* is a technique for defining the information generated and received by departments in a company. This is the first step toward understanding the nature of the information flow within an organization. Each department should be business-modeled prior to the development of any new applications. Business modeling uncovers potential overlaps in activity across the firm. Analysis of the model will point to opportunities for redefining and streamlining business procedures.

- *Data modeling* is a systematic way of identifying the data items that comprise the information flows defined in the business models. Lists of data called nominated entities are created initially. The lists are then simplified through a process called normalization, which groups data items in a way the allows each to be uniquely defined by one key. Data modeling builds a picture of the interrelationships among a company's data.

- *Process modeling* is used to document the way in which data is manipulated within an organization. A minimum of three procedure modules is written for each normalized entity within a data model. Each module contain the add, delete, or modification rules governing the way data will be processed in the system.

- *Enterprise modeling* is a method for integrating previously defined data and procedure models into a consolidated whole, which will serve as a means of sharing information across the company. Enterprise models are built iteratively, as project-level data and procedure models are integrated. Typically, an automated repository is used to manage the evolution and storage of the enterprise model. Most CASE (computer-aided systems engineering) tools provide automated repository capabilities.

To illustrate Information Engineering in use, the following case study walks through the IE family of methods and provides sample deliverables from each phase.

CASE STUDY

AN IE CASE STUDY

XYZ Corporation, a manufacturer of light fixtures, recently embarked on Information Engineering. After some initial planning discussions among business and IS management, XYZ decided that the Receiving Department would be the first business area studied. If the approach worked in Receiving, then IS would use IE for all other systems development across the company.

The IS Department assigned a project manager to coordinate the effort. He quickly commissioned two IS analysts and three business experts from Receiving to work on the project. The team began business modeling immediately.

BUSINESS MODELING

A consultant was hired to train the IE team in the business modeling technique. After three days of training, the consultant kicked-off the project with a two-day JAD (joint application development) session aimed at bounding and scoping a system development request.

After several weeks of business modeling, the team prepared the following summary, which described the content of Receiving's business model (presented in Figure 6–3).

The Receiving Department's main function is the receipt and acceptance of ordered goods from external vendors. Occasionally, the goods are damaged and must be returned. When goods arrive damaged, the product name and description are logged into a PC system and a Damaged Goods Report is generated. Copies of the report are sent to IS, Accounting, and Inventory Control.

Besides the Damaged Goods Report, Receiving generates the 3150 form; copies are sent to IS, Accounting, Billing, Inventory Control, and Order Entry. The 3150 form is an important document because it notifies the other departments that their goods have been received damaged.

There is an abundance of telephone activity in the Receiving area. Many departments call the Receiving Department to inquire about the whereabouts of orders. Most of the time, Receiving personnel are uncertain about projected delivery dates and will phone the vendors directly, regarding status. These calls are bothersome, and additional phone support will be required in the future.

As a final note, there are strong ties among Receiving, Inventory Control, and Order Entry. Inventory Control sends inventory numbers and Inventory Reports to Receiving each month. Receivers affix inventory numbers to each item as it's received. This helps XYZ keep track of physical inventory.

Order Entry sends Order Summary Sheets to Receiving each day. These summaries help Receiving schedule workloads for the coming weeks. If the scheduling process were automated, it would save two person weeks per month (the information is presently conveyed by FAX).

The business model documented all the communications that arrived in Receiving, including FAX messages, phone calls, reports, and forms. No piece of information processed by Receiving was left out, regardless of the medium in which it was sent.

A detailed business model is an extremely helpful management tool because an examination of business models across an organization can identify needless redundancies and point to opportunities for optimizing work flows.

Because this was XYZ's first business modeling effort, it was in no position to analyze work flows (no other business models existed). However, most firms find business modeling can help them eliminate costly overlaps in activity that lead to expensive management and maintenance of duplicate information systems.

DATA MODELING

The team began data modeling after completion of Receiving management's review and approval of the business model. Using consulting support for initial training and start-up, the IE team spent the next two months determining the data requirements of the Receiving Department.

Entity nomination was the first step in the data modeling process. Each form, report, and inquiry defined in the business model became a nominated entity. The team analyzed samples of the business model information flows to determine the data items within each entity.

Figure 6–4 presents five of the sample documents analyzed by the IE project development team. Figure 6–5 shows how an entity is nominated by transforming each component of a document—in this case a Monthly Order Summary—into a list of data items.

Once entities are nominated, they're normalized to reduce data redundancies. Redundant data makes systems difficult to maintain. Recognizing this, the IE team began to rigorously normalize their nominated entities.

DATA NORMALIZATION

The fruit of the team's labor appears in Figure 6–6. The team decomposed the nominated entity list on the left into the normalized entity list on the right. A perusal of the normalized list shows how the team organized the data so that each data item was defined by the key of the entity type where it resided.

For example, the data item EMPLOYEE-NO, the key of the normalized entity REQUESTOR, uniquely determined the value of the other data items in REQUESTOR (REQUESTOR-NAME, REQUESTOR-PHONE-NO and REQUESTOR-TITLE-NAME).

Data models that are organized so that each data item can be defined by the key of the entity are said to be in Third Normal Form. Third Normal Form data models are the easiest to enhance and maintain because redundant data is eliminated and related data is classified by entity (for easy access and manipulation).

DATA MODEL DIAGRAM

With the data well organized, the IE team set about defining the interdependencies among the normalized entities. A data model diagram (DMD) graphically depicts the nature of data dependencies. The DMD in Figure 6-7 was created to reflect the Receiving Department's data requirements.

A change in the flow of a relationship will significantly change the rules that define the data dependencies. Business rule 3 would be violated, for example, if the relationship between the VENDOR and ORDER entities were changed to allow one ORDER to be placed with many VENDORS.

The last step in the data modeling process was to review the DMD with user management. The team wanted to be sure it didn't make any wrong assumptions about the way data was related within Receiving. The team began process modeling following their DMD review.

PROCESS MODELING

Process modeling was the most time-consuming activity for the team to perform. It generally takes twice as long to develop the add, delete, and modify logic for each entity in a DMD as it does to create the DMD. The XYZ team's experience was no exception. Four months and two weeks of consulting support later, the process models for the Receiving Department project were done.

As Figure 6-8 illustrates, three process modules were created for each DMD entity. Each module contained English-like pseudocode that described the way the data was processed. The three modules for the REQUESTOR entity appear in Figure 6-9.

Once the modules were created, they were grouped together to form processing procedures. Figure 6-10 shows a processing procedure created for manipulating the REQUESTOR modules. The procedure contained four modules—one to manage the menu and three add, delete, and modify modules.

Upon completion of procedure modeling, the team was dissolved. The IS members were charged with converting the data model into a database system and the process models into structured COBOL programs. The Receiving department personnel resumed normal duties in their department and were called upon periodically to review implementation progress and to stress-test the application. The completed system reached production six months later.

RESULTS OF THE IE PROJECT

Besides building a system that truly met end user needs, XYZ Corporation established the foundation for future application development. All new systems will use Information Engineering and will harness user expertise during project design.

XYZ believes that the discipline introduced by the IE methodology will consistently result in higher-quality applications that will remain stable over time. Stable systems will reduce the maintenance backlog and allow

XYZ's Systems Department to spend more time creating automated solutions to business problems and less time repairing obsolete code.

WHAT ABOUT ENTERPRISE MODELING?

The IE project team didn't address enterprise modeling in the context of its analysis within the Receiving Department because it was the first project to use Information Engineering. However, the team's data and process models constituted the first contribution to XYZ's enterprise model. Subsequent development teams will refer to these models during their development efforts.

Figure 6–11 shows how the enterprise model was used. The data model created for the Receiving Department was the current enterprise model. A new project in the Human Resources area began. After business modeling, the Human Resources team examined the enterprise model for related data. The team extracted the REQUESTOR and LOCATION entities for their use. Following completion and review of the project data model, the Human Resources team added the new entities to the enterprise model. A new enterprise model was born.

XYZ will use IE again and again. In time, the enterprise model will contain the data needed to support XYZ in its entirety. Once that happens, the enterprise model can be used as a strategic weapon for determining which systems should be built. The ability to reuse data and its associated process models will help XYZ build systems faster than it's competition can.

The IE Advantage

What does a firm gain by adopting Information Engineering as its standard development approach? IE assists in achieving each of the major objectives of IS management: flexible systems, integrated applications, and interruption-free development. (See Figure 6–1.)

Flexible systems. Traditional, process-driven development tends to produce systems that tie data definition directly to program requirements. System modifications therefore require redefinition of databases as well as programs. This is not the case with IE. The modular nature of IE's data and process modeling logically separates data definition from program logic. Changes to an IE-based system can be readily made because the data requirements are thoroughly defined up front. Updates to the system are done by replacing obsolete process models with new ones; maintenance is as easy as defining new business procedures.

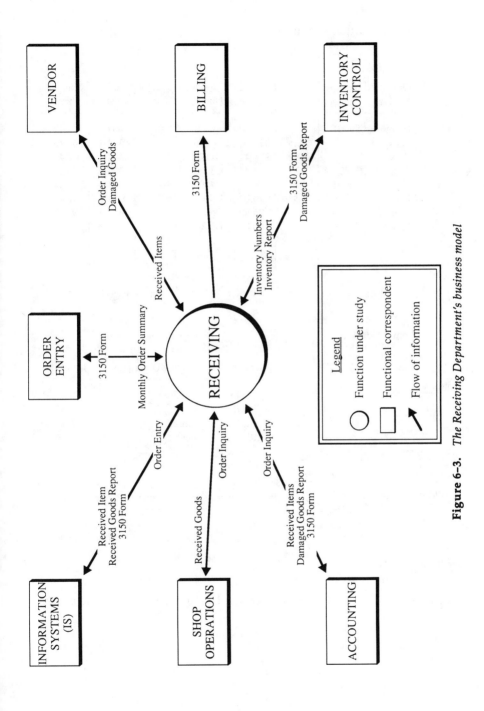

Figure 6-3. *The Receiving Department's business model*

111

Monthly Order Summary
June 16, 1988

Order Number	Ordered Product	Vendor Number	Qty	Unit Price
91334	Hammer	89001	2	$25.50
	Pens		6 cases	$15.00
	Tray		4 dz.	$ 4.44
91501	Tray	84070	2 dz.	$ 4.44
92000	Tray	89001	3 dz.	$ 4.44
	Iron		1	$70.00
92777	Hammer	78006	10	$25.50
92778	Saw	78006	1	$10.00

- End of page 16 -

May 21, 1988
Inventory Report

Inventory Number	Receipt Date	Location	Telephone Number
A0001	5-01	WH-1	X-423
B0020	5-08	WH-1	X-423
B1120	5-10	WH-1	X-423
C3333	5-17	WH-2	X-222
C4100	5-19	WH-S	X-444
D5000	5-20	WH-S	X-444
D5001	5-20	WH-1	X-423
D5002	5-20	WH-3	X-324

- End of page 1 -

**From the desk of
B. Brian Bummer
Computer Scientist
(212) 671-4424**

Date: *4-1-89*

To: *Mary Jones*

Re: *Order Inquiry*

Where is my copy of Lotail 123?

I Ordered it yesterday and have

yet to receive it!

B B B

Employee #: 1110

Damaged Goods Report
Period ending: March 31,1989

Order Number	Product Description	Unit Price
12345	Hammer	$ 27.91
16778	Iron	$ 35.65
18341	Chisel	$ 13.00
19111	Tray	$ 9.99

FORM 3150
88-APR-30

Order Number	Product Name	Projected Delivery
91234	Buzz Saw	88-05-01
91411	The Hammer	88-05-05
96633	Electroscrew	88-07-30
99445	Big Tray	88-12-01

Figure 6-4. *Sample of information generated by and sent to the Receiving Department*

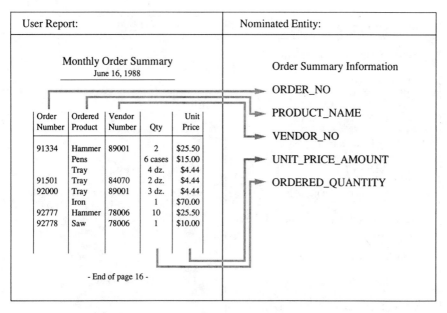

Figure 6–5. *Nominating an entity from user reports*

Nominated Entity List	Normalized Entity List

Order Summary Information
    ORDER-NO
    PRODUCT-NAME
    VENDOR-NO
    ORDERED-QUANTITY
    UNIT-PRICE-AMOUNT
 	
Inventory Information
    INVENTORY-NO
    LOCATION-NO
    RECEIPT-DATE
    REQUESTOR-PHONE-NO
 	
Damaged Goods Information
    ORDER-NO
    PRODUCT-NAME
    UNIT-PRICE-AMOUNT
 	
3150 Information
    PRODUCT-NAME
    PROJECTED-DELIVERY-DATE
    ORDER-NO
 	
Order Inquiry Information
    REQUESTOR-NAME
    REQUESTOR-TITLE-NAME
    REQUESTOR-PHONE-NO
    EMPLOYEE-NO
    PRODUCT-NAME
    ORDER-DATA
	Vendor
	    VENDOR-NO (key)
	
	Order
	    ORDER-NO (key)
	    ORDER-DATE
	
	Ordered Product
	    ORDER-NO
	  + PRODUCT-NAME (concatenated key)
	    PROJECTED-DELIVERY-DATE
	    ORDERED-QUANTITY
	    UNIT-PRICE-AMOUNT
	
	Location
	    LOCATION-NO (key)
	
	Requestor
	    REQUESTOR-NAME
	    EMPLOYEE-NO (key)
	    REQUESTOR-PHONE-NO
	    REQUEST-TITLE-NAME
	
	Inventory Item
	    INVENTORY-NO (key)
	    RECEIPT-DATE

Figure 6-6. *Entity nomination and normalization of Receiving Department information*

Data Model Diagram

Important Business Rules

1. One location can have many items and many requestors. However, each requestor and item can be from only one location.

2. A requestor can place many orders and an order will contain one or more products.

3. A vendor can deliver many orders, but an order can only be placed with one vendor.

4. One ordered product may become more than one inventory item (because products can be ordered in bulk).

5. An ordered product is entered into the system at the same time as an order.

6. Locations must be added to the system before requestors or items can be associated with them.

7. Vendors can exist in the system without any orders associated with them.

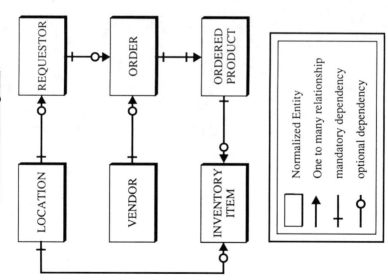

Figure 6-7. *Receiving's data model diagram*

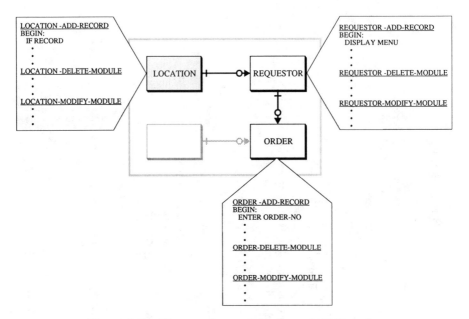

Figure 6–8. *The procedure modules for each DMD entity*

1: ADD-REQUESTOR-MODULE
****

This module ADDs REQUESTORs to the system.
****

Begin:
Display 'Enter Requestor Number'
Execute Edit Number Check
Check if: number exists
If so: Display 'Requestor Exists'
If not:
Display 'Enter Name'
Execute Edit Alpha Check
Display 'Enter Title'
Execute Edit Alpha Check
Display 'Enter Phone Number'
Execute Edit Number Check
Display 'Requestor Has Been Added'
End:

2: DELETE-REQUESTOR-MODULE
****

This module DELETEs REQUESTORs from the system.
****

Begin:
Display 'Enter Requestor Number'
Execute Edit Number Check
Get Requestor
If successful:
Find each Order
Execute Delete-Order-Module
Repeat until end of orders
Erase Requestor
If not:
Display 'Invalid Requestor Number'
Begin again
End:

3: MODIFY-REQUESTOR-MODULE
****

This module allows the user to update REQUESTOR information.
****

Begin:
Display 'Enter Requestor Number'
Execute Edit Number Check
Get Requestor
If Successful:
Start-Point-1
Display Requestor
Display 'Move Cursor to Field to be Changed'
Ready field for modification
Display 'Type Change'
If: field is Requestor-Name or Requestor-Title
Execute Edit Alpha Check
If not:
Execute Edit Number Check
Display New Requestor
Display 'Do You Wish to Make Another Change? Y/N'
If: entry = Y
Begin at Start-Point-1
or
If: entry = N
End
or
Display 'Enter Y or N, Please'
End:

Figure 6-9. *Process modules for REQUESTOR entity*

117

REQUESTOR-PROCESSING-PROCEDURE
****
This procedure allows the user to ADD,DELETE, and
MODIFY REQUESTOR information.
****

0: MENU-MODULE
Begin:
Display MAIN MENU PANEL
Display 'Enter Option'
Check If: ENTRY <= 3
If so: Execute Module Number ENTRY
Begin again
If not: Display 'Entry out of range'
Begin again
End:

1: ADD-REQUESTOR-MODULE
****
This module ADDs REQUESTORs to the system.
****
Begin:
Display 'Enter Requestor Number'
Execute Edit Number Check
Check if: number exists
If so: Display 'Requestor Exists'
If not:
Display 'Enter Name'
Execute Edit Alpha Check
Display 'Enter Title'
Execute Edit Alpha Check
Display 'Enter Phone Number'
Execute Edit Number Check
Display 'Requestor Has Been Added'
End:

2: DELETE-REQUESTOR-MODULE
****
This module DELETEs REQUESTORs from the system.
****
Begin:
Display 'Enter Requestor Number'

Page 1

Execute Edit Number Check
Get Requestor
If successful:
Find each Order
Execute Delete-Order-Module
Repeat until end of orders
Erase Requestor
If not:
Display 'Invalid Requestor Number'
Begin again
End:

3: MODIFY-REQUESTOR-MODULE
****
This module allows the user to update REQUESTOR information.
****
Begin:
Display 'Enter Requestor Number'
Execute Edit Number Check
Get Requestor
If Successful:
Start-Point-1
Display Requestor
Display 'Move Cursor to Field to be Changed'
Ready field for modification
Display 'Type Change'
If: field is Requestor-Name or Requestor-Title
Execute Edit Alpha Check
If not:
Execute Edit Number Check
Display New Requestor
Display 'Do You Wish to Make Another Change? Y/N'
If: entry = Y
Begin at Start-Point-1
or
If: entry = N
End
or
Display 'Enter Y or N, Please'
End:

Page 2

Figure 6-10. *Combining process modules into a processing procedure*

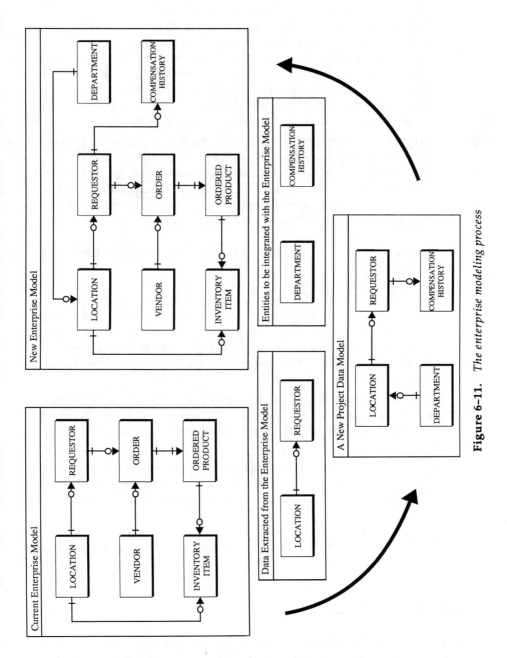

Figure 6-11. *The enterprise modeling process*

119

Integrated applications. In the past, the only way a firm could build integrated systems was by recognizing the fact that a new application required the same data as an existing one. In a flat-file world with no centralized database function to watch over data resources, such realizations were seldom made. Redundant files and stand-alone systems were the results. IE addresses the issue of data reusability through enterprise modeling (EM). Firms build integrated systems by practicing EM's methods of data extraction and iterative integration. EM is built into the IE method.

Interruption-free development. What better way to maintain the pace and continuity of a systems development project than by standardizing the analysis and design approach? The loss of a key player in an IE shop has no impact on the development team. The departing member is simply replaced by another highly skilled IE practitioner. Try to do that in a shop that's lacking any consistent development technique.

Besides these benefits, IE offers several subtle advantages to firms that enforce its use:

Rapid design. In time, systems are built quickly through the reuse of previously defined data and process models. A two- to three-year commitment to Information Engineering can yield an enterprise model that represents 80 percent of a firm's data. Consider how easily an application can be developed when 80 percent of the design already exists.

Lower IS expenses. Following the same line of reasoning presented above, systems that reuse portions of previously designed applications will cost less to build than systems developed from scratch.

Improved staff retention. Since IE is state-of-the-art, a good many staff members will become interested in learning about it—and stay on for additional training. Once the word gets out that a shop is using IE, other excellent new people will be attracted to the company.

How does an organization position itself to gain the advantages Information Engineering has to offer? Success begins with a commitment to IE implementation.

Institutionalizing IE

Information Engineering represents a tremendous shift from the way firms have gone about building information systems. Its adoption requires

IS professionals to change the way they do their jobs, and the mere suggestion that there might be a better way to develop applications is met with great opposition. After all, "The IS department has been building systems successfully for a long time without this IE stuff!" A well-rounded strategy for institutionalizing IE is in order. Here are the components of a good strategy.

1. Awareness program. IS managers knows that IE is a great way to build systems. But development staffs may not. Take time to raise staff awareness of Information Engineering before starting an IE-based project.

Develop a presentation that introduces the staff to the disciplines of IE. Present the materials in a nonthreatening way. Use old, familiar terms to explain new ones. Similarities between the old and the new will help staff members make the mental transition needed to understand the essence of IE.

A typical IE overview will take two to three hours and can be done several times during a year. Give each attendee a copy of the slides for reference. Distribute to attendees a flyer that summarizes key points brought out in the presentation. The IE awareness program will give each IS employee the opportunity to understand the firm's methodology direction.

2. IE task force. Establish a task force comprised of project managers, data administrators, and development personnel, soon after the completion of the IE awareness sessions. It should be chaired by the person responsible for introducing IE to the firm.

The charge of the task force is to oversee IE implementation, but the driving force behind it is to involve IS developers in the process. IS managers want the use of IE to be contagious.

The task force will be involved in:

- Defining training needs,
- Determining consulting requirements, and
- Coordinating IE policy evolution.

No facet of the implementation should be excluded from the task force's domain.

3. Pilot project plan. Like every new tool or technique, IE needs a test run before full-blown implementation. Determining which project is ripe for an IE test drive is less important than recognizing piloting as a necessary step in the institutionalization process.

▼

IE COMES TO AMOCO CORPORATION

In 1986, Amoco Corporation (see Figure 6–12 for organization structure) recognized the need to establish a standard systems development methodology across the organization. Ray Bell, data administrator within the corporate Information Services Department, set out to find an approach that completely supported the project development life cycle, was business-oriented, and possessed specific stages and tasks that could be measured and monitored. He chose Information Engineering.

A corporate policy was developed and distributed in early 1987:

> The Information Engineering methodology, in conjunction with the Information Engineering Facility (a computer-aided systems engineering tool sold by Texas Instruments), will be the approved and required methodology and toolset for use in the systems development function.

The policy went on to state that the Data Administration function would migrate out to client organizations throughout Amoco Corporation to help divisions apply the methodology. Bell and his staff of eight went to work.

By late 1989, Information Engineering had burgeoned within Amoco. Bell's team had helped build several key applications using IE. For example, a plant operations system was built in Amoco Chemical; Amoco Oil developed a credit card system; and an IE-based strategy plan was established in the Amoco Production Company. IE was there to stay.

With hard work and perseverance, Amoco Corporation weathered the IE storm. Up-front activities—tool and methodology training, establishment of new divisional data administration and IE coordinator positions, and pilot projects' facilitation—were completed successfully. All there was left to do was to enjoy the benefits of standardized development.

Currently, Amoco is engaged in cross-divisional planning sessions that will result in a global enterprise model. When built, this model will be used to drive the systems development priorities of the firm. Ray Bell and his staff are overseeing its evolution.

Source: Ray Bell, "Implementing the Information Age at Amoco," Strategic Data and Planning Forum '89, sponsored by Barnett Data Systems, Washington, DC, April 4, 1989.

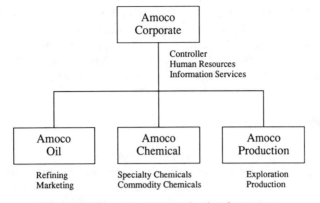

Figure 6–12. *Amoco's organizational structure*

The IE pilot project should be narrow in scope and implementable in three to six months. A project of any longer duration may not come to fruition. Longer projects tend to be postponed and cancelled far more frequently than those of shorter duration.

Regular monitoring of the pilot project will provide helpful insights into the trouble areas within IE. These insights are a valuable resource for defining training and consulting requirements.

4. Peer support program. The IE task force often sponsors an internal IE user group. Representatives from each IE project team comprise the user group. The group's biweekly meeting is a place where IE practitioners can bring their problems, share ideas, and determine solutions.

Once IE permeates the organization, the peer group will be the mechanism for resolving the data conflicts that arise when several development teams are building projects concurrently. The peer meeting facilitator will be responsible for identifying discrepancies across projects and driving project leaders to resolution.

A leading packaged goods company uses its IE coordination meetings to distribute updates in its standards and procedures documents and to notify project managers of upcoming IE training and seminar opportunities.

5. Policy creation and distribution. The creation and distribution of the Information Engineering policy is the last component of the institutionalization strategy. The policy will include a statement of company commitment to IE and will describe the major steps a project team should follow to conform to the standard.

As mentioned above, the IE task force will oversee the creation of the document and will coordinate the distribution of it to every member of IS. The policy goes out only under senior IS management's signature. There must be no doubt in anyone's mind that IE is the law!

Although there are no guarantees in life, the creation of an implementation strategy that addresses education, administration, and policy issues is sure to help the committed firm make IE work as intended. Awareness of the organizational impact IE has on an organization is another key aspect of gaining the advantages of the approach.

Organizational Impact

Anticipating the effect IE will have on a firm's development environment will help to smooth its transition to the approach. IS staff expectations must adjust as the infusion of new IE techniques transforms roles and responsibilities. The most typical changes are as follows.

New IS Positions

A fresh set of skills is necessary to create and manage the evolution of business, data, process, and enterprise models. Information engineers and enterprise model administrators (EMAs) are two new players on the IS team.

Descendants of programmer analysts, information engineers use IE techniques to determine user requirements and to specify systems designs. These professionals are senior developers who have mastered their craft and can act as methodology gurus to inexperienced project teams. Information engineers are good candidates for JAD facilitation and peer support representative roles.

Enterprise model administrators are typically members of the Data Administration or Database Administration staff. They have the responsibility of maintaining the enterprise model and will conduct design reviews, resolve data conflicts, and authorize access to the enterprise models. Enterprise Model Administration will chair the IE user group upon its inception.

One utilities company became so caught up with the idea of creating a new IS professional that it formed a "SWAT team" to act as internal IE consultants. The SWAT team is called in to bail out project managers who are having trouble applying the approach.

New User Roles

IE will not be successful without abundant user participation in systems analysis. Representatives from business areas must be involved in the creation of the IE models that support them. Business managers should take note of this trend and modify work schedules accordingly.

On the other hand, IS professionals accustomed to building information systems with minimum user input will have to adjust as well. They must recognize the need for forming partnerships with end users. Involving users in the awareness program and in the IE task force will facilitate the formation of these partnerships.

Focus on Design Standardization

Design standardization improves productivity. Information Systems professionals do better jobs when working from a standard set of specifications. Trouble arises when specifications differ among development teams. Confusion and uncertainty lead to mistakes.

Once each team begins to use IE development methods, database design and programming responsibilities become less challenging. Programmers focus on converting procedure models into programs and database designers focus on transforming data models into database systems.

The need to understand all the components of an application is minimized because of the quality of the design specifications. Programmers and designers have more opportunity to spend time perfecting their technical skills.

A Look Ahead

A well-established infrastructure has sprung up around IE and will continue to grow. CASE vendors have already jumped on the IE bandwagon. Established firms, like Knowledgeware and Texas Instruments, currently offer suites of technology that support the Information Engineering disciplines.

Consulting firms are responding to their clients' need for support as well. James Martin Associates and Pacific Information Management, Inc. are just two of the firms offering IE consulting and training services. The future holds more of the same, as industry giants like IBM begin to adopt IE terminology in their announcements of products, like AD/Cycle.

Availability of automation and consulting support will make the use of IE quite convenient in the future. So, too, will the improved availability of trained IE practitioners. As IE's popularity grows, we will see an influx of skilled professionals into the job market. In fact, "IE wars" will break out as companies vie to pirate experts from their competition.

University campuses will be a prime source of IE potential. Courses in the IE disciplines are beginning to become part of computer science curricula around the country. The Hartford Graduate Center, for example, offers a series of IE-related courses through its Professional Development Center. Firms may see the day when degrees are awarded in Information Engineering. After all, universities continue to form partnerships with industry and want their graduates to meet employer requirements.

The combination of these trends will eventually lead to industry standardization of IE, which will have significant impact on software vendors who market canned packages. These companies have to provide clients with the data and process models that underpin their product offerings. Clients, in turn, will make purchase decisions based on the content of the models.

Summary

Information Engineering will become the de-facto development standard of the 1990s. Firms are beginning to absorb the IE learning curve and to position themselves for managing the cultural revolution that takes place whenever change is introduced to an IS shop. As current trends continue, IE-based development will be the only approach for application building.

Key Points

1. Information Engineering (IE) is a family of data-driven analysis and design techniques that support the specification of automated systems.

2. IE is not a software engineering or project management methodology. It is made up of business modeling, data modeling, process modeling, and enterprise modeling disciplines.

3. Flexibility of maintenance, systems integration, and standardized development are the business drivers behind IE.

4. The benefits of IE include rapid design, lower cost, and improved IS staff retention and attraction. Organizational adjustments are required to gain these advantages.

5. An awareness program is one way to prepare a firm for the shift from current development practices to Information Engineering. Presentations and documentation highlight the program.

6. Task forces and peer support groups are formed to oversee the transition to IE. Peer support groups will become the mechanism for coordinating reusability of code and design.

7. New IS positions must be created, to fully utilize IE. The enterprise model administrator will manage enterprise model development.

Information engineers will take the place of senior analysts, assisting project teams in the application of IE techniques in development efforts.

8. Design standardization will simplify programming and database design, providing opportunities for professionals in those functions to continue to develop their technical expertise.

9. CASE vendors and consulting firms will make the move to IE much easier by offering methodology-specific automation and support.

10. Industry standardization of IE will revolutionize the software business. Software vendors will have to provide data and process models to clients.

References

1. James M. Kerr, "The Data-Driven Harvest," *Database Programming & Design,* May 1989, pp. 19–21.

7

Object Oriented Programming

That must be wonderful; I have no idea of what it means.

Molière, c.1650

This chapter introduces object oriented programming systems (OOPS), a new way for firms to craft program logic. OOPS bind code and data together into reusable modules that make information systems easy to modify and maintain.

Drawing an Analogy

In a March 1989 article, Lee Keough, senior editor of *Computer Decisions* magazine, drew an interesting parallel between object oriented systems and cubist art. He wrote, "If programming is an art, then the natural forebear of object oriented software design is the school of cubism" (1). What a wonderful analogy!

High analytic cubism, the most influential development in 20th-century art, is characterized by its assembly and reassembly of objects. A study of any vintage piece by Georges Braque or Pablo Picasso unveils a world of shapes bursting with excitement. (See Figure 7–1, Picasso's *Card Player*, for an example of the cubist art form.)

Like Picasso, who reused simple shapes to form new pieces of art, a programmer using object oriented techniques reuses code to form new applications. Figure 7–2 illustrates how existing objects can be combined to form new, more meaningful ones. Imagine each shape on the left of the figure as a chunk of data and code that is then combined to create an integrated system, similar to the bicycle on the right.

Object oriented programming focuses on building systems that reapply existing code chunks and program designs. We must come to grips

Figure 7-1. *PICASSO, Pablo.* Card Player.
Paris (winter 1913–14) Oil on canvas. 42¹/₂ × 35¹/₄. Collection, The Museum of Modern Art, New York. Acquired through the Lillie P. Bliss Bequest.

with this exciting new programming technique and determine where it fits into systems development.

A New Programming Paradigm

For years, IS has tried to build systems that were flexible and easy to modify. We've turned to third and fourth generation tools, like COBOL and Information Builder's FOCUS, for help. But the serial nature of these languages makes them extremely difficult to maintain. The logic is so

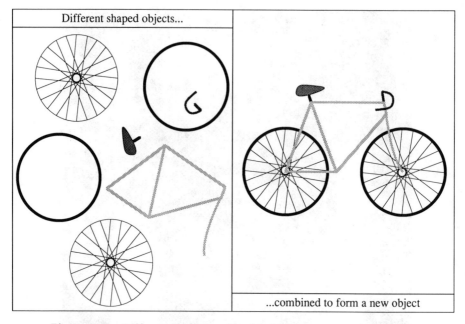

Different shaped objects...

...combined to form a new object

Figure 7-2. *Different objects combined to form a more meaningful one.*

interdependent with other code in the application that a seemingly simple program fix can take days to complete. A maintenance programmer has to examine each branch of an application program before implementing a change. If not done carefully, a one-line modification can bring an entire system to its knees.

Object oriented programming languages (OOPLs) change all that. OOPLs provide a way of integrating data definitions and processing rules into cohesive modules called objects. Each object in an object oriented programming system (OOPS) is a free-standing entity that can be combined with other objects to form a comprehensive application.

The maintenance burden is simplified in an OOPS environment because the programming logic is localized to the data it manipulates. An application change can be made to an object without affecting any other objects within the system. OOPLs avoid the programming nightmares that come with serial programs. A list of several prominent OOPL vendors appears in Figure 7-3.

At this point an in-depth explanation of OOPS terminology is in order. The differences between OOPLs and conventional languages can be somewhat esoteric without a strong foundation in the object oriented vernacular.

PRODUCT	VENDOR	TELEPHONE	PRICE
Actor	Whitewater Group	312-491-2370	$500
Advantage C++	Lifeboat Associates	914-332-4545	$500
C_Talk	CNS Corporation	612-944-0170	$150
C++	AT&T	201-221-2000	Call for more information
Eiffel	Interactive Software Engineering	805-685-1006	$2000-$9000
ExperCommon Lisp	Expertelligence	805-967-1797	$1000
Smalltalk 80	Parc Place Systems	415-859-1000	$1000
XLISP	Compuserve by: D.Betz	Compuserve ID 76704, 47	Free

Figure 7–3. *Prominent object oriented programming languages*
Source: *"Software Review,"* AI Expert, *January 1989, p. 70.*

Coming to Terms with OOPS

Like "nested if," "endless loop," and other terms in structured code systems, OOPS has its own phraseology that separates it from its predecessors. The following sections explain OOPS's key terms.

Objects

An OOPL's main ingredients, objects combine code and data definitions into cohesive modules that can be manipulated and meshed with other objects to form meaningful applications. Objects are the fodder used to feed object oriented systems (see Figure 7–4).

Encapsulation

In OOPS, objects are encapsulated (or encased) from each other. Because of encapsulation, objects exist and have meaning, without any relationships to other objects. An object oriented application is therefore easy to maintain and modify. Its objects can be retired or replaced without any interruption to the systems they comprise.

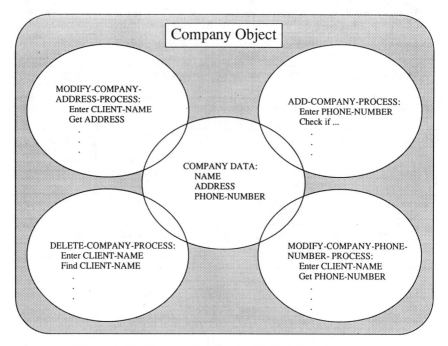

Figure 7-4. *The company object with its data and processes*

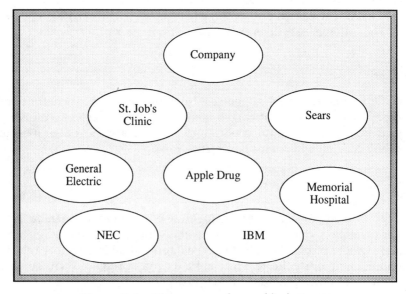

Figure 7-5. *The company class and its instances*

Classes and Instances

Objects can be grouped into classes—object categories that specify the data and process definitions for a particular object type. Each object within a class is called an instance. Instances will share common definitions.

Figure 7–4 for example, defines the company class. Each of its instances (presented in Figure 7–5) will possess client name, address, and phone number data, as well as common ADD, DELETE, and MODIFY logic.

Methods

The logic contained in an object is called a method. A method defines how data within an object can be manipulated. The ADD, DELETE, and MODIFY logic contained in Figure 7–4 are methods that determine how company data can be manipulated.

Messages

Methods are invoked by passing them the parameters that they need for execution. These parameters are called messages. Messages are passed between objects during program execution. Upon method invocation, a corresponding message may be produced that alters the content of one or more objects in the system.

The message in Figure 7–6 can be used to delete IBM from the list of instances presented in Figure 7–5. The message contains the target object name (IBM), the method to be invoked (DELETE-Company) and the argument (COMPANY = IBM).

Inheritance

Inheritance facilitates the reuse of previously defined objects. It allows objects to pass their attributes (methods and data definitions) on to other objects. Inheritance creates new objects out of old ones.

Class Hierarchies

Classes are grouped into class hierarchies to facilitate inheritance. The root of the hierarchy is called a parent. Lower levels within the hierarchy are called children. A parent can pass its attributes on to its children. Children can have their own attributes, and can inherit from children above them.

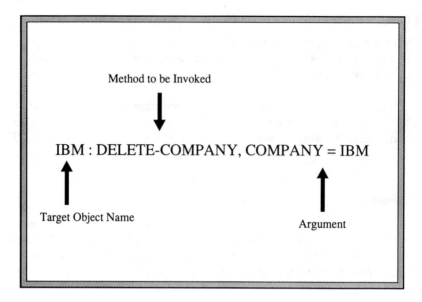

Figure 7-6   *A sample message used to invoke a method within an object oriented system*

Consider the class hierarchy presented in Figure 7–7. The parent object (company) contains the attributes (name, address, and phone number). The children (client and vendor) have inherited these attributes and even have some of their own (client contains total purchases, vendor contains volume discount).

What Does All This Mean?

OOPS means quicker systems development, for one thing. Inheritance turns each object into a valuable resource that can be reapplied in new development efforts. Picture a library full of reusable bundles of data and methods. When a new application is proposed, all that a development team would have to do is cull together the appropriate objects from the library. The object library in Figure 7–8, for example, contains six objects that are used time and again in the three systems shown in the diagram.

Because of the encapsulation feature of OOPS, a selected object can be refined to meet a system's particular processing need without any impact on other systems that use that object. The Vendor object, for example, appears in all three of the systems in Figure 7–8. Vendor may have different characteristics within these three applications, yet each can be traced back to the Vendor class defined in the object library.

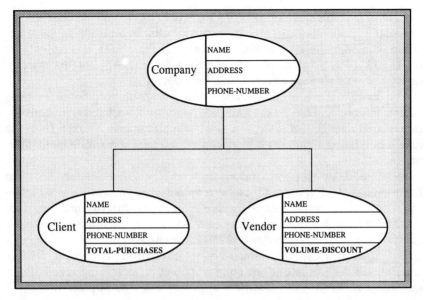

Figure 7-7. *Inheritance through a class hierarchy*

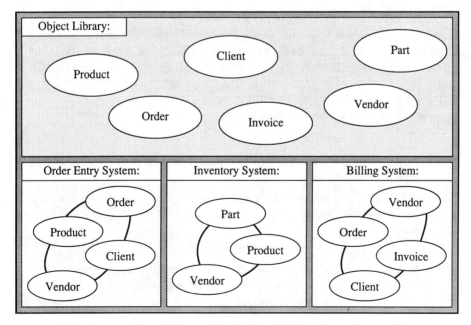

Figure 7-8. *Object library with objects culled together to form systems*

Ease of systems development isn't the only advantage of OOPS. Less expensive application maintenance also results. In addition to encapsulation, consider the benefit that comes with the ability to comfortably remove obsolete sections of code and data designs. Application maintenance becomes as easy as creating a new object.

The combination of inheritance and encapsulation helps systems evolve gracefully. The "freeze and fix" mentality associated with conventional languages (i.e., a system in need of maintenance is taken from the user while being repaired) is replaced with a real-time systems maintenance initiative.

OOPS adds up to a tremendous opportunity. Organizations that can harness these techniques will be better positioned to gain the productivity benefits that come with extensive systems modularity and program reusability. Applications that are easy to create and maintain can be competitive weapons in today's changing business climates.

But, there is a catch! We must create an environment where OOPLs can flourish. The simple adoption of an object oriented language will not guarantee success. A development approach must be in place that takes advantage of the strengths of object orientation.

The IE Connection

Chapter 6 focused on Information Engineering (IE), data-driven analysis and design methodology that is used to specify the data and processing requirements of a proposed system. Like OOPS, IE seeks to develop reusable code and design. It's only logical to draw a parallel between IE and object oriented programming. IE defines the "what" and OOPS defines the "how" of a development project.

As noted earlier, IE is composed of four interdependent analysis disciplines:

- Business modeling is used to determine the scope and boundary of a project proposal;
- Data modeling is used to discover the data required to support the business model;
- Process modeling is used to document the ADD, DELETE, and MODIFY rules for the data defined in the data model; and
- Enterprise modeling is used to create a repository of previously defined data and process models that promotes the reuse of application programs and database designs.

These disciplines can be employed to define the objects and methods of an OOPS application.

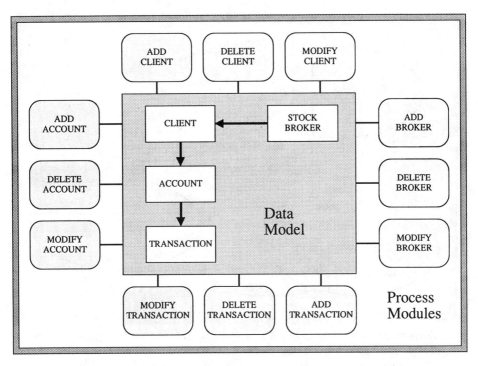

Figure 7–9. *A data model and its corresponding process models*

Figure 7–9, for example, shows a sample data model and its corresponding process modules (an ADD, DELETE, and MODIFY module for each entity defined in the data model). These models were used as specifications for the object oriented system represented in Figure 7–10.

The objects in Figure 7–10 contain the same data definition and process logic as the IE models. During OOPS implementation, the data and process (or methods) were bundled together into objects. The objects were then grouped into the system shown.

These examples illustrate how data model entities can be converted into objects and how process modules can be converted into methods. But how does IE promote reusability? How does it support inheritance? These are important aspects of object oriented applications.

Reusability Through Enterprise Modeling

Enterprise modeling iteratively integrates previously defined data models into a composite model. The enterprise model can be used by project design teams as a source of data and process definitions. A portion of the enterprise model can be subset for use by development teams at any

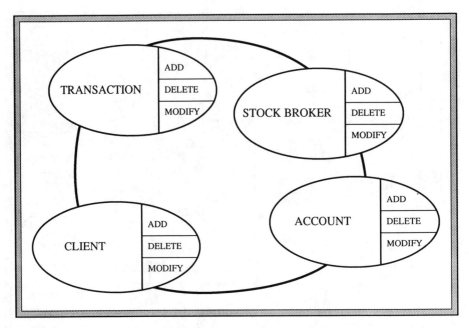

Figure 7-10. *An object oriented system using data and process models defined through Information Engineering*

time. Once completed, resultant data models are merged with the enterprise model, helping it to evolve (2).

The enterprise model serves the same function for systems analysts as an object library does for OOPS programmers. Programmers can look in an object library (where all objects within a system are stored) for objects to use in new applications. An enterprise model is the place where all data entities and process models are stored. Systems analysts can look there for data and processes to use in new development efforts.

Figure 7-11 illustrates the point. The enterprise model facilitates data and process model reusability through its merging and subsetting functions; the object library drives object reuse through inheritance and encapsulation. It makes sense to combine these two powerful concepts (enterprise modeling and object libraries) to form a new development environment in which OOPS can prosper.

Tying the Knot

Object oriented programming begs for a development approach that can help developers identify the objects that their firms care about. Information

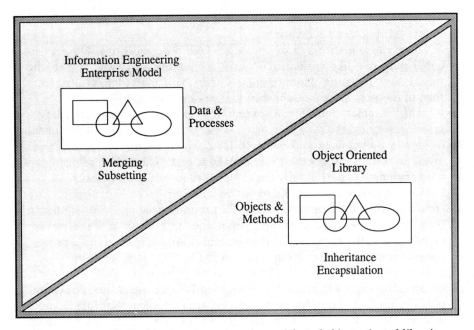

Figure 7–11. *Similarities between enterprise models and object oriented libraries*

Engineering is an extensive design methodology that can be applied to uncover an organization's information requirements. IE should be the development approach of choice among OOPS shops.

However, a methodology link isn't the only element missing from the OOPs arena. There are several weak spots in today's object oriented products. These weaknesses must be improved before OOPLs can explode in the marketplace.

Improvement Areas

Where are the OOPS-related programming tools, training programs, and interfaces?

Finding tools that complement an object oriented language is extremely difficult. A firm that wants to embark on OOPS must be willing to forego the bells and whistles that come with conventional programming environments. Object oriented development aids, fourth generated languages, recovery tools, and database management systems are few and far between.

The absence of these tools may prohibit organizations from achieving the productivity gains they might expect. Commercial programmers must build the toolsets they need to be productive, while waiting for OOPL vendors to heed the call. As more time is spent building tools, less time is spent building business systems.

There's also a shortage of packaged OOPS applications. Object oriented plug-ins, like spreadsheets and accounting software, are among the missing. A strong commitment to OOPS is difficult to make, knowing that, in a pinch, store-bought solutions are not available.

As if the lack of tools is not enough, the scarcity of trained OOPL programmers muddies the water more. Most of the available OOPS talent resides in universities and research labs, which means companies must invest in training to get their staffs up to speed. (The notion of hiring an object oriented expert to rally the troops is presently impractical.)

One Chicago-based company spent nearly two years trying to find someone who could manage an OOPS programming group it wanted to form. Finding no candidate with experience in both OOPS and project management, the company's management finally coaxed an area professor who had been conducting research in OOPS to join the firm.

Currently, only a handful of consulting firms offer OOPS training. Because the supply is limited, training tends to be expensive. For example, Technology Transfer Institute of Santa Monica, California, now offers a three-day OOPS seminar for $995 per person. It may not seem like a lot of money, but it can certainly add up when 200 programmers need training.

The interface issue represents another OOPS roadblock. Object oriented languages don't work well with conventional software products. Their file structures and internals are just plain different. Extensions must be made. How does a firm reconcile its existing software-base with this new programming paradigm? Should vendors be required to extend their products to accommodate OOPS? There are no easy answers.

These problems all boil down to infrastructure. Object oriented languages are available but the software tools, training programs, and appropriate interfaces are not. An object oriented infrastructure must emerge that supports object orientation.

Today, OOPS is where relational technology was a few years ago. Keep in mind that relational database tools were scarce back in the 1970s when the concept was pioneered; today, such tools are plentiful. Time was needed to let technology catch up with concept. OOPS needs some time, too.

In the Future

The time is coming when the basic facilities and services required for the growth and functioning of object orientation will exist. Vendors will

▼

OBJECT ORIENTED DBMS: THE NEXT FRONTIER

Just as relational database technology takes its place as corporate America's preferred database model, a new challenge is emerging—object oriented database management systems (or OODBMSs). OODBMSs manage objects the way relational databases manage tables. The differences between the two lie in the types of information that can be stored within them. Relational tools store character strings and integers. Object oriented databases store text, images, and graphics. An entire relational database can be viewed as an object within an OODBMS.

Although still an emerging technology (see Figure 7–12 for a list of selected OODBMS vendors), object oriented databases promise to revolutionize the way companies manage data. Just picture a world in which all the information that an organization cares about is stored in a single database.

Need to see the new product design? A quick database query, and a three-dimensional model appears on the screen. Realize that a critical part is missing? Check the database for its projected delivery date. Hasn't been ordered? Place the order.

The world could be that simple with the right technology.

Today's object oriented database tools still lack a few essential ingredients, like the precision of a mathematical model (or standard), ties to conventional languages (COBOL, FORTRAN, and so on), and efficient storage capabilities. However, significant research underway at places like the University of California at Berkeley and AT&T Bell Laboratories should lead to some practical solutions to these outstanding problems.

It won't be long before object oriented database systems establish a niche in the DBMS marketplace. Other technology vendors are sure to enter the growing OODBMS business, heightening competition and giving relational products a run for their money. Our firms will only benefit through the availability of better tools.

---

undoubtedly begin to develop the tools necessary to complement OOPLs. Object oriented technology is still new, but it's sure to improve in the coming years. Object oriented database systems are already beginning to emerge and to take their positions alongside relational tools.

Some off-the-shelf applications exist today. Products like Vision, a financial management system sold by Innovative Systems Techniques, Inc. of Newton, Massachusetts, have gained in popularity. Copies of the software have been sold to several leading investment banks and brokerage houses during the past few years (3).

The time will come when object oriented packages will flood the market. Software houses can benefit as much as we can, through object

COMPANY	PRODUCT	LOCATION
Servio Logic Development Corp.	Gemstone	Beaverton, OR
Ontologic Inc.	Vbase	Billerica, MA
Symbolics Inc.	Statice	Cambridge, MA
Graphael Inc.	Gbase	Waltham, MA

Figure 7-12. *Object oriented database vendors*

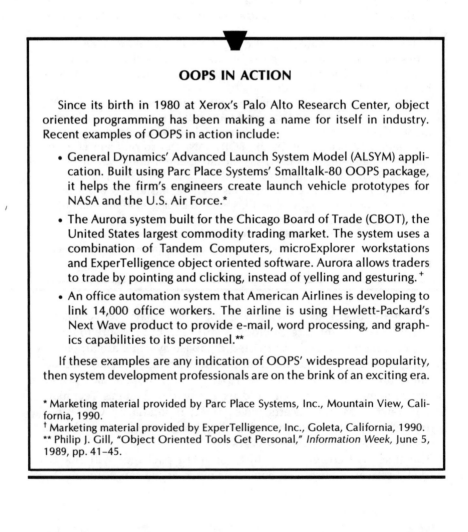

OOPS IN ACTION

Since its birth in 1980 at Xerox's Palo Alto Research Center, object oriented programming has been making a name for itself in industry. Recent examples of OOPS in action include:

- General Dynamics' Advanced Launch System Model (ALSYM) application. Built using Parc Place Systems' Smalltalk-80 OOPS package, it helps the firm's engineers create launch vehicle prototypes for NASA and the U.S. Air Force.*

- The Aurora system built for the Chicago Board of Trade (CBOT), the United States largest commodity trading market. The system uses a combination of Tandem Computers, microExplorer workstations and ExperTelligence object oriented software. Aurora allows traders to trade by pointing and clicking, instead of yelling and gesturing.+

- An office automation system that American Airlines is developing to link 14,000 office workers. The airline is using Hewlett-Packard's Next Wave product to provide e-mail, word processing, and graphics capabilities to its personnel.**

If these examples are any indication of OOPS' widespread popularity, then system development professionals are on the brink of an exciting era.

* Marketing material provided by Parc Place Systems, Inc., Mountain View, California, 1990.
† Marketing material provided by ExperTelligence, Inc., Goleta, California, 1990.
** Philip J. Gill, "Object Oriented Tools Get Personal," *Information Week*, June 5, 1989, pp. 41–45.

orientation. Vendors will spend the time needed to build software aids because not only can they use them, but they can sell them.

The second wave of OOPS (when an abundance of object oriented programming tools are available) will set a new standard for software packaging. Companies will be able to buy an application and the objects that underpin it. Consider the possibilities:

- Enhanced ability to extend canned applications to meet specific user needs;
- Unprecedented capability to integrate store-bought packages with a firm's existing systems architecture;
- New opportunity to build related applications out of newly acquired ones.

Won't they be a change for the better!

Further, there will be a flock of OOPS developers in years to come. Universities are beginning to graduate Smalltalk and C++ programmers. A firm that is serious about adopting object oriented programming techniques can stack its decks with college-grad new hires. When well managed, these young turks will make a fine contribution.

The learning curve expense will diminish as more vendors enter the marketplace. Expensive seminars, often the only source of OOPS training, will give way to on-site education offered by local consulting firms that have jumped on the OOPS bandwagon.

In time, conventional tools will be extended to accommodate OOPLs. Figure 7–13 lists several vendors that are planning to build interfaces between OOPS and relational database systems. As this trend continues, we can easily foresee an environment in which object oriented tools and standard software comfortably coexist.

COMPANY	LOCATION	PLANS
Informix Software Inc.	Menlo Park, CA	To support unstructured data types in RDBMS
Sybase Inc.	Berkeley, CA	To support unstructured data types in RDBMS
Data General Corporation	Westboro, MA	To develop object oriented front-end that makes calls to relational databases
Intellicorp Corporation	Mountain View, CA	To generate SQL code that extracts data from RDBMS for use in KEE
Hewlett-Packard Company	Palo Alto, CA	To develop an object oriented DBMS that can query a RDBMS

Figure 7–13. *Vendors planning to build interfaces between OOPS and relational technology*

Summary

Object oriented programming will bring great change to the development shops that adopt its use. OOPS concepts like objects, methods, encapsulation, and inheritance will require time to be fully appreciated. Programmers will have to unlearn all that they know about structured code, to work within an OOPS framework. However, the benefit will be worth the toil.

Object oriented languages don't come with all the "fixin's" just yet. But, in time, an entire infrastructure will build up around object orientation. Once fully evolved, OOPLs will be the cornerstone of a new development environment that is rich in reusable code and easily maintained systems.

Until then, we've got our work cut out for us. Learning curves must be absorbed and strategies devised that fold OOPS into the workplace. IS personnel should do all that they can to position their firms for the object oriented future that awaits us.

Key Points

1. Object oriented programming systems (OOPS) represent a new systems development paradigm. The concept focuses on building reusable code and designs.

2. Objects bind code and data together to form modules. These modules can be combined through OOPS techniques to form systems.

3. Systems maintenance is simplified in an OOPS environment because logic is stored with the data it manipulates.

4. Encapsulation allows objects to be retired or replaced without any interruption to other objects in a system.

5. Inheritance facilitates the use of previously defined objects by allowing them to pass their attributes on to other objects.

6. Parallels exist between OOPS and Information Engineering (IE). IE should be used to define specifications for object oriented implementations.

7. Combining enterprise modeling with object libraries is a necessary step in establishing a development environment that leverages object orientation to its fullest.

8. OOPS-related programming tools, training programs, and interfaces to existing application software are needed for OOPS to grow.

9. The next few years will show tremendous advances in OOPS infrastructure. OOPS facilities and services will emerge.

10. Object oriented database management systems (OODBMS) will be the next database frontier. Their ability to manage diverse data types (images, graphics, text, and so on) will provide OODBMS vendors with a niche in the DBMS marketplace.

11. Firms should begin to prepare themselves now, for the object oriented world that lies ahead.

References

1. Lee Keough, "Objective: Better Software," *Computer Decisions,* March 1989, pp. 37–40.

2. James M. Kerr, "Corporate Data Models Flourish from the Bottom Up," *Computerworld,* May 11, 1987, pp. 71–78.

3. David Stamps, "Taking An Objective Look," *Datamation,* May 15, 1989, pp. 45–48.

8

CASE Technology

Because it's there!
George Mallory, 1923

There's a new technology in town! It's called CASE. We mentioned it briefly in Chapter 2. CASE stands for computer-aided systems engineering. CASE software offers automated support to programmers and system designers. It does for application developers what the electronic spreadsheet did for accountants: It helps them perform their tasks faster and more effectively than ever before.

CASE technology conjures up different images in the minds of Information Systems personnel. Some think of the workstation components that are used to graphically depict data and process specifications. Some think of CASE as a near magical tool that, when invoked, generates bug-free code and database designs. The fact is, there's a collection of applications and together they make up CASE.

Figure 8–1 lists the types of applications that CASE encompasses. Product features and functionality will vary by vendor. Some CASE tools are considered stand-alone and perform a single function; others

Data Model Diagramming Aids	Systems Testing Facilities
Process Model Diagramming Aids	Reverse Engineering Tools
Code Generation Packages	Re-engineering Tools
Database Generation Packages	Design Repositories

Figure 8–1. *Various facets of CASE technology*

146

are integrated and provide a breadth of project life cycle support. Regardless of the architecture, the basic thrust remains the same: CASE helps systems developers build better systems.

The CASE Development Environment

Imagine a systems development environment in which a project manager can log-on to a workstation, review the company's existing systems designs, identify portions of those designs that can be used by a project team, press a button, and generate an application for users. It seems futuristic, but CASE provides such a mechanism.

A full-function CASE architecture is presented in Figure 8–2. Not every CASE tool is as comprehensive. However, companies should strive to establish a CASE environment that is comprised of front-end, back-end, and encyclopedia technology. These three tiers automate the project development life cycle.

The front-end tier of the architecture is made up of workstation tools that support the creation of data and process models. The encyclopedia

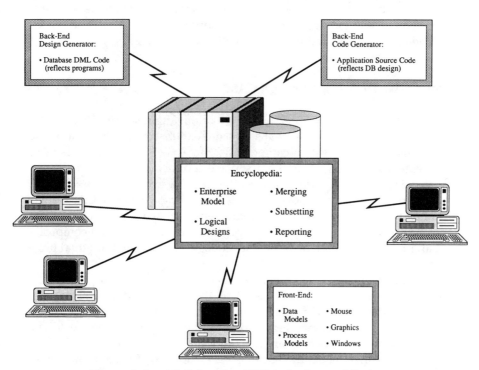

Figure 8–2. *A full-function CASE technology architecture*

tier is a mainframe-based tool that manages the evolution of the enterprise model and is a central storage space for all workstation designs. Code and database generators comprise the back end of the architecture. Application generators convert data and process models into databases and structured program logic.

As Figure 8–2 indicates, the workstation tools use mouse, graphics, and windowing technology to make the front-end toolsets easy to use. Ease of use is an important CASE feature. It's great to be able to generate applications automatically, but the tools must be easy to use or developers will reject them.

The encyclopedia, the core of a CASE architecture, takes advantage of the mainframe's processing power. Its shareable workspace helps project design teams integrate system components that were individually developed across several workstations. Project managers can coordinate the work of each of their analysts through the encyclopedia. Capabilities are built into the tool so models can be merged, subsetted, and reported on.

The back-end tools reside on the mainframe as well. Data and process models are passed to the generators through the encyclopedia. The encyclopedia and generators work hand-in-hand to ensure that generated applications perform optimally. Generated designs are modified by changing the underlying data and process models back at the workstation. Enhanced models are sent to the mainframe where they are regenerated and implemented in the production environment.

Enterprise Modeling Through CASE

As discussed in the chapter on Information Engineering (Chapter 6), enterprise modeling is the means by which an IS organization can reuse previously defined system components. Since CASE technology is used to create the components in the first place, it only makes sense to manage enterprise model evolution through the CASE encyclopedia.

Figure 8–3 illustrates how enterprise modeling works in a CASE environment. The encyclopedia is subdivided into two logical levels. The enterprise level possesses the enterprise model (an integrated composite of all project models). The project level possesses all the individual project models.

Project teams develop designs at their workstations and promote finalized models to the project level of the encyclopedia. Each project team uses the code and design generators to transform their models into applications. Once completed, copies of the models are moved to the enterprise level where they are merged with the enterprise model.

The enterprise model in Figure 8–3 is comprised of three project data models. Enterprise model data is shared by new development projects

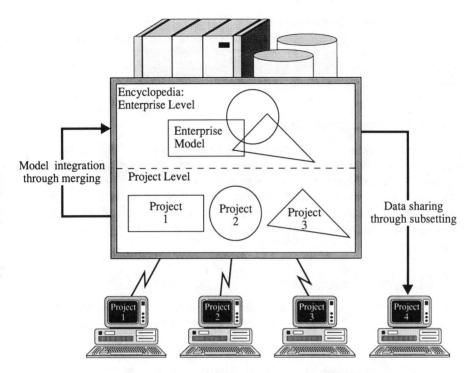

Figure 8–3. *Enterprise modeling through an encyclopedia*

through a subset feature in the encyclopedia. Project 4 in the figure, for example, can use any portion of the enterprise model by identifying and subsetting pertinent data constructs. Once Project 4 is complete, it will be promoted to the encyclopedia and eventually merged with the enterprise model.

CASE technology's merging and subsetting features help project teams reapply portions of existing systems and thereby leverage past development investments. However, enterprise modeling isn't the only benefit that comes with the implementation of CASE technology.

Benefits of CASE Technology

It's easy to see that an automated development environment will improve the level of service IS can provide its companies. Time requirements, systems quality, and development costs are the measures by which IS is judged. For example, Royal Insurance of Charlotte, N.C., acquired the Information Engineering Workbench from Knowledgeware, Inc. and began to achieve phenomenal results. Karl Kerschner, a research consultant at the firm, said Royal cut 30–50 percent off of every project that used the tool (1).

CASE helps IS raise the grade by accomplishing several tasks, as described in the following sections.

Reducing Development Time

The time it takes to build systems is reduced when developers use CASE technology to define requirements and generate applications. The up-front analysis time is put to good use when data and process models are converted into databases and programs with a click of a mouse. CASE helps to speed-up delivery of critical applications to the business community, by automatically generating code from system specifications.

Reducing Maintenance Time

CASE-generated systems can be readily enhanced and modified by letting the technology do the work. Systems specifications are self-documenting when defined through CASE technology. CASE tools provide reports and graphics, which serve as adequate documentation. A maintenance programmer can access the design documentation through the tools interface and view all the information that exists about a particular system.

Programs that need mending can be changed by redefining the process models that underpin them. New functionality can be introduced to existing systems by creating new process models and generating new programs. CASE helps us to rapidly adjust systems to meet changes in business direction.

Improving Communications

A communications gap exists between systems development and end user personnel. Often, the systems delivered to users aren't quite the ones they requested; something gets lost between business specifications and systems implementation. CASE narrows the communications gap by providing the means of representing user requirements diagrammatically through a front-end tool.

When Constitution Health Network (CHN) of North Haven, Connecticut, began its first CASE project, Al Mignone, a vice president of planning and development, got excited. Mignone immediately assigned one of his people to the project. The team of IS and user personnel brought the system in six months ahead of schedule. Now every project at CHN is built jointly (2).

Improving Project Management

Very large projects are often developed by decomposing them into smaller, implementable components. The integration of these components can become a nightmare without a framework in place that helps to coordinate each development effort. CASE technology keeps track of system components as they evolve, simplifying the burden of managing large systems integration.

Improving Application Quality

Rigorous development techniques improve the quality of resultant systems. CASE's built-in error detection prohibits practitioners from interposing inconsistencies into their designs, ensuring application reliability. CASE helps to build better systems by introducing rigor into the design process.

When Cytrol Portable Data Corporation's development staff grew to 135, Hank Childers, manager of advanced software engineering, knew it was time for a change. He brought CASE tools into the group, to introduce some discipline to the Edina, Minnesota-based software house. Now, all of Cytrol's code is built through CASE (3).

Enhancing Job Satisfaction

CASE is a "hot" technology. Nearly every systems developer has heard of it. Aggressive, forward-thinking staff members eagerly await CASE implementation, so they can learn it and get a first-hand appreciation of its capabilities. CASE helps retain valued employees—professionals who might otherwise leave, seeking exposure to advanced technologies.

Lowering Costs

Over the long haul, all these benefits add up to lower costs in building and maintaining systems. Time is money and plenty of it is saved when firms quicken the generation of code and designs, better manage project integration, and improve systems quality and documentation. CASE lowers costs by saving time and improving IS's ability to deliver the right systems to a demanding user community (see the Barton Group Survey on page 156).

Evaluation and Acquisition

As mentioned earlier, there are a myriad of CASE offerings in the marketplace (see Figure 8–4 for a partial list of CASE products and vendors).

PRODUCT	VENDOR	DESCRIPTION	PRICE
CASE 2000 Design Aid	Nastec Corporation 313-353-3300	Process and data modeling toolset	Contact vendor for further information
Corvision	Cortex Corporation 617-894-7000	Provides tools for converting specifications into systems	$50,000
Excellerator	Index Technology 617-491-2100	PC-based analysis and design aid	Contact vendor for further information
4-Front	Holland Systems 313-995-9595	An integrated set of tools for systems development and design	Contact vendor for further information
Information Engineering Facility	Texas Instruments 214-575-4404	An integrated set of analysis, design and construction tools	$90,000 and up
Information Engineering Workbench	Knowledgeware, Inc. 404-231-8575	Modularized set of analysis, design and construction tools	$10,000 and up
Life Cycle Productivity System	American Management Systems, Inc. 703-841-606	An integrated set of tools for systems development and project management	$175,000 to $275,000
Netron/CAP Development Center	Netron, Inc. 416-636-8333	Custom application generator for IBM, DEC and Wang environments	Contact vendor for further information
PACBASE	CGI Systems, Inc. 800-PAC-1866	Full life cycle automation toolset driven from centralized dictionary	$20,000 to $100,000
Telon	Pansophic Systems 312-572-6000	COBOL code generator for IBM mainframes	$130,000 to $285,000

Figure 8-4. *A partial list of CASE vendors*
Source: *Data Sources,* Vol. II. New York: Ziff-Davis Publishing Co., 1989.

IS management is constantly inundated with marketing brochures that tout the strength of one product or another. How do they know which tools to consider? IS must establish a minimum set of CASE requirements before evaluating product offerings.

Figure 8–5 lists some questions to consider when defining CASE needs. It's important to know where the tool will be placed organizationally, on what platform it will run, and the amount of financial resources that will be made available for CASE acquisition. The time may not be right for CASE, if IS lacks the money or human resources needed to manage it.

Issues regarding system design methodologies, productivity measurements, and complementary toolsets must also be addressed. The introduction of the wrong CASE tool is worse than having none at all. Companies must be sure that the products they select fit in the existing environment. Otherwise, CASE software may become dust-ridden shelfware.

Besides the obvious logistics, IS managers who are interested in CASE should ponder some of the organizational subtleties that may influence the outcome of a CASE implementation in their firm. Knowing how developers are evaluated, and anticipating resistances to the technology, may provide opportunities to better position their CASE recommendation.

1. Who will manage the implementation of CASE within the firm?

2. Do any budgetary constraints exist? Will they have an effect on software acquisition this year?

3. What is the firm's technology platform? What hardware and operating system environments are used in the organization?

4. How well conceived is the development environment? Is methodology and life cycle training available to all personnel?

5. Are there productivity standards in place? Are they achieved?

6. What other tools do developers use?

7. How are developers evaluated? Can CASE be tied to yearly objectives?

8. What is the firm's stance on consulting support?

9. How will CASE be piloted?

10. What resistances to CASE can be expected? From whom?

Figure 8–5. *Questions to consider when defining CASE needs*

CASE Evaluation Committee

After the implementation questions are answered, a CASE evaluation committee should be formed. The committee should be made up of five or six individuals from the IS shop. Data administration, database administration, and project development representatives must be included. They will be the staff groups most affected by a CASE acquisition.

If possible, invite one or two of the individuals who might resist CASE to participate on the committee. Those who have the greatest influence within the company are especially important to harness. Committee participation heightens awareness and can change sour attitudes toward CASE.

The committee should follow the steps to software acquisition outlined in Chapter 2 (see Figure 2–6). The group's first major deliverable will be the establishment of evaluation criteria. It's important for the firm to decide what it's looking for in a CASE toolset. Once the criteria are established, each can be ranked by order of importance and given a relative weighting factor. An evaluation form, like the one in Figure 8–6, should be developed as a reference point when examining vendor offerings.

The form in Figure 8–6 is divided into eight major sections. Vendor and product information is at the top of the form, a discretionary rating factor is at the bottom. The sections in the body of the form are broken down by: front-end tools, back-end tools, encyclopedia, technical platform, vendor rating, and customer rating.

Each product evaluated can be rated on this 1000-point scale. Critical criteria are given a weight of 35; less important features are weighted at 5 or 15. The form provides a place to measure customer feedback as well. Up to three current users of the tool can be surveyed for their reaction to the product. A discretionary rating allows the individual committee member to fold personal taste and instincts into the evaluation.

Once all the candidate tools are reviewed and rated, the committee will make a final decision and negotiate the acquisition of the selected CASE product. Before the tool is installed, however, the firm should have a pilot project defined that will act as a test for the technology.

Piloting CASE

The optimal pilot project requires a short period of time to complete and involves the development of a nonmission critical application. A project that can be wrapped up in three to six months and is of relative importance to the business (but not critical to a firm's success) makes an excellent CASE pilot candidate. Projects like personnel management or

CASE Technology
Evaluation Form

Date: _____   Rating: _____

Product Name: _____   Contact Person:_____
Vendor Name: _____   Telephone Number:_____

Front-End Tools:		Back-End Tools:	
Data Model	____ of 35	Code Generation	____ of 35
Process Model	____ of 35	Design Generation	____ of 35
Model X-Reference	____ of 35	Screen Writing	____ of 35
Graphics	____ of 35	Report Writing	____ of 35
Flexibility	____ of 15	Code Efficiency	____ of 35
Reporting	____ of 15	Integrated Testing	____ of 15
Mouse	____ of 5	Code Portability	____ of 5
Windowing	____ of 5	**Sub-Total**	**____ of 195**
Sub-Total	**____ of 180**		
		Technical Platform:	
Encyclopedia:		IBM Workstation	____ of 35
Model Merging	____ of 35	DOS	____ of 35
Model Subsetting	____ of 35	IBM Mainframe	____ of 15
Consistency Checking	____ of 35	MVS	____ of 15
Versioning	____ of 15	OS/2	____ of 5
Security	____ of 15	Other: _____	____ of 5
Reporting	____ of 15	_____	
Model -to-Design		_____	
X-Reference	____ of 15		
Sub-Total	**____ of 165**	**Sub-Total**	**____ of 110**

Vendor Specific:		Customer Feedback:		
			Great	Fair
Reputation	____ of 35			
Support	____ of 35	1. _____	____	____
Training	____ of 35	2. _____	____	____
Price	____ of 35	3. _____	____	____
Customer Base	____ of 5			
Sub-Total	**____ of 145**	**Sub-Total**	**____ of 105**	

Discretionary:			
Sub-Total	**____ of 100**	**Total:**	**____ of 1000**

Figure 8–6. *A CASE evaluation form*

▼

THE BARTON GROUP SURVEY

In 1989, the Barton Group, Inc., an IS consulting and training group in Andover, Massachusetts, conducted a survey of CASE users. More than 100 project managers and CASE practitioners from 55 firms participated in the study. The focus was to determine the effect of front-end CASE tools (those supporting analysis and design) on successful projects.

Some key findings from the Barton Group survey appear in Figure 8–7. It's apparent from these results that CASE contributed to the quality and timeliness of project deliverables, improved development team productivity and communication, and enhanced IS's ability to meet user needs.

It is interesting that none of the responses to the key questions (see Figure 8–7) broke the fourth quartile. This implies that CASE played a role in project improvements but was not the sole reason for stated gains. Factors like a team's experience in business, methodology, and development also affect project success.

The Barton Group summarized that:

> To improve productivity, the organization and culture must change. If the goal is to produce systems more quickly and productively, addressing the environmental factors . . . is probably the best approach. To produce systems with the same effort, but higher quality of the design and documentation, the best approach seems to be the use and enforcement of structured methods with CASE and JAD.

This conclusion is compelling, given the survey's focus on CASE technology's front-end. However, a study that would investigate the productivity gains of back-end tools, like code generators, might show a more significant productivity benefit.

Even so, the Barton Group's survey makes it difficult to argue against the idea that CASE offers an advantage over manual development approaches. Their findings legitimize the notion that CASE, when backed by an enforced methodology, produces results.

Source: The Barton Group, "Survey of CASE Users," Andover, MA, 1989.

office supply management systems are preferred over money management or product development applications.

Once a project is selected, one of the project leaders from the CASE evaluation committee should be assigned project management responsibility. After all, committee members will understand CASE capabilities better than others who are not involved in product evaluation. A

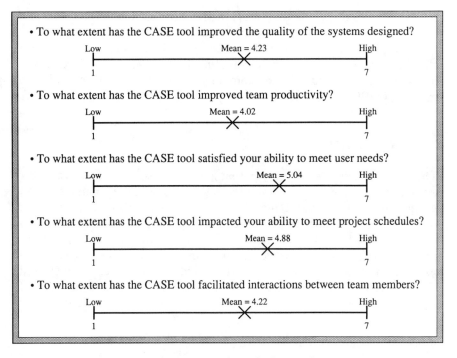

• To what extent has the CASE tool improved the quality of the systems designed?

Low   Mean = 4.23   High
1   7

• To what extent has the CASE tool improved team productivity?

Low   Mean = 4.02   High
1   7

• To what extent has the CASE tool satisfied your ability to meet user needs?

Low   Mean = 5.04   High
1   7

• To what extent has the CASE tool impacted your ability to meet project schedules?

Low   Mean = 4.88   High
1   7

• To what extent has the CASE tool facilitated interactions between team members?

Low   Mean = 4.22   High
1   7

Figure 8-7. *Key questions from the Barton Group survey*

committee member can drive the team to results by knowing how to avoid technology limitations.

A staff of developers should be placed on the project and provided proper training. Consultants, already knowledgeable in the tool's use, can be used as well. There's nothing wrong with a little "hand holding" while the development staff is absorbing the product's learning curve.

Besides managing the development effort, the pilot's project manager must also continually perform the following tracking aspects of the pilot:

• Assess the cost savings associated with the project;
• Define guidelines for using the tool;
• Determine whether the tool lives up to expectations;
• Estimate training requirements.

These findings should be regularly reported to the evaluation committee for its review and action.

If the product runs amok and the tool proves to be less functional in practice than in theory, the company should return the tool for a complete refund. There's no reason to be stuck with a product that doesn't fit users' needs. There's always time to examine another tool.

If the pilot is successful, and the tool is deemed viable, the company should examine the infrastructural issues that underpin CASE technology's success or failure in the company. Provisions must be made for ongoing CASE support and nurturing.

Infrastructural Issues

The introduction of a technology that generates code and manages project modeling may be very threatening to development managers and programmers. They may believe that CASE tools will replace them on the organization chart. Be prepared to address the issue.

It's true that a fully functional CASE environment will require less programming expertise. However, programming personnel aren't eliminated. In fact, programmers are motivated to become better analysts and CASE practitioners. CASE doesn't mean staffs get thinner; it means that more work gets done.

CASE Management Group

A CASE management group should be formed to soften the culture shock and manage CASE implementation. The CASE group can be part of a data management area, a development center, or a separate group within applications development. (See Figure 8–8 for possible organizational designs.)

The CASE management group charter should include the sponsoring of CASE awareness sessions. The group can aim these sessions at the systems development community as a way to promote the benefits of CASE while dispelling any rumors about staff reductions. Session attendees should walk away knowing that their roles may change but their jobs are secure.

Besides the awareness sessions, CASE management personnel will have to document and publish CASE guidelines and standards for their firm. The standards document should include elements like naming conventions, operating procedures, and review requirements. Every systems developer should be presented a copy for reference.

Further, the CASE management group should coordinate biweekly meetings among users of the CASE toolset. Similar to the IE project coordinators' meeting described in Chapter 6, the CASE project review meeting provides a forum for CASE users from within the firm to get together with their fellow developers and discuss issues, concerns, and successes.

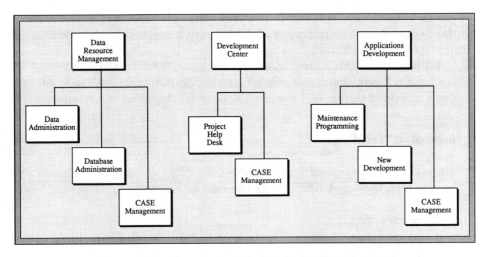

Figure 8–8. *Organizational designs for CASE management*

In time, the CASE management group may participate in systems planning within the company. Technological advances, like enterprise modeling and application generation, should be folded into the strategic plan. Business leaders must be exposed to the potential that CASE promises, so that they can drive its use and foster its growth within the concern.

Training Requirements

Every company feels the need to expand the training of systems development and user personnel. Programmers and designers must be taught how to use the tools, and users must be shown the importance of participating in application development efforts.

Training departments should offer CASE toolset training on a regular basis. Project managers who are just starting out in CASE must be able to receive a one- to two-day overview of the technology. Case studies and product demonstrations are helpful. They give project leaders a chance to ponder the implications of managing a CASE-driven project, without having to risk the embarrassment of mismanaging a real-life situation.

User training is also a must. Fortunately, CASE provides systems developers with the time to conduct a thorough analysis of user requirements. However, users are often not prepared to dedicate the level of participation needed in a CASE-driven project. Users should be informed of their obligations well in advance.

Courses on automated-JAD (AJAD; see Chapter 3) and CASE terminology must be standard fare in the training department. Users should be shown how a project evolves using CASE and what their role will be during project development. In this way, there are no surprises when a developer asks for an interview and whips out a portable workstation to capture the specification.

With product administration and training needs addressed, an organization must look ahead and consider the implication that CASE technology's emerging trends will have on the new development environment.

Emerging Trends

There are three areas within the CASE technology arena that appear to be changing the way CASE will be used in the future:

1. Reverse engineering
2. AD/Cycle
3. Dual repository strategies

IS executives must understand these trends, to properly position their firms for the CASE explosion of the 1990s.

Reverse Engineering

Until recently, CASE vendors offered only tools that would assist in the analysis, design, and construction of new systems. There was little or no support offered to maintenance programmers, the people charged with maintaining existing applications. This trend is shifting as CASE users begin to demand tools that will assist in the modification and enhancement of the installed base.

Reverse engineering tools represent a category of CASE technology product that is aimed at converting old applications into new integrated database systems. As Figure 8–9 denotes, reverse engineering tools can be included in the CASE environment and made to work with classical front-end and back-end CASE technology.

Figure 8–9 illustrates how an enhanced CASE architecture will operate. Old applications will feed the reverse engineering toolset their data and will process logic definitions. These definitions may be file layouts and source code or database schemata and program logic. Either way, the reverse engineering toolset transforms existing system definitions into data and process models that can be read by standard CASE tools. Once transformed, these project models can be passed to the encyclopedia, where they can be acted upon by the back-end application generators.

The introduction of reverse engineering tools to the CASE architecture will not affect how new development takes place. User requirements are still captured in the front-end toolset and new applications are

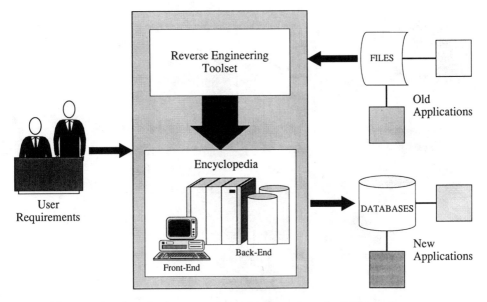

Figure 8–9. *Introducing reverse engineering tools to the CASE environment*

still generated from the back end. The only element that changes is CASE technology's ability to support maintenance activities.

AD/Cycle

AD/Cycle is IBM's CASE solution. It is a set of integrated CASE products that conform to IBM's SAA (systems application architecture) standard. IBM's announcement of AD/Cycle in September 1989 marked the company's commitment to computer-aided systems engineering and legitimized CASE technology in the eyes of its many skeptics.

The planned AD/Cycle architecture appears in Figure 8–10. The toolset centers around Repository Manager/MVS, which was available in June 1990. It is IBM's encyclopedia. The front-end tools include IBM's Developmate (a business modeling and prototyping tool to be made available in December 1990) and several offerings from business partners, including the following companies and their products:

- Bachman Information Systems' Bachman Re-Engineering product set
- Index Technology's OS/2 version of Excellerator
- Knowledgeware's PS/2-based Information Engineering Workbench

The back-end tools include a new release of IBM's cross-system product (Version 3, Release 3, was available in June 1990).

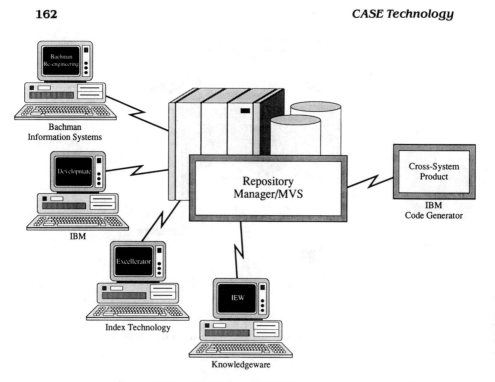

Figure 8-10. *IBM's planned AD/Cycle Architecture*

The fact that IBM is jumping on the CASE bandwagon is evidence enough that it is worth investing in. IS's biggest challenge is now deciding whether to wait for the IBM product line to mature (debugged and fully functional) or to begin to absorb the CASE learning curve with another product that can be interfaced with IBM's Repository Manager.

Dual Repository Strategies

In the face of IBM's AD/Cycle announcement, many user firms that have already acquired a comprehensive CASE tool are considering what can be done to salvage their investment. Besides functioning as IBM's CASE encyclopedia, the Repository Manager will also act as a much needed DB2 directory. This little wrinkle makes it very difficult for companies using DB2 to ignore AD/Cycle, even if a CASE tool is already in place.

Therefore, some companies are considering dual repository strategies. An architecture for a development environment that combines a CASE tool encyclopedia and Repository Manager can be created so that

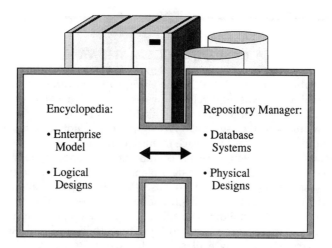

Figure 8–11. *A dual repository strategy*

the enterprise model and logical designs are kept in the encyclopedia and the physical designs and the database systems reside in the Repository Manager.

The architecture, as depicted in Figure 8–11, is straightforward. The only challenge that remains is the creation of the import and export functions that will transport information into and out of the repositories. This can be done with some simple programs that read data from one repository into a file that can be loaded into the other repository. It is perhaps a small price to pay to rescue a significant CASE investment.

While these emerging trends represent future changes in the CASE marketplace, the wise IS organization will begin planning today for their arrival. A firm that is prepared for the "ebb and flow" of technology will be able to make the impossible happen.

The Impossible Can Happen

The effective use of CASE technology can make the impossible happen. Automated project development allows small teams of people to build large integrated applications. The monotonous rigor of a development methodology can be simplified through integrated error detection built into the CASE development architecture. Expansive encyclopedias, which drive application generators, facilitate the creation of reusable code and designs. CASE is the vehicle through which IS will make significant gains in its pursuit of a truly productive work environment.

A CASE OF SUCCESS AT TWA

Trans World Airlines (TWA) began a frequent flier program in 1981. The original system was built in IMS and was designed to manage 100,000 members. By 1987, membership had risen to 4 million people. It was time for a new frequent flier system. TWA simply could not respond to the tremendous change that took place in enrollment since 1981.

Cloene Goldsborough, Director of Information Management at TWA, took charge. She spearheaded a data planning exercise that pointed to the need for an integrated client database. Goldsborough's challenge was to find the right set of tools and approaches to deliver the desired client system and assist in rebuilding the ailing frequent flier application.

TWA began to look for integrated CASE tools to lend a hand. After an evaluation of commercially available products, the Information Engineering Facility (IEF) from Texas Instruments was selected. The COBOL code and DB2 design generators fit well with TWA's stated DBMS direction (relational).

The IEF has served the airline well. The frequent flier system was rebuilt using the IEF. The 40-table DB2 database contains huge amounts of data (more than 30 million rows within some tables) and supports 58 on-line transactions.

Down the road, TWA plans to attack other client-related applications, using the IEF to drive the design and integration of each new system component. The result should lead to the client database that TWA seeks as the cornerstone of its strategic data plan.

It's exciting to see CASE technology being applied in the development of strategic systems. TWA is proving that advantages can be realized through the adoption of advanced tools and techniques. The fact that a major airline staked its future on CASE is strong testament that CASE is a legitimate application development approach.

Source: John Desmond, "DB2, TI's IEF in the Mainstream at TWA," *Software Magazine,* September 1989, pp. 40–41.

Summary

This chapter focused on computer-aided systems engineering (CASE). CASE technology automates what the systems developer does. It provides a way to assist in the analysis, design, and construction of software applications.

Shorter development life cycles, reduced programming cost, and improved systems quality are a few of the primary reasons companies are jumping on the CASE bandwagon.

Key Points

1. CASE technology encompasses an assortment of tools, including code generators, encyclopedias, reverse-engineering packages, and process and data modeling applications.

2. A full-function CASE development environment is composed of three tiers: a front end, a back end, and a centralized encyclopedia.

3. Enterprise modeling can be automated through CASE. The enterprise model is managed along with its component project models within a CASE encyclopedia.

4. Companies that use CASE can minimize the time needed to build and maintain systems, improve application quality, and reduce project development costs.

5. Before a firm acquires a CASE application, an evaluation committee should be formed to investigate the myriad of CASE offerings in the marketplace.

6. A CASE pilot project should do more than evaluate a product. It should assess cost savings, define user guidelines, and estimate training requirements.

7. A CASE management group should be formed to manage CASE implementation within a firm. The group can be part of a data management area, a development center, or the application development group.

8. User training, as well as technical training, is needed to make CASE a success. Business personnel must understand their new role in systems development activities.

9. Emerging trends like reverse engineering and IBM's entrance into the CASE marketplace will influence the burgeoning CASE industry. Firms must be prepared for the changes that will come.

10. CASE can make the impossible happen. It will be the vehicle through which IS achieves its productivity goals.

References

1. Jan Snyder, "Counting the Ways CASE Helps," *Computerworld*, Spotlight No. 46, June 6, 1988, p. s14.
2. Peter Scisco, "Users Start Cozying Up to Systems Development," *Computerworld*, Spotlight No. 46, June 6, 1988, p. s15.
3. Amy Fiore, "There's a Time to Buy and a Time to Wait," *Computerworld*, Spotlight No. 46, June 6, 1988, p. s2.

9

New Development Environments

The world must be made safe for democracy.

Woodrow Wilson, 1917

Project development life cycles (PDLCs) are the framework for blending the methodologies, tools, and techniques that a firm applies when building information systems. PDLCs broadly define the steps to be taken during application development; they form a platform on which all the elements of an IS shop rest (see Figure 9–1).

The traditional or classical life cycle that most firms follow today appears in Figure 9–2. It's divided into two major phases: the logical design phase, which analyzes and specifies the project requirements, and the physical design phase, which implements the required application. The

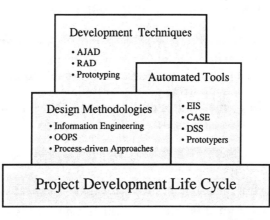

Figure 9-1. *An applications development environment with the PDLC as a platform for IS methodologies, tools, and techniques*

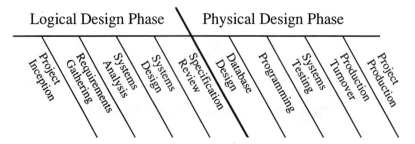

Figure 9–2. *The classic project development life cycle*

PDLC starts with a project proposal and ends with the creation of a production system.

The classical life cycle used to support every development project within IS. However, the introduction of innovative technologies and methods like CASE and Information Engineering has changed the way applications are built and has made the traditional PDLC obsolete. A new and improved life cycle is needed.

Improving the Life Cycle

The development environment of the 1990s will support highly productive development techniques. It will be flexible enough to adapt to improved ways of building systems. Users will become active participants in the development process because of a renewed commitment to better manage information assets. Firms will be seeking ways to effectively leverage their IS investments. The PDLC will be stretched to accommodate these development environment changes.

The changes will be so sweeping, in fact, that a single PDLC will not suffice. A development environment that encompasses several PDLCs will evolve. Each PDLC will harness unique combinations of tools and techniques aimed at supporting particular project types.

The multi-PDLC environment of the future will include the following elements:

Information Engineering life cycle, which supports the development of integrated, transaction-driven systems;

Prototyper's life cycle, which supports rapid systems development;

Management Information life cycle, which supports the establishment of ad-hoc inquiry applications;

Executive and decision support life cycle, which supports the creation of EIS and DSS projects;

System realignment life cycle, which supports the tailoring of existing application to new business needs.

With this environment in place, firms can immediately categorize every systems request and establish project teams that will evolve applications along the dimensions of one of its suite of PDLCs.

About the Life Cycles

Each PDLC has its own focus and is uniquely different from every other PDLC. Understanding the differences will enable firms to better incorporate the life cycles into their development environments.

Information Engineering Life Cycle

The IE life cycle, presented in Figure 9–3, reshapes the front-end of the PDLC. The requirements gathering, systems analysis, and systems design steps of a traditional life cycle give way to the IE cycle's business, data, process, and enterprise modeling disciplines. Even the nature of specifications reviews shifts from an evaluation of typewritten program requirements to an examination of graphical models.

The IE life cycle can be improved by folding in a variety of IS tools and techniques like JAD, prototyping, and object oriented programming without significantly changing the content of its steps.

Figure 9–4 illustrates the ease with which CASE can be added to the IE PDLC. Even though CASE greatly improves a developer's ability to build integrated applications—by providing automated modeling and generation capabilities—the life cycle remains unchanged.

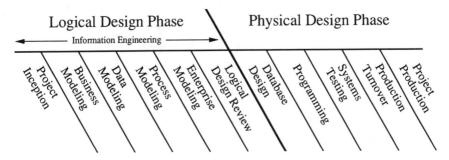

Figure 9–3. *The Information Engineering life cycle*

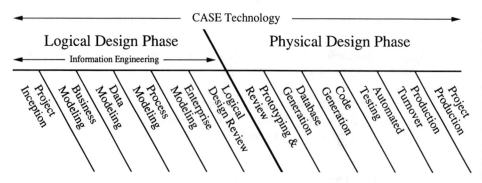

Figure 9-4. *Fitting CASE technology into the IE life cycle*

Prototyper's Life Cycle

Where the IE life cycle gives developers a framework to build integrated, transaction-driven systems, the prototyper's life cycle seeks to provide an environment to develop applications quickly.

The prototyper's life cycle appears in Figure 9–5. Because it is comprised of only physical design processes, the prototyper's life cycle is significantly different from both the traditional and IE life cycle approaches.

It's no wonder that the prototyper's life cycle is void of a logical design phase: Its focus is the rapid development of applications. Systems can be built quickly when a project team begins its effort by defining a model of the physical system (i.e., prototyping) instead of analyzing requirements and modeling data needs.

The prototyper's life cycle lends itself to the techniques outlined in Chapter 3 (AJAD, RAD, and prototyping). Undoubtedly, firms run the

Physical Design Process

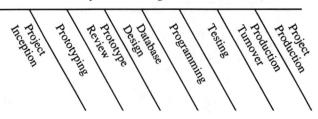

Figure 9-5. *The prototyper's life cycle*

"QUICKIE"	APPLICATION DESCRIPTION	AREA OF IMPACT	IMPLICATION
MBO System	Cross-references action plans to management objectives	Strategic Planning	Helps managers align their areas with management objectives
Job Training System	Classifies in-house training courses by job category and tracks employee attendance	Training & Development	Assists in career pathing and personal development
Preferred Vendor System	Maintains a list of preferred vendors by product and service category	Purchasing & Contract Administration	Helps managers and consumers of services seek vendors with established reputations
IS Problem Log	Logs problems encountered in the IS production environment	IS Customer Support	Improves IS's ability to solve production problems
Accent On Quality System	Logs quality improvement ideas across firm	Company-wide	Focuses attention on quality and facilitates the involvement of all employees in productivity improvement

Figure 9-6. *Some high-impact "quickies"*

171

risk of confronting all of prototyping's pitfalls—a team's ego involve-ment with the prototype, the "smoke and mirrors" syndrome (see Chap-ter 3), and a general inability to integrate the prototyped system with the rest of the application architecture.

However, the prototyper's life cycle does have a place in a firm's devel-opment environment. It can be used to construct high-impact "quickies," those stand-alone applications that require less than four months to build and have a lasting impact on the way a business functions. Figure 9–6 lists a few "quickie" systems.

Many "quickies" are used to justify IS's existence. Their successful implementation can demonstrate IS's ability to respond to business needs quickly. Management Information applications offer another way to re-new commitment to IS endeavors.

Management Information Life Cycle

Figure 9–7 presents the Management Information life cycle. Its logical design phase begins with a request for an ad-hoc inquiry capability to be folded into an existing database. If the database meets the need (as deter-mined by the subject area review and data identification steps), a solution is prototyped and programmed into the database environment. If the database does not possess the information requested, a full-scale physical design effort is needed (i.e., IE life cycle).

Today, very few IS shops are prepared to implement the Management Information life cycle. It would require the establishment of an MIS environment (like the one described in Chapter 5) that supports both operational systems and subject area databases. (See Figure 9–8 for a review of the MIS environment.)

As more firms migrate toward the Management Information Center concept, the Management Information life cycle will become extremely important. Until then, a majority of firms will rely on decision support

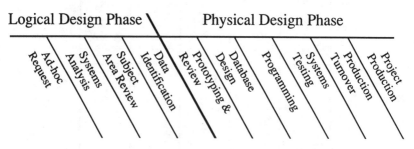

Figure 9–7. *The management information life cycle*

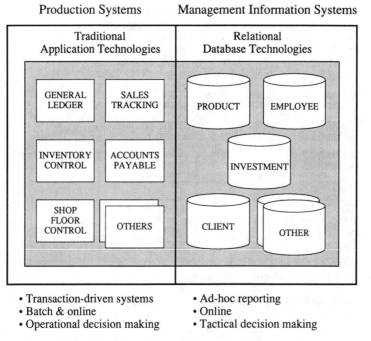

Production Systems   Management Information Systems

- Transaction-driven systems   • Ad-hoc reporting
- Batch & online   • Online
- Operational decision making   • Tactical decision making

Figure 9-8. *The Management Information Center environment*

and executive information life cycles to provide business managers with the insights they need to run the company.

Executive and Decision Support Life Cycle

As mentioned in Chapter 4, DSS and EIS applications are developed in the same way. Decision and information domains are defined, software tool-sets are identified, and system interfaces are established. The difference between DDS and EIS is in their audiences: a DSS focuses on middle management needs, while an EIS addresses senior management concerns.

Because of this uniqueness in focus, the Executive and Decision Support Life Cycle (EDSLC) must be flexible enough to accommodate various degrees of end user involvement. The EDSLC depicted in Figure 9–9 will apply regardless of the level of executive participation in the design. However, the acceptance testing step of the physical design phase becomes extremely important in situations where intermediaries (instead of executives) are used to build the system's prototype.

Executive and decision support systems that are not thoroughly tested may need to be enhanced down the road. A systems realignment life

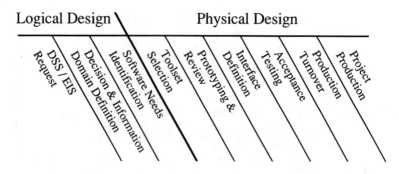

Figure 9-9. *The executive and decision support life cycle*

cycle dedicated to the embellishment of existing systems (EIS, DSS, or otherwise) is a necessary part of the development environment.

Systems Realignment Life Cycle

Projects involving significant enhancements to existing applications are the focus of the systems realignment life cycle. However, simple maintenance activities, like changing source code or adding a field to a database record, do not require a unique life cycle and are not supported by the systems realignment life cycle.

The life cycle steps are presented in Figure 9-10. The process involves the review of existing system models and the regeneration of code and designs to meet new information requirements. The use of CASE technology is assumed, but firms that have not adopted CASE can still apply the systems realignment life cycle. However, these firms will have to handcraft new code and designs to meet evolving user needs, and that's much less efficient than an automated means of construction.

The systems realignment life cycle rounds out the multi-PDLC environment. It enables companies to better address their maintenance woes

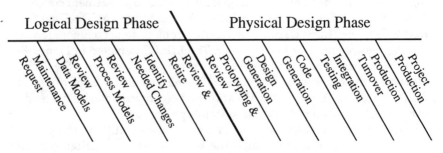

Figure 9-10. *The systems realignment life cycle*

by providing a framework for keeping old systems current with today's business needs. The next step toward establishing a premier systems development shop is to create ways of managing projects through the myriad of newly formed life cycles.

Using CASE Technology to Pull It Together

There's no doubt that the intelligent use of CASE software can provide a means of pulling together the multi-PDLC environment. CASE is the only systems development technology that can be applied universally across all PDLCs. (See Figure 9–11 for a matrix that cross-references the components of a development environment.)

CASE encyclopedias are central storage devices for all systems designs. They are used to manage the evolution of enterprise models and to drive the generation toolsets of CASE technology's back-end. The coordination capabilities of an encyclopedia make it an important project management tool.

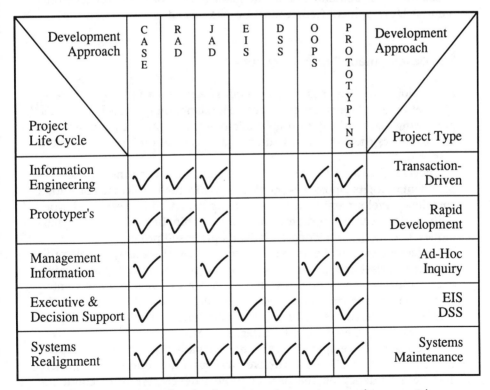

Development Approach / Project Life Cycle	CASE	RAD	JAD	EIS	DSS	OOPS	PROTOTYPING	Development Approach / Project Type
Information Engineering	✓	✓	✓			✓	✓	Transaction-Driven
Prototyper's	✓	✓	✓				✓	Rapid Development
Management Information	✓		✓			✓	✓	Ad-Hoc Inquiry
Executive & Decision Support	✓			✓	✓		✓	EIS DSS
Systems Realignment	✓	✓	✓	✓	✓	✓	✓	Systems Maintenance

Figure 9–11. *A project development environment cross-reference matrix*

By using CASE in every application development effort, firms can easily orchestrate the integration of multiple projects across any and all of their PDLCs. Project managers need only reference the encyclopedia to review a project's status or plan the next coordination meeting.

Parallel development efforts are made easy through the use of the technology. An integrated sales tracking and product design system that is being built using the Information Engineering life cycle can be coupled with an EIS application under construction in the executive and decision support life cycle.

This kind of cross-project integration is too cumbersome to manage using manual techniques. Most shops would tackle both efforts as stand-alone projects and try to retrofit them after they've been released to production—a messy solution to a stated business need.

The multi-PDLC environment of the future could put new demands on an already overworked IS organization. The acquisition of a comprehensive CASE toolset that provides front-end modeling support, an integrated encyclopedia, and application generation facilities makes a good deal of sense. However, progress is not made with technology alone. Resources must be dedicated to the management of the PDLC environment. A Development Center must be established.

The Development Center Concept

A Development Center is a designated, specially staffed area where IS application developers can go to receive guidance on subjects like PDLCs, processing standards, design methodologies, and project planning. The Center serves the entire IS community as a central project management resource.

The Development Center is a staff function, reporting to the vice president of IS; its employees provide newly formed project teams with à complete development itinerary. Development Center personnel work with project leaders to define the right combination of IS tools, techniques, and methods needed to deliver a proposed project.

Project management elements—programming checklists, sample project plans, toolset and methodology training guides, a variety of IS reference manuals—can be made available through the Development Center. A project manager can even have a project plan reviewed to determine the feasibility of staffing, scheduling, and milestone projections. (See Figure 9–12 for a list of Development Center services.)

Because the Development Center has virtually no operational responsibilities (i.e., it is not asked to deliver systems, only support them), there may be a tendency on the part of project developers to discount the Center's value. Many project teams may not understand the advantage of

A Development Center...

- Provides project planning guidance
- Maintains a library of IS documentation
- Develops programming checklists
- Participates in long-range systems planning
- Coordinates methodology and toolset training
- Facilitates synergy among IS functions
- Conducts seminars on system development techniques
- Reviews project schedules and staffing estimates
- Consults on IS development projects
- Documents the PDLC environment

Figure 9–12. *Development Center services*

using the Development Center, and may opt to go it alone, rationalizing their decision on the grounds of avoiding needless overhead. However, it does not have to be that way.

Full IS development staff participation can be ensured through the implementation of a rotational program in the Development Center. Every six months a group of project development personnel can be randomly selected from across the firm, to serve in the Development Center. Of course, provisions must be made to postpone the appointments of key personnel working on critical applications. Each person selected will be asked to spend six to 12 months on the job before being reassigned to his or her previous position.

Rotational programs help development personnel to better understand the significance of the Development Center and provide the Center with a source of fresh project management ideas. Project developers from around the company will be more inclined to turn to the Center for guidance when they and their contemporaries may be employed there.

But watch out for the pitfalls. A New York City-based firm implemented such a program. Project managers were notified a year in advance that they must appoint one of their people to a nine-month assignment in the Development Center. The effort failed because the

▼

PDLC DOCUMENTATION

Firms must take the time to document each and every one of their PDLCs (see Figure 9–13) so that development staffs have reliable reference materials to use during project development. Like most forms of IS documentation, the PDLC guides are often hastily put together or not written at all, which leaves a gaping hole in many development environments.

Excerpts from an in-house project development life cycle guide, currently in place at a Fortune 500 firm, are presented in the Appendix. The guide should be reviewed for its content. The examination of a good PDLC model may be the catalyst needed to ensure proper documentation down the road.

ABOUT THE GUIDE

The PDLC guide shown in the Appendix focuses on the Information Engineering life cycle. Each IE life cycle step is documented in a separate section of the guide. The Table of Contents shows the adoption of a standard section format; the instructional sections begin with an introduction and purpose statement and end with a recapitulation.

Standard formats make PDLC guides simple to use and understand. Devices like indexes and glossaries facilitate easy access to pertinent information. The guide shown contains the firm's data architecture strategy in its Overview section. Other related guidelines and procedures can be presented in the PDLC documentation.

On page 12 of the guide, in the Business Modeling section, you'll find an Activity/Participant Table. A similar table appears in every subsequent section of the guide. It lists the major deliverables from that life cycle step (i.e., Business Model Diagram, Function Correspondence Table) and specifies the level of participation needed from the various members of a development team (i.e., the creation of a Business Model Diagram is the primary responsibility of the Project Manager).

This kind of summary information is important because it reduces each life cycle step to its simplest terms. The recapitulation at the end of the sections also provides good information as do the sample business model diagrams and function correspondence tables, which act as quick reference sources for development teams on the go.

Most PDLC guides will also contain the forms and reports needed to round out the audit trail. The Database Request Form that the company uses to schedule the migration of a test-level database to a production environment is on page 139 of the guide. Having such forms at the fingertips of development personnel will ensure their use and make the life of the project developer and the EDP auditor much easier.

As mentioned earlier, the Glossary at the end (pages 143–148 of the guide) is a useful tool. It can document key terms that may not be familiar to development personnel and can provide a mechanism for presenting company-specific jargon. For example, the term X-Test Analyst (on page 148 of the guide) is definitely specific to the company, yet its definition is stored in the PDLC glossary.

Life cycle documentation is required in order to establish a stable development environment. Firms must gain appreciation of its importance and strive to create quality PDLC reference materials. Information presented in the sample PDLC guide demonstrates the proper level of detail needed to make guides useful to development personnel. Keys to success include the use of glossaries, indexes, diagrams, tables—and simple, straightforward language.

personnel appointed tended to be the project managers' least productive employees. The Development Center was disbanded after 18 months.

Development Centers and their rotational programs can serve their organizations well. However, they need the active support and direction of senior IS executives. The problem described above could have been avoided if the personnel were hand-picked by the MIS chief.

PDLC Phase:

    LOGICAL DESIGN PHASE

PDLC Step:

    DATA MODELING

Deliverables:

    DATA MODEL DIAGRAM

Participants:

DA	- Primary
DBA	- Review
P/M	- Participate
P/A	- Participate
USER	- Participate
U/MGR	- Review

Figure 9–13. *Sample PDLC documentation*

What Lies Ahead?

The future is calling for change! The introduction of new IS tools and techniques is requiring firms to reconsider their stance on project development life cycles. A multi-PDLC environment is on the horizon. Organizations must prepare to make needed shifts toward its adoption.

Infrastructural elements like PDLC documentation and the establishment of Development Centers will ease the transition toward a new way of managing systems construction. CASE technology will act as a linchpin by providing a means for managing several development efforts through a central storage device known as an encyclopedia.

We're heading into some exciting times. Don't be left behind with antiquated approaches to building applications. Begin to plan for the 1990s. Create new frameworks for systems development. Begin today. The competition won't wait.

Summary

This chapter challenges the classical project development life cycle (PDLC). It argues that firms should reconsider the steps they take to build and maintain systems because tools and techniques like CASE and Information Engineering are redefining IS's capabilities to meet user needs.

Key Points

1. A project development life cycle is a framework for combining the methodologies, tools, and techniques used for building information systems.
2. Changing development approaches are causing shifts in the classical life cycle. A multi-life cycle environment may be required.
3. Project development efforts can be categorized into:
   Integrated, transaction-driven systems
   Ad-hoc inquiry application
   Rapid development efforts
   EIS or DSS projects
   Maintenance activities
4. Project-specific life cycle include:

Information Engineering life cycle	(transaction-driven)
Management Information life cycle	(ad-hoc)
Prototyper's life cycle	(rapid)

      Executive and decision support life cycle   (EIS/DSS)

      Systems realignment life cycle   (maintenance)

5. CASE technology, and its encyclopedia, can be used to integrate all development efforts within a firm.

6. Development Centers provide life cycle guidance and project development leadership to IS professionals from across the firm.

7. Development Centers can use rotational programs to ensure acceptance.

8. Life cycle guides should be made available. They will act as reference sources to project developers in the field.

9. Quality life cycle documentation is marked by the use of diagrams, tables, and glossaries. It is written in easy-to-read language and should be available to every member of the IS organization.

10

Electronic Data Interchange

The only thing to fear is fear itself.
Franklin Delanor Roosevelt, 1933

No discussion of information resource management would be complete without an exploration of electronic data interchange (EDI). EDI, the mechanism for electronic trade among companies, relies heavily on both intracorporate (within one company) and intercorporate (among separate companies) networking technologies.

EDI applications eliminate the labor-intensive paper flow that often swamps today's businesses and replace the paper with a set of standard computer transactions that are passed between information systems within partner sites.

Orders and invoices are traded instantly, vendor inventories and price lists are perused with a touch of a button, and funds are transferred without a trip to the bank. The implications of EDI are obvious:

- Processing costs go down as the personnel used in order entry and customer support are removed from the equation;
- Payment periods shorten because funds are automatically moved among client and vendor accounts;
- Business relationships improve as customers receive better support and vendors achieve higher productivity.

EDI systems streamline transaction processing and provide better information for decision making.

How EDI Works

There's nothing magical about the way EDI systems function. The architecture is designed to convert one company's automated transactions into a format that can be used by another company's business applications. Figure 10–1 illustrates the way a typical EDI environment works.

Trading Partner 1 places an order through its acquisition system. The resulting transaction is passed through a transaction converter, which is software that transforms the order into a standard format. The standard format transaction is sent to Trading Partner 2, where it is read by the transaction converter at Partner 2's site. The converter transforms the standard transaction into a format that can be interpreted by Partner 2's order entry system. The order is placed, and a confirmation is delivered to Trading Partner 1 through the same channels.

Variations of the architecture are used to perform inquiries, post proposals, transmit reports, send bills, and so on. The biggest challenge facing firms interested in EDI is not tweaking the architecture—it's defining the business agreement among trading partners.

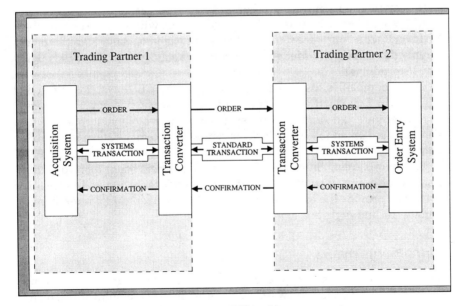

Figure 10-1. *EDI architecture*

Trade Agreements

Companies wishing to do business electronically must be prepared to agree on a myriad of technical and business issues. Decision areas range from hardware platforms to discount practices. The whole nature of business dealings changes when EDI is brought into the picture.

Instantaneous information transfer among companies can change the way businesses operate. Just-in-time (JIT) manufacturing, shorter order cycles, and improved trend analysis are just a few of the results achieved through EDI. However, a few details must be worked out before the electronic trading environment can really take shape.

Technical Issues

Trading partners must have similar communications hardware and software, in order to communicate electronically. The hardware is used to generate and receive information passed between business partners; the software is used to convert in-house transactions into a format that can be passed to partners. Conversion software also transforms transactions received from external partners into a format that can be read internally.

Agreeing on which tools to use is often very difficult. Companies are driven to technology decisions by different factors, including functionality, cost, and preference. The tools that are right for one partner, therefore, may not be right for the other.

Many suppliers who want to lock in customers will offer to develop the EDI architecture and give it to key clients (for example, American Hospital Supply developed an order entry system and gave it to the hospitals that buy its products).

Other companies insist that suppliers use their EDI systems. Pratt & Whitney in East Hartford, Connecticut, for example, has developed several inventory and order control systems for use by key suppliers. The suppliers are asked to use the Pratt & Whitney system in return for Pratt's continued business.

When an agreement cannot be reached, partners often turn to third-party vendors for a solution. Third-party vendors, acting as intermediaries, can provide the tools needed to execute electronic data interchange among trading partners.

Third-Party Vendors

Third-party EDI vendors come in different shapes and sizes. Some provide the conversion software. Some provide the communications technology. Some offer their clients both. Firms wishing to use third-party vendors should inquire about the services and products they offer.

Figure 10–2 lists a handful of EDI software providers. Most vendor offerings target only one hardware platform. Not every vendor will have the software that is needed in every installation. Take the time to explore options with multiple vendors.

EDI service providers, like the ones listed in Figure 10–3, can usually package together the hardware and software needed to implement EDI at any site. Of course, the full-service solutions that these vendors offer will, on average, be more expensive than straight EDI conversion software acquisition. Firms must weigh price differentials into their decision making.

There's no doubt that third-party solutions are convenient—plug 'em in and move on. However, consider every alternative. Firms save the costs of developing internal expertise and building the EDI system at the

- Chase Manhattan Corporation
  212-552-5762

- American Business Computer
  313-855-4520

- Control Data
  216-5295-5420

- Ordernet Services
  614-459-7500

- EDI Incorporated
  301-670-0811

- Intec Systems
  417-739-4214

- ACS Network Systems
  800-426-3836

- Trax Systems
  714-661-7661

Figure 10–2. *A partial list of EDI software vendors*
Source: Phyllis K. Sokol, *EDI: The Competitive Edge.* New York: McGraw-Hill Book Co., Intertext Publications.

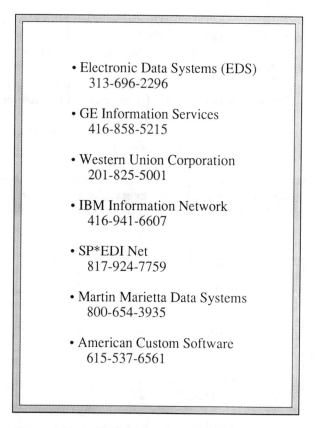

Figure 10-3. *A partial list of EDI third-party software providers*
Source: Phyllis K. Sokol, *EDI: The Competitive Edge.* New York: McGraw-Hill Book Co.,
Intertext Publications.

expense of buying the software (and maintenance) and having limited
control over new releases.

As if the technical issues aren't demanding enough, the business issues offer even stiffer challenges.

Business Issues

New discount arrangements should be formulated. Orders from interconnected clients are less expensive to process than orders from those who
aren't electronically linked. It's only right to pass on some of the savings to
those that trade through EDI.

Further, businesses should reexamine payment discounts. The standard "2/10, net 30" (2 percent discount on payments received within 10
days of invoice, full amount due in 30 days) is just about obsolete in an
EDI environment. Maybe discounts should be extended to include a
same-day payment discount.

The other side of discounting is order placement and change. Ordering guidelines must be established early in the trading relationship and must define time limits for changing and cancelling orders. Vendors should not have to absorb the cost of filling an order that is cancelled at the last minute.

Windows of operation comprise a third negotiation point. Electronic correspondents from different parts of the country (or the world) work in different time zones. Time-zone differences sometimes put a kink in the EDI-trade game. Mutually agreed-upon times for trade are needed along with a mechanism for processing transactions generated outside of the operations window.

Once these technical and business issues are addressed, an agreement is drafted and signed by executives from partner firms. The agreement outlines the nature of the EDI trading arrangement, specifies the technology to be used, and states the business rules that will govern trading practices among the companies.

With a trade agreement in place, firms can develop an EDI implementation plan and begin to build their new trading environment.

Some Are Already There

A great many companies are already trading electronically. The firms listed in Figure 10–4 are just a few of the enterprises exploiting EDI

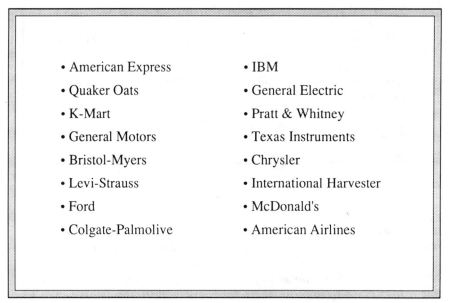

- American Express
- Quaker Oats
- K-Mart
- General Motors
- Bristol-Myers
- Levi-Strauss
- Ford
- Colgate-Palmolive

- IBM
- General Electric
- Pratt & Whitney
- Texas Instruments
- Chrysler
- International Harvester
- McDonald's
- American Airlines

Figure 10–4.   *Some of the firms currently using EDI*

▼

EDI SEEN IN FORD'S FUTURE

The Common Manufacturing Management System (CMMS) is the $20 million brain child of Ford Motor Company. Ford's MIS chief, S. I. Gilman, is tying together dozens of Ford plants throughout North America and providing an electronic connection to hordes of suppliers—improving internal and external communications are two reasons behind this ongoing EDI development effort.

A rewrite of Ford's aged material control systems was determined to be a necessary component of the CMMS development plan. Order entry, control, and assembly coordination systems have to be consistent across Ford's 50 parts factories and 20 assembly plants, in order for the project to be fully realized.

Thirty-five of the auto company's programmers, along with a bundle of Arthur Andersen consultants, have been assigned the chore of coding both the new manufacturing system and the EDI software necessary to transfer information among the Ford factories and their suppliers.

When the programming is finished in the early 1990s, the Ford Company will have a single, standardized order/inventory system that will govern the manufacturing processes throughout the enterprise. Hundreds of Ford suppliers will be able to pass order and shipment information directly into the centralized CMMS application—helping the company to better manage overhead and schedule assembly runs.

Once CMMS is in place, Ford can continue to parlay its technology investment by implementing JIT manufacturing practices in its assembly plants. JIT will lower costs by reducing inventories and quickening order processing.

With Japanese firms breathing fire to keep away their competitors, the time is right for American companies to explore the advantages that technology has to offer. Ford's use of EDI in its Common Manufacturing Management System positions the company well to compete in the global marketplace.

Source: J. B. Iida, C. Von Simpson, and B. Caldwell, "Ford Jumps Starts EDI," *Information Week,* November 21, 1988, pp. 12–13.

technology in support of a wide range of applications, including order processing, invoicing, product design, and customer service.

Further, many of the world manufacturers view EDI as an essential component of their JIT inventory strategies. Businesses are scrambling to put EDI in place to improve their suppliers' abilities to deliver parts to

▼

McDONALD'S INTRACORPORATE NETWORK

What's this? Big Mac gives way to ISDN! Not exactly. However, McDonald's does plan to use integrated services digital network (ISDN) technology to tie its 10,000 stores together into one big happy network by the turn of the century.

ISDN enables companies to transfer data and voice through the same phone lines. It provides easy access to the company network by standardizing the interfaces between the computer and the communication devices. More importantly, it can be used to implement EDI applications.

The fast-food chain wants to parlay ISDN technology into a bottom-line improvement. Its goal is to pump sales, marketing, and inventory information (generated by each store) into headquarters, where it can be assimilated and used to:

- Monitor sales,
- Track inventory,
- Enhance forecasting, and
- Define marketing strategies.

McDonald's believes that the insight into company operations that this EDI application will facilitate justifies the millions it will invest in ISDN technology over the next 10 years.

Illinois Bell and AT&T, McDonald's telephone and long-distance carriers, are working diligently to make McDonald's successful. Both companies recognize the McDonald's effort as a testing ground for their ISDN-related services and a showcase to potential customers down the road.

From McDonald's viewpoint, intracorporate networking is another weapon in its never ending war with Wendy's and Burger King. Last week, McNuggets; this week, EDI! What will the "Golden Arches" think of next?

Source: R. Layne and C. Medford, "McDonald's Serves Up Global ISDN Strategy," *Information Week,* February 15, 1988, pp. 36–37.

---

them in time for product assembly—a practice that lowers production costs by reducing inventory requirements (see the discussion of EDI at Ford, page 188).

Cross-company communications is not the only way EDI can be used. Several organizations like McDonald's (see above) are using EDI to help integrate their internal, decentralized operations, which is another reason why EDI's popularity continues to grow.

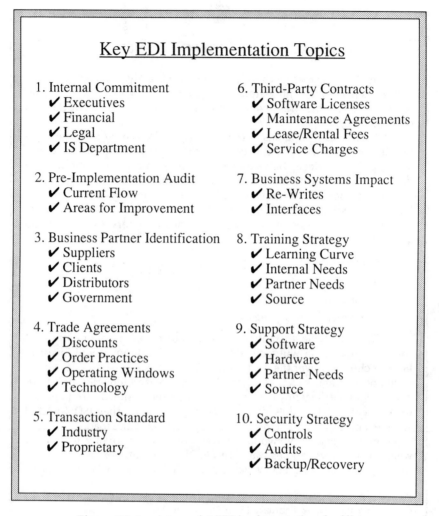

Figure 10–5. *A ten-point EDI implementation checklist*

A Word of Warning

Electronic data interchange is not a panacea. It will not improve ill-conceived business procedures and it will not refurbish poorly designed systems. These kinds of inefficiencies can only be reconciled by firms prior to EDI implementation.

In fact, the introduction of EDI into a chaotic business environment will probably worsen the situation by accelerating the rate of information transfer. Eventually, poorly designed procedures (whether manual or automated) will become overburdened and fail, leaving the enterprise in a precarious situation.

This pitfall can be avoided if time is invested in the development of a comprehensive EDI implementation plan. Pre-implementation audits, training strategies, and transaction standards are some of the elements of a good implementation plan.

EDI Implementation Plan

The checklist presented in Figure 10–5 specifies key EDI implementation topics. It can be used as a guideline for developing effective implementation plans. Companies must be prepared to address the following issues to ensure success.

Internal Commitment

As Figure 10–6 illustrates, many facets of the enterprise must come together to make EDI work:

- Corporate executives define the requirements
- Legal drafts the agreement
- Accounting determines the controls

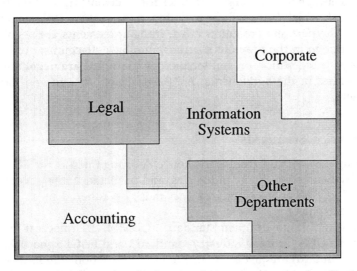

Figure 10-6. *Piecing together the functional area commitments for effective EDI implementation*

- IS implements the technology
- Other departments use the system

A sound implementation plan will include an awareness program that educates decision makers about the benefits of EDI and the commitment needed to see it through.

Pre-implementation Plan

With the proper commitment secured, firms should plan to conduct a pre-implementation audit of the current business flow. The audit will determine the information that is generated and received by the function(s) that will use the EDI application. It will document where the information is sent and who sends information to the function(s).

A technique such as business modeling (as explained in Chapter 6) should be employed. Business modeling allows the firm to graphically depict the flow information, making it easier to analyze the current work environment and to specify areas that need improving before EDI implementation.

Business Partner Identification and Trade Agreements

Firms must identify the business partners that will use the EDI application when it's developed. Customers, distributors, suppliers, and the government are the primary candidates for electronic trade. Take time to distinguish which firms will be included in the system implementation.

Once the partners are determined, trade agreements are negotiated. As mentioned in the previous sections, purchase discounts, order practices, operating windows, and technology platforms are negotiated and documented in the agreements. All parties meet to sign and date the contracts.

Transaction Standards

Knowing the users up-front is the key to defining the way the EDI application will function. Some industries, and particularly the government, have widely accepted standards that must be adhered to, in order to trade electronically.

ANSI-X.12 (a government standard), COMMNET (medical industry standard), UCS (grocery industry standard), and EAGLE (hardware industry standard) are just a few of the EDI transaction standards in use. Firms must decide whether they will adopt an industry standard or develop a proprietary standard that only they and their trading partners will use.

Third-Party Contracts

If a third party is used to provide the EDI solution, then the implementation plan should call for the documentation of any licenses, agreements, fees, or service charges. In fact, all third-party contracts should pass through the legal department before signature, to protect the firm from dishonest vendors who might take advantage of an unassuming client.

Business Systems Impact

Usually, only a handful of existing business systems will be affected by the implementation of EDI. Some programs may need to be rewritten to work with EDI; others will require the development of an interface so that they can pass information electronically. Either way, maintenance activities should be specified in the EDI implementation plan so that resources can be allocated effectively.

Training and Support Strategies

Training and support are important elements of the EDI implementation plan. Mechanisms must be in place to ensure that EDI applications are used properly and technology problems are resolved quickly. Otherwise, firms stand the risk of losing their EDI investment.

Quality EDI training and support strategies specify the requirements for the total trading environment (internal and trading partner needs) and recommend the source(s) of the training and support services.

Security Strategy

No EDI implementation plan would be complete without the specification of a security strategy. Controls, audits, and backup/recovery processes are essential components of any good system, and EDI applications are no exception.

A mutually agreed-upon security scheme must be defined to protect the interests of all the trading partners. No one wants a security breach to be the downfall of the enterprise. Security should be discussed during EDI implementation.

Keep in mind that the creation of an EDI implementation plan does not a successful project make. Firms must face the barriers to EDI and find ways to overcome the resistances to electronic trading.

Understanding Resistance

There are many reasons why companies don't embrace EDI. The lack of a single, accepted, transaction standard keeps many firms from jumping on the EDI bandwagon. The EDI standardization challenge, as depicted in Figure 10–7, may put firms in the precarious position of supporting multiple EDI interfaces. Rather than assume the burden, these firms resist EDI.

Costs become another factor that impedes EDI use. The incremental costs of additional communications hardware, software, and trained personnel are often prohibitive. But the hidden expense of modifying existing systems (to work with an EDI application), coupled with the cost of supporting business partners (who may be ill-equipped to support their end of an EDI system), makes electronic trade a pricey proposition.

However, as mentioned before, using a third-party provider can alleviate some of these problems. Third parties still cost money, but they can manage the interface issues and provide the hardware, software, and personnel needed to implement EDI.

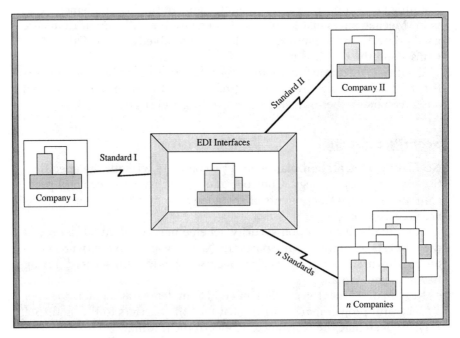

Figure 10-7. *The EDI standardization challenge*

Standardization and costs aside, management is the primary cause of EDI resistance. Most executives don't appreciate the significance of intercorporate communications and may not be aware of the benefits of the following EDI features:

Online business. Providing real-time banking, trading, and shopping services to clients will ultimately lock in customers and lock out competition.

Economies of scale. Bulk purchasing and mass production lower the cost of goods sold. Ordering and production economies can be achieved by using the trend information provided by EDI applications.

Backward and forward integration. A popular business strategy is to acquire suppliers (backward integration) and/or distributors (forward integration). Companies that do this control their entire manufacturing and sales process. EDI enables companies to enjoy the same benefits without expending the capital needed to buy suppliers and distributors outright.

Electronic marketing. Firms can conduct marketing surveys and execute advertising campaigns through EDI. Electronic marketing helps companies target their markets while differentiating their product through online services.

Once executives understand the opportunities that EDI offers, they will dedicate the necessary resources to make EDI work for them.

What Will the Future Bring?

As Figure 10–8 illustrates, the future will look like one great, big, electronic trading ground. Manufacturers will be tied to their suppliers, suppliers will be linked to R&D shops, R&D shops will be connected to federal and state governments, and so on. Eventually, EDI will be the only way to commercially trade.

Further, international EDI standards will emerge. American companies that want to take advantage of Europe's common market (discussed further in Chapter 12) will more than likely adhere to the EDIFACT (EDI for Administration, Commerce, and Transport) standard or will run the risk of developing potentially obsolete proprietary software.

Artificial intelligence (AI) will also play a role in EDI's future. AI will become the core of the EDI control center. It will administer security and be folded into applications where appropriate. In fact, the EDI/AI combination may be the beginning of a new era, one in which computers talk to computers without any human intervention.

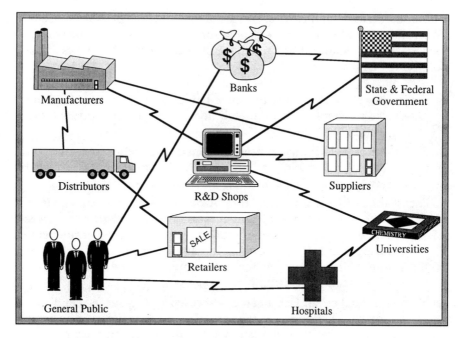

Figure 10-8. *The interconnected world of the future*

Summary

Electronic data interchange offers firms the capability to transact business online. Electronic trading leads to internal operating efficiencies, improved business relationships, and, ultimately, competitive gains. In time, EDI will be the only way firms will converse. Companies should begin to plan the use of EDI today.

Key Points

1. Electronic data interchange (EDI) is a mechanism for electronic trading among companies.

2. EDI applications eliminate paper flow and replace it with online transactions that lead to operating efficiencies, economies of scale, business integration, and improved business relationships. These help companies stay competitive.

3. The EDI architecture is made up of transaction converters that transform business applications into standard transactions that can be passed electronically.

4. Trade agreements should be developed among trading partners. Agreements should specify the technical architecture (hardware and software) as well as the business architecture (discount and ordering practices) that will be used by all trading partners.

5. EDI is not a panacea. It will not correct poorly designed business procedures or repair dysfunctional software.

6. An implementation plan should be developed before a firm embarks on EDI. Elements like pre-implementation audits, third-party contract negotiations, and security strategies are contained in the plan.

7. A lack of transaction standardization, coupled with high start-up costs, keeps many firms away from EDI. However, management commitment to the technology can overcome those resistances.

8. In the future, EDI will be a prerequisite of all businesses. Companies won't stay in business without it.

11

Information Systems Planning

The end justifies the means.

Hermann Busenbaum, c. 1650

Information Systems Planning is a discipline used to formulate a long-range strategy for the deployment of IS technology. An Information Systems Plan (ISP) specifies the database, application, hardware, communications, and personnel architectures needed to help the business achieve its mission.

Most ISPs require six to nine months to define. They are developed by members of the IS community, demand extensive business management involvement, and are driven by an executive-level committee. An ISP's underlying objective is to align IS goals with strategic business initiatives so that every IS activity contributes to the bottom line.

What's in a Plan?

Information Systems Plans are made up of the five basic components described in the following sections (1).

Business Summary

The company mission statement, goals, and objectives are presented in the business summary. Subjective assessments of the economy, expected regulatory shifts, and management attitudes (i.e., aggressive risk taking versus conservative direction setting) may also be included as background information to support predictions of where the company may be in the future.

Data Management Plan

This section of the ISP contains a broad statement of the basic data needed to support the business. A completed enterprise model, representing all modeled data within the company, will not be available. (As discussed in Chapter 6, enterprise models require years to build.) However, a sketch of the high-level data requirements can be presented in the data management section of the ISP.

Along with a statement of data needs, the data management plan will outline the tools and methodologies that the firm must adopt to manage data properly. Items like DBMS policy, CASE recommendations, and methodology selection are included in this section as a guide for accepted data management practices.

Application Development Plan

The application development plan identifies the systems that must be developed to help the firm meet the goals specified in the business summary. Systems are classified by life cycle type (outlined in Chapter 9) and priority.

Also included in this section are project descriptions, projected delivery dates, and programming language recommendations. If existing systems need to be expanded to meet future business needs, that's specified in the application development plan as well.

Technology Needs Assessment

The technology needs assessment defines the hardware and communications technology required to deliver the systems outlined in the application development plan. It points to trends in the high-tech marketplace, defines corporate standards (i.e., SNA, OSI, and so on), and identifies upgrade requirements for the installed base of technology.

The technology needs assessment section includes recommendations on workstations, minicomputers, and mainframes, as well as emerging technologies like CD-ROM, imaging, and microwave communications. However, the basic thrust of the section is to define a flexible work environment that will meet processing needs today and can grow into the environment of tomorrow.

Personnel Plan

With the physical environment defined, all that remains is to determine the personnel needed to develop and maintain the data, applications, and technology platforms. The personnel plan specifies the staffing requirements, training programs, and recruiting processes that will create a corps of qualified technical professionals.

Some ISP personnel plans even go so far as to recommend the human resources programs required to develop and retain the technical staff. Recommendations may include dual career pathing, mentoring programs, and performance evaluation standards, all geared toward getting the right people for the job at hand.

Figure 11–1 presents a sample of the kind of information documented in an ISP. Vendor products, development methodologies, and programming languages are just some of the systems development elements recommended. A full-fledged ISP can contain hundreds of pages of explanations and detailed justifications.

A plan of this magnitude requires extensive management participation. Business managers' perspective on how technology can be put to better use is a necessary ingredient to the recommendations set forth in the plan. As with other IS initiatives, selling the ISP concept is the first step toward gaining the commitment needed for success.

Selling the Concept

Unless blessed with well-informed and forward-thinking leadership, most organizations will have to begin the ISP process with an awareness campaign. Business management must be convinced that the time and resources expended on ISP are worth the bother.

There are a multitude of ways to sell the concept. Some firms begin with an initial study in a specific area of the business. Its aims are to identify opportunities to apply technology in ways that improve productivity, to cut costs, and to better meet business objectives. The results of the study are then presented to senior management as an example of how better systems planning leads to a better business.

Other approaches include one or a combination of the following activities:

- Conducting ISP awareness sessions throughout the firm
- Hiring ISP experts to lecture on the subject
- Facilitating visits to companies that practice ISP
- Inviting business managers to ISP seminars.

Each activity is focused on attaining senior management commitment to planning.

PLANNING ACTIVITIES	SECTION COMPONENTS	SAMPLE DELIVERABLES
Business Summary	- Statement of Business Goals and Objectives - Critical Success Factors - Target Dates	- Improve Sales by 20% - Achieved thru Introduction of New Product - Target: Mid-June
Data Management Plan	- Matrices X-Referencing Business Functions to Data Requirements - Definition of Data Management Tools (i.e. DBMS, CASE, etc.) - Definition of Methodologies	- The Marketing Dept. needs Client and Product Information - DB/2, FOCUS and IEF will be the DM Tools - Information Engineering
Application Development Plan	- Prioritized Systems List - Programming Language Definition - Development Shells (i.e. Expert Systems, Windowing Tools)	- Integrated Accounting System to be developed before Sales System - Languages: C and COBOL - Shells: Windows/386
Technology Needs Assessment	- H/W Plans (i.e. PC's, Mainframes) - Peripherals Recommendation - Special Equipment Plans - LAN Recommendation - Gateway Requirement Definition - Bandwidth Manager Technology	- IBM 3090 and PS/2 Model 70 - Epson Printers and Plotters - Terradata DB Machine - IBM Token Ring - PS/2 Gateway Drivers - IBM IDNX
Personnel Plan	- Personnel Requirements for IS - Recruitment Plans - Training Plans	- 6 DBAs with DB/2 Expertise Needed - Recruitment: Local Search Firms - Training: In-House Windows Class

Figure 11-1. Components of an Information Systems Plan

▼

A STRATEGIC PLAN FOR THE
SOCIAL SECURITY ADMINISTRATION

Dorcas Hardy, commissioner of the Social Security Administration (SSA), and Herbert Doggette, Jr., deputy commissioner of SSA operations, attempted to overhaul the antiquated systems that supported their agency. These systems churn out 40 million checks each month. The trick for Hardy and Doggette was to continue to distribute checks in a timely fashion, while revitalizing the applications environment. They had their work cut out for them.

In the spring of 1988, the SSA published a strategic plan. It included some startling statistics. A 30 percent increase in elderly Americans is expected by the end of the century, but the labor force that funds the SSA benefits to the elderly is projected to grow by only approximately 10 percent annually. The implication is obvious. The SSA must do more with less.

Like any good manager, Hardy looked to technology to lend a hand. The SSA's $700 million strategic plan spans 10 years and calls for:

- The installation of 22,000 IBM terminals to handle claims processing;
- The use of smart cards for direct benefit deposits;
- The support of electronic data interchange among other agencies, like the Internal Revenue Service; and
- The harnessing of expert systems for disability settlement processing.

These strategic objectives might seem a bit aggressive for an organization steeped in dumb terminals and disparate technologies. However, the synergy stirred by the strategic planning exercise positions these goals for success.

Obviously, the targeted changes won't happen overnight. But the partnership between the business function (Hardy) and IS (Doggette) is sure to carry the Social Security Administration into the 21st century.

Source: C. Von Simpson, "Social Security in the Year 2000," *Information Week,* April 18, 1988, pp. 38–42.

ISP Steering Committee

Once the ISP concept is understood and committed to by all, an ISP steering committee must be formed. The committee will appoint an ISP team to conduct the study, monitor its results, resolve conflicts as they occur, and approve or reject the proposed plan.

The committee is staffed by middle and senior business managers. Representatives from every functional area within the company should be assigned to the committee. One manager, acting as the chairperson, will be required to keep the group focused.

Other members of the committee include senior IS managers and the ISP team leader. Usually, the ISP team leader will be asked to act as the group's secretary, documenting and distributing minutes, publishing agendas, and scheduling future meetings. It's the leader's job to be sure that the committee meetings run smoothly.

When the ISP is finished, the steering committee will remain active as an IS advisory board that provides ongoing direction to the IS staff throughout ISP implementation. The advisory board will ensure that IS continues to support the most pressing business needs.

ISP Team

The ISP steering committee will define a four- to six-person ISP team. This team, made up of IS personnel, is charged with conducting management interviews, synthesizing and analyzing interview results, formulating plans for each component of the ISP, and presenting a formal recommendation to the ISP committee.

An ISP leader will be identified by the committee. That individual will act as a project manager for the team, ensuring that work is done on time and is of the highest quality. The ISP steering committee empowers the ISP leader to do what is needed to make the ISP successful.

Because this is an important role, the ISP leader must be respected by both the IS and business communities, possess strong communication and negotiation skills, and be learned in both business planning and ISP techniques. (See the discussion of business planning practices, below.) Any less skilled leader is sure to invite trouble.

Recognizing that few individuals possess the full complement of required skills, many firms look to external consultants to play the role of leader. This practice can be dangerous because ISP project control can often be lost to money-hungry consultants who are more interested in enjoying a long-term engagement than in delivering a timely ISP.

Not every consulting company is out to turn a buck; there are many that have integrity. However, an alternative to using a consultant as a leader is to use one as an assistant to an internal ISP leader. The "right" consultant will have the skills that the ISP leader may lack, yet is there only to support the leader through the ISP process.

The other members of the team are considered project staff. They do what the team leader needs done. They will act as scribes or facilitators

COMING TO GRIPS WITH
BUSINESS PLANNING PRACTICES

Systems professionals who will be asked to spearhead ISP efforts should be in tune with the approaches businesses use to set strategic direction. Being knolwedgeable in these approaches will help the ISP practitioner to define better recommendations because of enhanced sensitivity to the concerns of business managers.

There is a myriad of business planning techniques. Here's a brief explanation of some of the more popular ones.

WOTS-UP ANALYSIS

WOTS-UP analysis answers the question: "What's the nature of our company's situation?" WOTS stands for weaknesses, opportunities, threats, and strengths. Organizations that practice this technique systematically define elements about the business that fit into each of the four categories. The senior management team uses the lists to define strategic goals and initiatives for the business.

For example, if high employee turnover is a weakness, then an improved employee retention program may become an initiative. Similarly, if a firm's reputation is its primary strength, then marketing strategies would be based on promoting the name. The focus of WOTS-UP analysis is overcoming weaknesses, exploiting opportunities, thwarting threats, and leveraging strengths!

INDUSTRY ANALYSIS

"How can we better compete in this industry?" is the question that is answered through industry analysis. This technique examines the markets a company competes in along several key dimensions, including:

Projected industry growth rate

Ease of entry into the industry

Substitutability of products

Product dependencies (i.e., support, complementary products)

Bargaining power of suppliers and customers

Assessing these and other industry-related elements help firms define marketing and product plans.

ETHICAL AUDIT

"Will they still respect us in the morning?" is the question that the ethical audit tries to answer. Ethical auditing delves into social issues involving individual rights, fairness, and societal norms. It is a way for executives to "gut check" their strategies before executing them.

Ethical audits examine issues such as:

Right to life

Equal opportunity

Ecological impact

Freedom of speech

Religious practices

Cultural differences

as they apply to a proposed strategic plan. Ethical audits act as a firm's conscience, helping it to distinguish between right and wrong.

FINANCIAL ANALYSIS

Every company performs some form of financial analysis every day, whether in the bookkeeping it does or the financial forecasts it projects. Financial analysis comprises the steps that lead to the bottom line. When the smoke clears, financial analysis answers the question, "Can we afford it?"

Firms analyze their financial performance by applying a series of equations or ratios aimed at measuring profitability, liquidity, leverage, and activity. Ratios used in financial analysis include:

Gross profit margin

Return on equity

Fixed asset turnover

Current ratio (assets/liability)

Debt-to-asset ratio

Average collection period ratio

The results of this analysis help decision makers come up with a plan of attack that their companies can financially sustain.

Source: Alan J. Rowe, Richard O. Mason, and Karl E. Dickel, *Strategic Management & Business Policy.* Reading, MA: Addison-Wesley Publishing Co., 1986.

during the interview process, be asked to merge and analyze findings, and put together the final management report.

ISP staff members should be good analysts, be trained in interview techniques, be able to communicate well in both written and verbal forms, and have a knack for translating business requirements into systems opportunities.

Subject Matter Experts

Most ISP teams lack the full complement of IS expertise needed to develop a thorough plan. The ISP leader, in conjunction with the head of the IS department, reserves the right to use experts from within the IS function to help in the development of a consistent ISP.

Database, methodology, advanced hardware, and communications specialists act as internal consultants to the team. They are regularly asked to review interview findings and analyze ISP matrices (see page 210), in order to assist the team in defining the tools and approaches needed to build the strategic systems recommended in the plan.

Sometimes these subject matter experts from the IS community resent having to play second fiddle to the ISP team. They can become jealous of the management exposure that the team is getting. To combat this, subject matter experts can be invited to pertinent ISP team and ISP committee meetings, to present their views and opinions. This technique helps to share the glory of the ISP experience.

Gathering Information

With the team assembled, it's time to begin gathering the information required to devise the plan. There are several ways to gather information from the business community. However, a combination of brainstorms, executive interviews, and JAD workshops is an effective way to gain insights into what the business needs in an ISP.

Brainstorming

Brainstorming is an easy way to get the ISP effort off to a good start. It's done in a one- or two-day meeting (favorably off-site, away from the distractions of the office). The focus of the session is to let the executives from the functional areas within the company lay out their plans and aspirations for the future so that the ISP team can begin to appreciate the direction in which the business is heading.

There are ground rules for the brainstorming session:

1. Everyone must participate openly. There's no holding back.
2. No one will be excused from the session. Participants must be present for all discussions.
3. No substitutes can be sent. Executives are required to be there (they may bring managers who work for them, if they please).
4. There are no wrong answers. The session is aimed at expressing beliefs. All issues raised are noted, but none can be challenged. Every comment is considered a legitimate one. There is no filtering. Candor is expected.

These ground rules should be presented by the session leader (ISP team leader) upon kickoff.

Once the rules are laid out, the session begins. The session leader breaks the ice with questions like:

What are your area's major goals this year? Over the next three years?

What do you see as potential roadblocks?

How will you measure success?

What are your critical success factors?

Members of the ISP team document the answers as they are presented. (One member of the team keeps a running list of the responses in a notebook, while another member summarizes answers on a blackboard or flip chart for all to see.)

When it appears that all the questions regarding direction and goals are fully explored, the session leader begins to examine where the executives stand regarding the use of technology. Leading questions like these are asked, to prod participants into expressing their ideas about automation:

Where can technology be put to use in your area?

If you could have a magic box that contained all the information in the world, what would it tell you?

What's the most time-consuming activity you perform?

Following the brainstorming session, a brief summary is developed by the ISP team and distributed to participants. Executives are asked to make time for a more in-depth discussion of their area's needs and expectations. A schedule for the follow-up interviews is communicated.

Executive Interview

The executive interview is a way for the executive to reexamine any of the issues raised at the brainstorming session and to share additional insights that may apply. Questions like the following are explored:

What are your major priorities?

What changes do you expect in coming months and years that may affect you?

How do you plan to deal with these changes?

The information gathered during the brainstorming is used as a catalyst for discussion.

Because the interviews are far more directed than the conversations in the previous session, less of the executive's time is required. Most executive interviews need only two or three hours. Like the brainstorming session, the interview is best scheduled away from the executive's office and is followed up by a summarizing memo.

Once the executive interviews are complete, all the information generated is assimilated by the ISP team. Rough-cut sketches of the data, applications, and technology platforms are derived. JAD workshops are then scheduled with personnel from the business community. The purpose is to confirm the team's findings before they are formally presented to the ISP steering committee.

JAD Workshop

Each executive interviewed is asked to gather a handful of troops to participate in a half-day workshop. The focus is to review the rough-cut data, applications, and technology plans as they apply to the executive and his or her staff.

The workshop is aimed at demonstrating the relationship between the information shared (by the executive during the brainstorm and interview) and the technical recommendations formulated by the team.

Figure 11–2 exemplifies the interdependence of the business summary information and other ISP components. A simple statement of a business goal leads to data, applications, technology, and personnel plans that would not have been defined if the ISP team hadn't understood the goal.

Any blind spots that may exist in the executive's and/or the ISP team's mode of thought can be uncovered by the other JAD participants who have had minimal or no involvement in the ISP process to date.

With the recommendations "bullet-proofed," the team can prepare the final report. Items that weren't included before are developed and

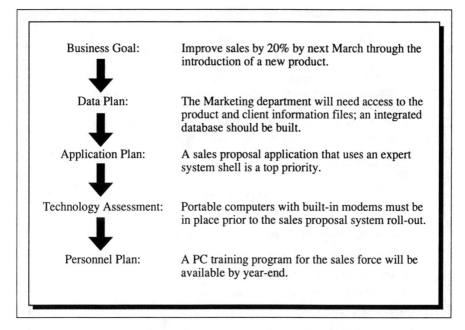

Figure 11-2. *Contents of an ISP driven from a stated business goal*

presented to the ISP steering committee along with supporting documentation. These might include:

Cost/benefit analysis,

Project priorities, and

Contingency plans.

Keeping ISP Alive

ISP work doesn't stop with the completion and approval of the plan. The finished product must be kept up-to-date with changes in business direction and technology advancements. If the company decides to pursue a new line of business, then the systems development priorities should change to support the new endeavor. Similarly, if a new technology that is sure to be of great value to the organization is introduced into the marketplace, then it should be folded into the master plan.

There are several steps a firm can take to keep ISP alive:

1. Appoint a "belly button," a responsible person who will oversee ISP. A position can be created to keep the ISP current. The ISP

▼

MAKING SENSE OF MATRICES

The information-gathering and ISP development process seems to be quite simple: sell the concept, form a team, ask some questions, and develop a plan. However, a bit of analysis that takes place behind the scenes makes the process extremely challenging. As mentioned earlier, the time between the brainstorming session and the final presentation (to the steering committee) can take six to nine months. A chunk of that time is spent in a matrix analysis.

MATRIX ANALYSIS

A series of matrices, developed throughout the ISP process, cross-references the following elements of the business:

Business processes to functional areas

Functional areas to data needs

Information systems to business goals

Data needs to information systems.

The matrices are used to identify and prioritize the applications (i.e., databases, programs, and technology) needed to support the business.

PROCESS-TO-FUNCTION MATRIX

The process-to-function matrix shows the processes each functional area within the firm performs. It's used to trace activities to departments and uncover redundancies (activities performed in more than one area) that exist across the company.

A sample process-to-function matrix is presented in Figure 11–3. Analysis of the matrix raises several questions:

Should purchasing be centralized?

Should Human Resources and Legal be merged into one department?

Can an integrated system be built to support the advertising and sales functions?

Answers to these questions, and others, are explored during the JAD sessions and ISP committee presentations.

FUNCTION-TO-DATA MATRIX

The data needed to support the enterprise is identified in the function-to-data matrix. This matrix maps functional areas according to the data they manipulate. The function-to-data matrix is used to determine potential data-sharing opportunities, as well as to demonstrate the importance of information to the performance of business activities.

Figure 11-4 presents a sample function-to-data matrix. It shows that client and order data is used by the advertising, accounting, and sales functions, for example. Perhaps this data can be integrated into a single database that can be used to support all three functions. It's up to the ISP team to derive other recommendations through further analysis.

SYSTEMS-TO-GOALS MATRIX

The systems-to-goals matrix is developed to match the recommended systems against the business goals defined in the brainstorming and interview sessions. It uncovers shortcomings in the existing applications while helping the ISP team prioritize its systems recommendations.

A sample systems-to-goals matrix is presented in Figure 11-5. It separates the systems that will primarily contribute to the achievement of specified business goals from the ones that contribute to a lesser extent.

The information presented in the figure would lead an ISP team to recommend the development of the quality control, parts inventory, and computer-integrated manufacturing systems over the others. These three applications help to achieve more goals than the others combined. However, that recommendation may be premature.

DATA-TO-SYSTEMS MATRIX

This matrix is used in unison with the systems-to-goals matrix. It identifies application integration candidates. It would be premature to rank any systems recommendations until the data-to-systems matrix has been analyzed.

The sample matrix presented in Figure 11-6, for example, shows that the integrated accounting system would act as a strong foundation for other systems development because it requires all the data types identified. If the accounting system were tackled first, it would establish the database platform needed by the other applications. Subsequent systems development is that much easier with a solid database environment in place.

When all the matrices are completed and analyzed, the ISP team develops a list of the top five systems (the "Top 5") that must be developed to help the firm achieve its mission. Figure 11-7 presents the "Top 5" for the matrices presented earlier. Review the list for an explanation of the ranking criteria.

FUNCTION / PROCESS	Advertising	Accounting	Sales	Production	Human Resources	Legal
Sales Forecasting	PR		P			
Order Processing			PR	R		
Product Marketing	PR		P			
Billing		PR	R			
Inventory Management			P	PR		
Purchasing	P	P	P	P	P	P
Hiring					PR	PR
Contract Negotiation		R			PR	PR
Severance Processing					PR	PR
Financial Forecasting	R	PR	R			

PR - Primary Responsibility
P - Participatory Involvement
R - Review Process

Figure 11-3. *A sample process-to-function matrix*

DATA FUNCTION	Client	Vendor	Product	Employee	Order	Material	Invoice	Contract	Shipment
Advertising	X				X				
Accounting	X	X			X		X		X
Sales	X		X		X		X		
Production			X		X	X			X
Human Resources				X				X	
Legal		X		X				X	

Figure 11-4. *A sample function-to-data matrix*

SYSTEMS \ DATA	Cut Inventory Costs	Create Consolidated Accounting Statements	Improve Product Pricing Process	Improve Sales Through Client Commitment	Improve Quality	Cut Purchasing Expenses	Streamline Payroll Process	Shorten Time-to-Delivery to a Week Or Less
Billing/Invoicing		C		C				
Integrated Accounting		PR						
Quality Control				PR	PR			C
Work-in-Process			PR					C
Expert Sales Forecasting				PR				C
Computer-Integrated Manufacturing	PR		C	C	C			PR
Payroll		C					PR	
Parts Inventory	C		C		C	C		
Expense Budgeting						PR		
Capacity Planning	C			C				C

PR - Primary to achievement
C - Contributes to achievement

Figure 11-5. *A sample systems-to-goals matrix*

DATA \ SYSTEMS	Client	Vendor	Product	Employee	Order	Material	Invoice	Contract	Shipment
Billing/Invoicing	X								
Integrated Accounting	X	X	X	X	X	X	X	X	X
Quality Control			X		X	X			X
Work-in-Process	X		X		X	X			
Expert Sales Forecasting	X		X						
Computer-Integrated Manufacturing			X		X	X			X
Payroll				X	X				
Parts Inventory			X			X			
Expense Budgeting				X		X			
Capacity Planning			X		X	X			X

Figure 11–6. *A sample data-to-systems matrix*

SYSTEMS RANKING	EXPLANATION
1. Integrated Accounting	Defines the database platform needed by the other applications
2. Computer-Integrated Manufacturing	Satisfies two major business goals and supports three others
3. Quality Control	Satisfies two major business goals and supports another
4. Parts Inventory	Supports four business goals
5. Capacity Planning	Supports three business goals

Figure 11–7. *Top 5 mission-critical systems*

manager plays a staff role, reporting to the CIO (or equivalent). The ISP manager's primary tasks are to implement and monitor an ISP change management program and to conduct quarterly ISP reviews for the IS Advisory Board. (As pointed out earlier, the ISP steering committee remains active after the initial ISP study. They become an advisory board that ensures that the ISP stays up-to-date.)

2. Implement an ISP change management program. The change management program would be the primary way for IS project leaders to report shifts in project focus. New system priorities can be identified and reflected in a revised ISP. As mentioned above, the ISP manager would be responsible for making the changes and distributing the results.

3. Develop an ISP tracking system. A system, developed under the direction of the ISP manager, can be developed to track and report on ISP implementations. The tracking system can take the shape of an Executive Information System (so senior management can keep track of ISP shifts) or of a stand-alone database that would be made available for use by IS managers across the company.

4. Conduct quarterly reviews. Conducting quarterly ISP reviews with the ISP Advisory Board is a good way to maintain momentum. The reviews give senior management a chance to fully appreciate the benefits of the ISP and allow the IS Department to keep a high-powered channel of communications open with senior management.

With mechanisms in place to keep the Information Systems Plan teeming, the organization can be assured of improving.

Summary

Information Systems Planning is a rigorous process that focuses business leaders to take a long, hard look at their operations and consider ways to improve them through the timely development of mission-critical systems. The planning experience opens the door for improved communication between IS staff and the business professionals they support, and helps to facilitate the establishment of user-driven systems priorities. ISPs chart a course for the future and enable companies to exploit technology for competitive gains.

Key Points

1. Information Systems Planning is done to formulate a long-range strategy for the deployment of IS technology.

2. ISPs are composed of five facets—business summary, data management plan, applications development plan, technology needs assessment, and personnel plan—and require six to nine months to develop with the proper business management involvement.

3. An awareness campaign marked by ISP lectures, company visits, and management attendance at off-site seminars is expected to gain executive commitment to systems planning.

4. An ISP steering committee is formed to oversee the development of the plan. Upon plan approval, the committee becomes an IS advisory board that monitors ISP implementation.

5. The steering committee establishes an ISP team to develop the plan. It is embellished by consulting and IS subject matter experts.

6. Business planning practices should be understood by ISP team members, to help planners develop better plans.

7. A combination of brainstorms, executive interviews, and JAD workshops is used to gather the information needed to create an ISP.

8. Matrix analysis is a technique used to synthesize the information gathered during the brainstorms, interviews, and JADs.

9. Following approval, ISPs should be kept current to reflect changes in the business environment and technology advancements. Some of the techniques used to keep ISP alive include:

   The creation of an ISP manager position,

   The implementation of an ISP change management program,

   The development of an ISP tracking system, and

   The scheduling of quarterly management reviews.

With these devices in place, how can a company help but be successful in Information Systems Planning?

References

1. James M. Kerr, "A Blueprint For Information Systems," *Database Programming & Design*, September 1989, pp. 60–67.

12

A Simple Challenge

Everything should be made as simple as possible.
Albert Einstein, 1943

What follows is a simple challenge, a vision of the future that helps to tie together many of the ideas presented in this book. It is intended to provide further insight into the way businesses will use and manage technology in the 1990s.

Dawn of a New Era

Gone are the days of implementing technology for technology's sake. The time has come for IS departments to buckle down and begin nurturing their relationships with the business professionals they support. It's the only way for the IS investments of the 1980s to pay dividends in the 1990s and beyond.

Practices that encourage user participation in systems development will gain popularity. JAD and RAD approaches will continue to evolve, while IS steering committees and various IRM-related awareness sessions become more common. The focus will switch from improving hardware performance to harnessing end user involvement.

As Figure 12–1 suggests, new partnerships between IS and business professionals will form. Business executives will drive systems planning efforts because the new breed of IS managers will show how Information Resource Management can make a distinct difference on the bottom line.

A more participative business community is only part of the picture; quality service is another. IS will continue to improve its ability to respond to user demands while concentrating on building stable and timely applications more quickly and less expensively than ever before.

Figure 12–1.　*A new IS/business partnership is emerging*

Automation of Automation

Competition is dictating the pace at which businesses change. Systems must change along with their companies. Organizations that aren't using automated means of building applications by 1995 won't be in operation by 2000. Hand-crafted code is not flexible enough to bend with the demands that will be placed upon it in the years to come.

As depicted in Figure 12–2, IS shops will become automation factories that churn business requirements into usable software for a code-hungry business world. Therefore CASE, OOPS, and Information Engineering play heavies in IS's future.

CASE tools that generate object oriented systems will represent the next wave of application development technology. Their use will be an essential element of the "reusable code and design world" of tomorrow. Information Engineering will provide the rigor and discipline to ensure that the tools are used in a way that promotes systems shareability.

IS Specialty Shops

As the systems development shops of the 1980s evolve into automation factories, new "specialty shops" will open within IS. These specialty

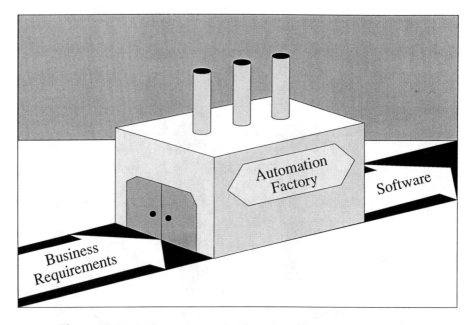

Figure 12–2. *In-house automation factories will automate automation*

shops will gear their services to particular types of users, providing better support to the business community.

Development Centers, Executive and Decision Support Centers, and Management Information Centers will have a definite place in tomorrow's IS world. Each will develop specific types of systems and follow a unique life cycle development approach.

Wheel of Systems

As Figure 12–3 suggests, firms will have a multitude of development life cycles from which to choose. A particular cycle will be selected for each project proposal brought to IS. In this new "Wheel of Systems" game, the challenge of the future will be selecting the appropriate approach for a given project proposal.

Although not every member of the IS Department will have the occasion to use each life cycle approach (for example, members of the E&DS Center may never build anything but E&DS applications), all the members of the IS development community should be exposed to every PDLC method. This exposure will give an organization the flexibility it needs to accommodate fluctuations in user requirements.

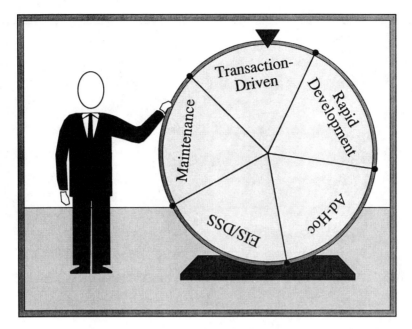

Figure 12-3.   *"Wheel of Systems" will be the development game of the future*

Application Globalization

EDI applications will become the cornerstone of American Eurostrategies, as systems built in the United States are distributed to business partners overseas (see Figure 12–4). Companies like Ford and Kellogg, which have established a European presence through the deployment of proprietary software, will face extreme competition from latecomers who take advantage of newly available telecom services.

However, by the mid-1990s, communications will no longer be a distinguishing competitive factor in the world. Instead, firms will measure success by their ability to manage the subtle challenges of language, customs, currency, and personal preferences in the global marketplace.

A New and Improved IS

To be effective, executives in charge of systems development will need to spend more time understanding the businesses they support. A new and improved IS function will emerge as business knowledge becomes a valued commodity within IS.

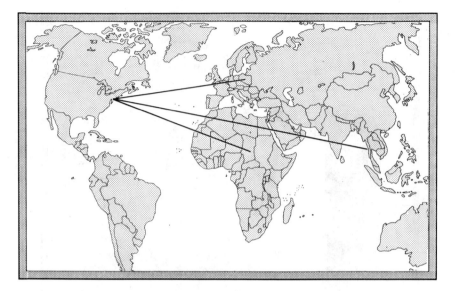

Figure 12–4. *The global marketplace of the 1990s will globalize systems*

Business training will become a major focus for the IS community. IS professionals will need to better understand the businesses they support, in order to deliver the right systems in a reasonable timeframe.

Rotational programs that cross-train IS personnel by transferring them into open positions in business units will become very popular. So, too, will the user liaison roles that are espoused by proponents of Management Information Centers. Both will be major contributors to improving the IS/Business partnership.

Enhanced Stature

The emphasis on cross-training will prepare corporate America to accept the inevitable—a senior executive team comprised of CEO, CFO, COO and CIO. Figure 12–5 suggests that tomorrow's companies will place as much importance on the management of information, automation, technology, and corporate communications as they do on the management of sales and finances.

Of course, this enhanced stature within the corporate hierarchy will not come without its share of new responsibility. Investment accountability is a key responsibility that can make or break a company.

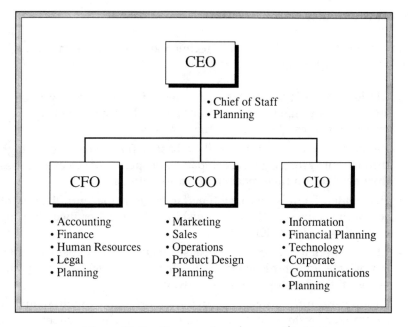

Figure 12-5. *Tomorrow's senior executive team*

Investment Accountability

Historically, IS has seldom been held accountable for its technology investments. However, those times are changing. Competition is shortening the margin between business success and failure. Even the wealthiest of concerns can no longer squander scarce resources on efforts that promise little or no return.

Since IS will be required to defend its budgets, CIOs will have financial and marketing experts on their staffs to help justify investments and measure return. These experts will be available to help other IS managers position new technologies and will report results to the keepers of the purse strings.

Does that mean that IS won't get the financial resources it needs to help the firm achieve its mission? On the contrary, "Cost control, not containment" will be the 1990s' investment slogan. Executives will be reminded that they must spend money to make money. CIOs will lead the cry, calling for significant investments in new technologies to revamp their departments.

New Technologies

Innovative software and hardware technologies will make the scene in the 1990s. Firms will grow interested in the following hot technologies:

- CD-ROM tools, because they provide an inexpensive way to store and distribute high volumes of information, helping firms keep communication lines open for real-time processing.
- Database machines, because they hasten the processing of high throughput systems, giving companies the performance capabilities they need to run their most critical applications.
- Distributed DBMSs, because they facilitate the decentralization of computing power without diminishing IS control or incurring the costs of excessive redundancies.
- Client-server architectures, because they are less expensive than mainframe and minicomputer architectures, which don't tap the power of the desktop machine anyway.
- Groupware applications, because they offer the functionality of centralized systems but are designed to run on a client-server architecture.
- Image processing technologies, because they promise ways to capture and manipulate huge amounts of paper-based information, freeing-up resources dedicated to data entry.
- Object oriented DBMSs, because they enable the storage and management of image, sound, and multidimensional arrays, which represent a significant amount of information required for decision making.
- Integrated CASE technologies, because they simplify the development and maintenance of information systems needed to support the business.

As with the other changes forecasted, the implementation of these technologies is sure to meet some resistances.

Resistance to Change

Change rarely comes without a struggle. People affected by change often feel threatened (see Figure 12–6). Undoubtedly, plans for a new IS will be met with tremendous resistance from the IS professionals who want to continue working within the old paradigm.

There will be some who:

Figure 12-6. *The challenge of change*

Fear that the introduction of CASE, EIS, and DSS technologies will eliminate their jobs;

Refuse to champion new tools and technologies because of trepidation of failure;

Believe that store-bought solutions cannot work and will want to continue to build systems from scratch;

Cling to the old way of doing business because of anxiety over the unknown;

Actually sabotage projects aimed at introducing change;

Engage in all of the above.

But don't lose hope. There are ways to overcome these resistances and make the necessary progress to achieve a first-class IS organization.

Overcoming Resistance

IS leaders charged with implementing change should consider:

- Managing expectations by reminding "nay-sayers" that change takes time;

- Preselling ideas to key business managers who might support and champion promising tools and techniques;
- Piloting new concepts before taking steps to fully implement them;
- Choosing pilot projects that can be done in a short period of time and are not crucial to the success of the business;
- Proving feasibility by delivering small successes early in implementation;
- Including top-notch training as part of every implementation plan.

Although there are no absolute guarantees, these techniques will help to diminish many of the impediments to change. As the new replaces the old, IS will be better prepared for tomorrow's business challenges.

Summary

Although the changes suggested herein are not as dramatic as those proposed by others, who foresee phenomena like thinking robots that answer the phone and respond at the customer support desk, the decade ahead promises to be both exciting and challenging.

Big Company, Inc.
Balance Sheet
December 31, 1999

Assets:		Liabilities:	
Cash	11100	Notes Payable	75500
Information	**8500**	Accounts Payable	600
Notes Receivable	1400		----------
Land	16600	Total Liabilities	76100
Office Equipment	29000		
Trucks	8000	Owner's Equity:	
Goodwill	6500		
	----------	Irene Ruepp, Capital	4000
	80100		----------
	======		80100
			======

Figure 12–7. *Information, the new item on the balance sheet*

IS departments will continue on their evolutionary paths and will make progress. New technologies like CASE and database machines will find a home in tomorrow's corporate structures. Advanced development techniques, such as AJAD and RAD approaches, will continue to engage user participation in systems designs. CIOs will head-up planning programs, and innovative organizational designs will provide businesses with unprecedented levels of technical support.

IS will make so much progress in the 1990s that, by the year 2000, firms will truly be tracking their information assets on balance sheets (see Figure 12–7), and CIOs will be the auditors.

Key Points

1. The 1990s will usher in the dawn of a new era. User-driven approaches will mature and new IS/business partnerships will form.

2. Automation factories that exploit CASE technology and advanced development techniques will become a wave of the future.

3. IS specialty shops geared toward end user computing and rapid application development will gain popularity. IS departments will be reorganized to accommodate the business needs of the future.

4. Specialty shops will give rise to new development approaches. Multiple project life cycles will emerge. Firms will have the luxury of selecting a unique set of tools and techniques to apply in each design effort.

5. Application globalization will force firms to develop systems with their international trading partners in mind. So far, this is not a task American companies are accustomed to.

6. A new IS professional will emanate from the rank and file because of the popularization of cross-training and user liaison programs.

7. CIOs will gain stature in the 1990s, and will be given the same respect as other senior business officers.

8. Advanced technologies will continue to mature, and many tools, like CD-ROM and client-server architectures, will find a home in corporate America.

9. Many of the changes forecasted will be met with resistance from IS personnel. Techniques like piloting and expectation management can be used to overcome these resistances.

Appendix

Excerpts from a Project Development Life Cycle Guide

TABLE OF CONTENTS

FOR

PROJECT DEVELOPMENT LIFE CYCLE

REFERENCE GUIDE

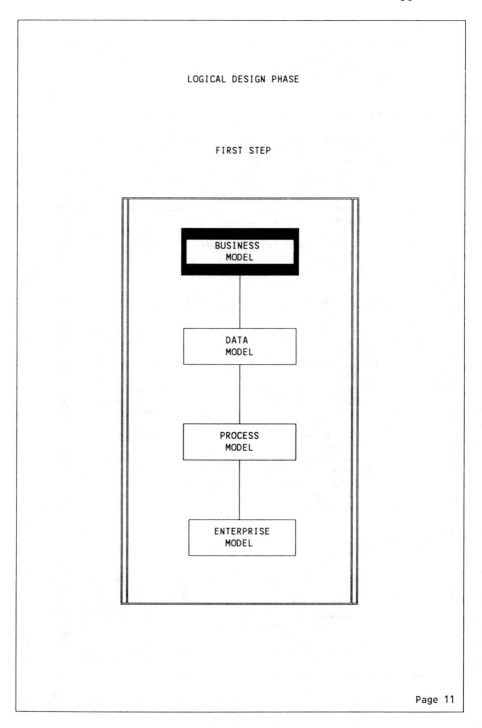

LOGICAL DESIGN PHASE

FIRST STEP

BUSINESS
MODEL

DATA
MODEL

PROCESS
MODEL

ENTERPRISE
MODEL

III. BUSINESS MODELING

A. INTRODUCTION

Business modeling is the first step in the logical design phase of the Information Engineering Methodology. It serves as the foundation for data modeling. In this task a framework for identifying the information generated and received by a business function is established.

Although not supported by CASE-SW, business modeling is a necessary first step for defining the scope and boundary for a systems development project. Business modeling deliverables are used in subsequent IE analysis stages.

Business modeling typically requires two to four weeks of full time analysis.

Business modeling produces the following deliverables:

1) Business Model Diagram
2) Function Correspondence Table

Activity/Participant Table:

ACTIVITIES	PARTICIPANTS					
	CT	DBA	UM	U	PM	IS
BUSINESS MODEL						
Business Model Diagram	R	R	R	P	PM	P
Function Correspondence Table	R	R	R	P	PM	R

B. PURPOSE

The purpose of business modeling is to determine the boundaries of a user's project request. It is a means of identifying and documenting data utilized by a specific business area. A diagram that documents the flow of information within a business area is created.

The business model diagram not only serves as a system design deliverable but also as a guide for redefining and streamlining current business processes. Some companies even use business models for training new employees.

C. BUSINESS MODELING COMPONENTS

Business models are comprised of three components:

    1) Function under study
    2) Information groups
    3) Functional correspondents

1. Functions

> A function is a domain of business expertise authorized to
> perform particular activities aimed at supporting the
> achievement of a business mission.

Business functions participate with other functions in a
community where each one buys (receives) facts which it
requires, and sells (or sends) facts required by other
business areas. Every business unit within an organization
corresponds to a function. For example, Marketing,
Accounting and, Product Development are all functions
within the XYZ.

Functions within the span of interest define a business
boundary while functions outside that span are ignored.
For example, if the function under study is Personnel, all
the functions related to it are part of the business
boundary. That is while Payroll, and Recruiting may be
part of the boundary, Finance, may not be included. This
is because Finance passes no information to and receives no
information from Personnel.

Some business areas within a company may be very large and
difficult to model. Those areas should be subdivided into
smaller functions and modeled separately. For example, the
Accounting department within a company may be cumbersome to
model. It can be sub-divided, into three smaller
functions: General Ledger, Accounts Payable and Accounts
Receivable. Once completed the three models can be merged
together to form a composite business model.

2. Correspondents

Correspondents are the customers which send information to
or receive information from the function under study. There
are two types of correspondents defined in a business model.

Internal -- An internal correspondent is a business area
within the company which passes information to/from the
function under study (i.e. another department or division
within the firm).

<u>External</u> -- An external correspondent is a business area outside the company which passes information to/from the function under study (i.e. clients or vendors).

3. Information Group

An information group is any data sent or received by the function under study. Information groups include reports, forms, computer printouts, memos, phone calls and electronic messages. More often than not, information is passed both ways between a function and its correspondents. The collection of information groups passed between a function under study and a correspondent is called a conversation.

D. BUILDING A BUSINESS MODEL

Business modeling begins by asking the users a few questions:

What information does your area generate?
What information does your area receive?
Where do you get the information?
Where do you send the information?

The answers reveal two important aspects of a business. One, the data that the business makes use of. Two, the target and source of this data. The boundary of the project is determined by defining related functional areas and the information that must be processed by the business. The project team will then try to automate the processing of the information defined.

Figure 2.1 is a legend of the symbols used in a business model diagram. Figure 2.2 represents a sample business model graphic.

The function under study is AGENCY SUPPORT. Also, represented are :

o The CLIENT area which periodically sends client information forms to the AGENCY.

o The CONTRACT ADMINISTRATION area which mails commission checks to the AGENCY.

o The UNDERWRITING area which receives applications from the AGENCY on a as needed basis.

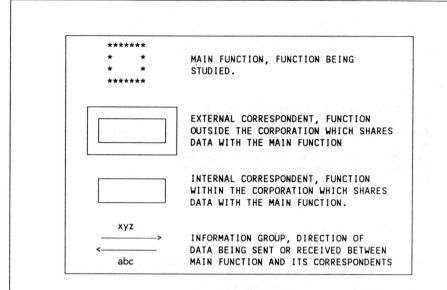

```
*******
*     *      MAIN FUNCTION, FUNCTION BEING
*     *      STUDIED.
*******


 _____    EXTERNAL CORRESPONDENT, FUNCTION
|  ____  |   OUTSIDE THE CORPORATION WHICH SHARES
| |    | |   DATA WITH THE MAIN FUNCTION
| |____| |
|_____|


 _____    INTERNAL CORRESPONDENT, FUNCTION
|        |   WITHIN THE CORPORATION WHICH SHARES
|        |   DATA WITH THE MAIN FUNCTION.
|_____|

    xyz
 _____>   INFORMATION GROUP, DIRECTION OF
<_____    DATA BEING SENT OR RECEIVED BETWEEN
    abc      MAIN FUNCTION AND ITS CORRESPONDENTS
```

Figure 2.1 Symbol Table

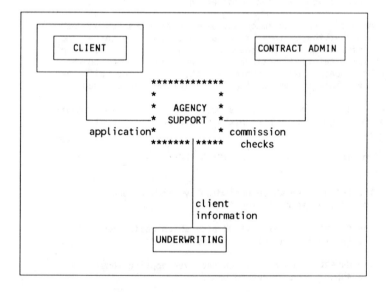

```
 _____                        _____
|  _____  |                      |              |
| | CLIENT| |                      | CONTRACT ADMIN|
| |_____| |                      |_____|
|_____|
     |          *************             |
     |          *           *             |
     |          *  AGENCY    *            |
     |_____*  SUPPORT   *_____|
                *           *
 application*   *           * commission
                ******* ***** checks
                       |
                       |
                   client
                   information
                    _____
                   | UNDERWRITING |
                   |_____|
```

Figure 2.2 Sample Business Model

E. BUSINESS MODEL DIAGRAM

A business model diagram is the graphical representation of the function under study and its correspondents. The graph also depicts the information groups produced during the execution of business activities. When complete, the business model diagram represents all the facts required to support the function under study.

The function under study is represented as an octagon (8 sided polygon). It is drawn in the center of the chart.

The correspondents are drawn as rectangles. Internal correspondents are depicted as single-lined rectangles. External correspondents are depicted as doubled-lined rectangles. These are drawn around the octagon.

An arrow drawn between the function being studied and its correspondents designates the direction of the information flow. The information groups are the labels on the lines (see Figure 2.2).

F. FUNCTION CORRESPONDENCE TABLE

As the business model diagram is developed, a function correspondence table is created. It documents the business model in textual form.

The entries on the table are:

Main Function - the name of the function under study.

Information Group - the names of the data being sent or received between the function under study and its correspondents

To/From - Designates whether the information is generated or received by the function under study.

Correspondent - the names of the business areas which interact with the function under study.

Information Group Definition - briefly defines what information is contained in the information group.

A Function Correspondence Table Form is presented in Figure 2.3. This form should be used to document Business Modeling activities at the XYZ

Main Function:			
Info Groups	T/F	Correspondent	Info Group Definition

Figure 2.3   Function Correspondence Table Form

G. ISSUES AND ASSUMPTIONS

Business modeling often uncovers areas of uncertainty within
business areas. A list of issues and assumptions should be
accumulated as business modeling progresses. These may be
statements of facts or mode of operations which are unclear.
The list will be reviewed periodically by appropriate business
management. Resolutions that lead to more efficient or
profitable practice will be sought.

These results will be documented and distributed to the project
development team. User management can use the resolutions as a
way to streamline business practice within the area they manage.

For example:

Fact:

> Function 'Y' sends function 'X' a set of 3 reports each
> week. Function 'X' sends those reports to function 'Z'.
> Function 'X' never uses or looks at the reports sent by
> 'Y'.

Issue:

> Shall the flow of these reports change so that 'Y' sends
> them directly to 'Z'? This will eliminate a mail service
> activity which does not concern or profit function 'X'.

Resolution:

> Eliminate the activity. There is no value added through
> this process. This is a time consumer that is better left
> outside of the function's purview.

H. SUMMARY OF BUSINESS MODELING

o Begin a development effort by business modeling.

o Define and name the correspondents.

o Identify the data that is sent to and received from the
  function under study.

o Document your findings in a business model diagram and a
  correspondence table.

o Resolve all issues and assumptions.

The following example illustrates the deliverables from a
business modeling exercise.

PC SUPPORT BUSINESS MODEL

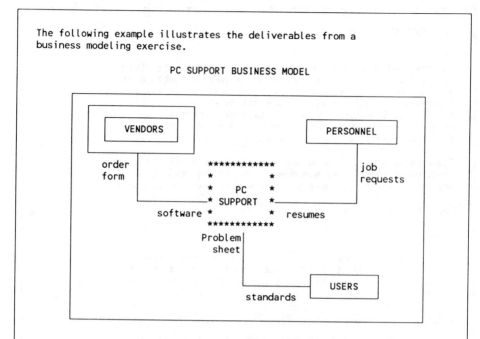

FUNCTION CORRESPONDENCE TABLE

Main Function: PC SUPPORT			
Info Groups	T/F	Correspondent	Info Group Definition
Software	from	VENDORS	PC software products
Order Form	to	VENDORS	A request for product form
Resumes	from	PERSONNEL	Individual curriculum vitae
Job Request	to	PERSONNEL	A job request form
Standards	to	USERS	Operational procedures
Prbl Sheet	from	USERS	Log sheet of problem areas

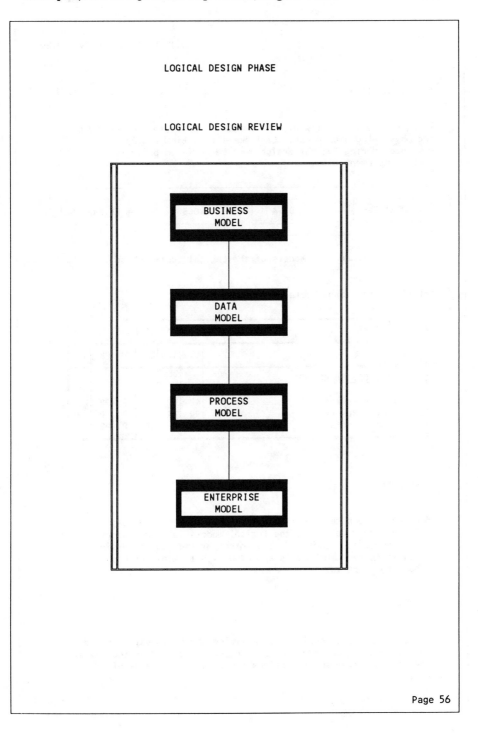

LOGICAL DESIGN PHASE

LOGICAL DESIGN REVIEW

BUSINESS MODEL

DATA MODEL

PROCESS MODEL

ENTERPRISE MODEL

A. INTRODUCTION

A logical design review will be conducted prior to implementing the physical design phase. Each model (see Figure 6.1) developed during logical design must be reviewed prior to system implementation.

| BUSINESS | — | DATA | — | PROCESS | — | ENTERPRISE |

Figure 6.1 Models of the Logical Design Phase

Activity/Participant Table

ACTIVITIES	PARTICIPANTS					
	CT	DBA	UM	U	PM	IS
LOGICAL DESIGN REVIEW						
Prepare Package	NP	NP	NP	P	PR	PR
Conduct Review	PR	PR	P	P	P	P
Re-Work (optional)	NP	NP	NP	P	PR	P

B. PURPOSE

In order to reap the benefits of IE's physical design features, it is necessary to review the logical models for consistency and adherence to standards. The intent of the logical design review is to have the models approved by a team of business and methodology experts.

C. OVERVIEW

The review process consists of analyzing the business, data and process models. CASE-SW generated reports are used in the review. They act as system specifications for subsequent phases of design.

The review team (comprised of Project Personnel, User Management and TMOS DBAs and CASE Technology specialists) examines the models for correctness, conformance to standards and completeness. If re-work is needed it is identified during the review and will be implemented prior to approval.

D. LOGICAL REVIEW PROCESS

When the project team has completed its analysis and developed the deliverables listed in Figure 6.2, the team leader schedules a review meeting.

Business Model:	Business Model Graphic Function Correspondence Table
Data Model:	Normalized Entity List Entity Relationship Diagram
Process Model:	Process Hierarchy Diagram Process Dependency Diagram Process Action Diagram

Figure 6.2 Deliverables to be Reviewed

1. Review Participants

The following personnel participate in the logical review session:

CASE Technology Specialist:

This individual has final approval of the logical design. CASE specialists are responsible for identifying areas for improvement in the design.

User Management:

These people are responsible for verifying that the models presented reflect the business area's requirements.

DBA:

>   These people are responsible for transforming the
>   logical data model into physical databases.

Project Personnel:

>   These people are responsible for developing the code
>   and implementing the system.

2. Responsibilities

Specifically, the review team:

>   o Reviews the business model for correctness and
>   completeness.
>
>   o Examines the data model for accuracy.
>
>   o Verifies that the ERD correlates with the PAD.
>
>   o Verifies that the PHD correlates with the PDD.
>
>   o Determines that the attributes and entity names
>   conform to naming conventions and that each entity
>   has a proper key.

Two reviews are usually needed for approval of the logical
models. The first review identifies areas for improvement.
The second review verifies that all requested changes have
been correctly implemented.

Once verified the Logical Design Review Form (on the next
page) is completed and signed by the Director of CASE
Technology, the user and project management personnel.
Physical design begins following approval.

3. Reports

The following logical design reports are available through
the CASE-SW and should be used in the review.

Model Content Report:

>   Lists all objects in a model (ID, type, code,
>   description and properties).

Debugging Report:

>   Identifies problems encountered in CASE-SW models.

```
                        LOGICAL DESIGN REVIEW
                               FORM


PROJECT MANAGER: _____  DATE: __ /__ /__

PROJECT:_____  DATA MODEL: _____

==================================================================

CASE Technology use Only:

Review Comments: _____
_____
_____
_____
_____
_____
_____
_____
_____
_____
_____
_____
_____
_____
_____
_____
_____
_____
_____
_____
_____

==================================================================
Approvals:
   CASE Technology Center: _____     Date: __ /__ /__
   Project Manager: _____  Date: __ /__ /__

==================================================================

Date Received:      __ /__ /__        Date Reviewed:   __ /__ /__
Date Implemented:   __ /__ /__        Date Notified:   __ /__ /__

==================================================================



```

Entity Definition:

> Includes entity descriptions and pertinent entity
> details such as attributes within entity types.

Attribute Definition:

> Includes attribute descriptions and pertinent attribute
> details such as field lengths and character types.

Function Definition:

> Includes details about the functions and processes of a
> specific model.

These reports are used by system managers and business
users to facilitate the review process.

E. RECAPITULATION

Logical models (business, data and process) are reviewed prior
to physical implementation. Any flaws identified during the
review with users, DBA and CASE technology personnel will be
documented on the Logical Design Review Form. The project team
is expected to make the appropriate changes. Once implemented,
the models are again reviewed. Physical design begins upon
approval.

XII. PRODUCTION TURNOVER

A. INTRODUCTION

Production Turnover is the last step in the physical design
phase of the project development life cycle. It is conducted
after Application Design Review completion. In this task the
CLISTs and Procedures are migrated from the Test to the
Production environment.

Production Turnover is done in three steps:

    1) Submission of Database Request Form to DBA
    2) Submission of TSO Application Fact Sheet to DP Services
    3) Submission of TSO Application Fact Sheet to Security
       Administration

The DBA group reserves space for the system. The DP Services
group schedules backup/recovery run jobs. The Security
Administration group assigns user IDs.

Activity/Participant Table

ACTIVITIES	PARTICIPANTS						
	SA	DBA	UM	U	PM	IS	DS
Prepare Turnover Procedure	NP	NP	NP	P	PR	PR	NP
Request for Turnover	NP	NP	NP	P	PR	R	NP
Prepare DASD	NP	PR	NP	NP	P	P	NP
Prepare IDs	NP	P	NP	R	PR	P	PR
Execute Turnover	PR	NP	R	R	R	R	R
	R	R	R	R	PR	P	PR

* SA = Securtiy Administrator   DS = DP Services

B. PURPOSE

This process defines the rules and regulations for migration
CLISTs and Procedures from Test to Production environments.
It's intended to aid systems developers in the evolution of
their applications. Production Turnover standards are to be
upheld by the entire IS community.

C. OVERVIEW

The Production turnover process insures a protected
environment for the production applications. This
environment will not interfere with the Test development
environment and will prevent the contamination of important
business information.

D. OPERATING PROCEDURES

Application programmers may use CLISTs and Procedures to
execute their DBMS-SW applications. In program development,
CLISTs reside in TSO.CLISTS dataset, and Procedures reside in
the application programmer's development dataset. When a

project is ready for migration to the Production DBMS-SW
environment, the Applications group is to fill out the
Database Request Form (DBA014).

The request to move CLISTs from TSO.CLISTS to
COMM.PROD.CLISTS, and to move the Procedures from the
application programmer's development dataset to
SYS1.TSO.PROCLIB should be made to the Database Processing
Services group through the TSO Application Fact Sheet (form
SA03). The Test CLISTs will be deleted from TEST.CLISTS by the
Database Administration group at this time, and the Quality
Procedures will be deleted from SYS1.TSO.PROCLIB by the
Database Processing Services group, as requested.

The TSO Application Fact Sheet (SA03) is also to be filled
out by the Applications group, and submitted to the Security
Administration group, to indicate the connection of userids.

The CLISTs and Procedures are to reference Production
Libraries. There should be no references to libraries
beginning with DBMS.TEST, COMM.TEST, SYSPP.CV.TEST,
SYSPP.DBTS, SYSPP.CV.DBTS. Those CLISTs and Procedures that
do reference Test, or Development libraries will not be moved to
Production.

The forms appear on the following pages.

Form DBA014

DATABASE REQUEST FORM

Project: Date Requested

Requestor: SID #:

Approvals:

USER: DSM:
IDS SPA: DBA PA:
IDS PA: DBDI MANAGER:

REQUEST DATABASE: REQUESTED AVAILABILITY DATE

------ TEST
      ----- NEW ----- EXISTING   --------
------ QUALITY *   --------
------ PRODUCTION   --------

* Indicate clist (s) to be copied to quality clist library

BRIEF DESCRIPTION: _____
_____
_____
_____
_____
_____

CHANGES TO EXISTING DATABASES:

 SCHEMA   --------------
 SUBSCHEMA (S)   --------------------------

If applicable: Attach Logical Database Design Package
                 Attach requested Database changes

Persons to be contacted in case of DB problems:

1. _____   2. _____

Form SA03

TSO APPLICATION FACT SHEET

Project: _____   Date Submitted: _____

Requestor: _____   Date Required: _____

User Management Approval: _____

Project Management Approval: _____

User ID's Requested: _____ (total qty)

User Names: Current ID:

_____   _____
_____   _____
_____   _____
_____   _____
_____   _____
_____   _____
_____   _____
_____   _____
_____   _____

For SA Use Only:

  Priority: High: _____ Medium: _____ Low: _____

  Assigned To: _____

E. IN CASE OF FAILURE

The systems development groups are responsible for the
contents of CLISTs and Procedures. If there are any changes
to the requirements of the CLISTs and Procedure, as used by
DBMS-SW the DBA group will communicate them to the
development teams during Production Turnover.

A diagnosis of a failure can be made by the errors obtained
during program execution within the production environment.
Users may experience abend code 1239 if they are allocating
production libraries, while executing a test schema. If the
Test database is updated, instead of the production one,
contact the DBA group immediately.

F. RECAPITULATION

o Production Turnover is the last phase of the PDLC
o Forms SA03 and DBA014 must be completed
o DB space, Backup/Recovery Procedures and User IDs are
  supplied through the process
o The content of CLISTs and Procedures are the developer's
  responsibility
o Contact DBA in case of improper DBMS update
o All parties must conform to this standard

GLOSSARY

ANALYSIS TOOLSET:

Refers to the CASE-SW tools that support the data and process modeling disciplines of Information Engineering.

AUTOMATED JOINT APPLICATION DEVELOPMENT (AJAD):

A development technique that combines users and IS personnel for the purpose of building an information system. CASE tools are used during the process to capture systems requirements.

ATTRIBUTE:

Data items contained within an entity or an information group.

BUSINESS MODELING:

The first step of the logical design process. It is a discipline which defines a particular business function and all the information which it generates and receives.

BUSINESS MODEL GRAPHIC:

A graphical representation of a business model which depicts the function under study, its related correspondents and its information groups.

CASE:

Computer Aided Software Engineering is a body of productivity tools such as design analyzers and code generators which automates systems analysis, systems design and program generation.

CASE-SW

A CASE tool based on the IE methodology. It is produced and sold by Mephis Instruments.

CODE GENERATOR:

A software product that converts process models into COBOL code with embedded SQL.

CONVERSATION:

Collection of information groups passed between a function under study and a correspondent.

DATA ARCHITECTURE:

A set of interdependent data structures that support the firm's business activities.

DATA CONSTRUCTS:

A set of entities and relationships within a data model. A data model
is a set of data constructs.

DATA DICTIONARY:

A mainframe software product that stores information about data,
including field lengths and record definitions.

DATA MODEL:

A diagram that represents the interrelationships among normalized
entities.

DATA MODELING:

Second step in the logical design phase. It is a discipline for
defining data requirements in terms of entities and relationships.

DBMS-SW:

A database management system sold by Mephis Instruments.

DEPENDENCY ANALYSIS:

Study of the interdependence between processes.

DESIGN GENERATOR:

A software product that converts data models into DBMS-SW databases.

DESIGN TOOLSET:

Refers to the CASE-SW tools that support the conversion of logical models
into physical designs.

ELEMENTARY PROCESS:

The lowest level of decomposition for a process. Also known as a
procedure module.

ENCYCLOPEDIA:

Synonymous with repository, it is the mainframe component of the CASE-SW
where models reside. All data and process models are stored here.

ENTERPRISE MODELING:

Fourth step in the logical design phase. It is a discipline which
represents a composite of all project data models within the company.
The model resides on the mainframe and is available for viewing and use
through CASE-SW.

ENTITY:
A set of related attributes. (i.e. CLIENT, POLICY, AGENT).

ENTITY HIERARCHY DIAGRAM (EHD):

A diagram which represents an entity in relation to its subtypes.

ENTITY NOMINATION:

A data modeling activity which defines the data items that compromise
the information groups discovered in business modeling.

ENTITY RELATIONSHIP DIAGRAM (ERD):

Synonymous with data model, a graphical representation of the
interrelationships among normalized entities.

EXTERNAL CORRESPONDENT:

An organization outside of the enterprise that passes information to or
receives information from a functional area within the company (i.e.
STATE GOVERNMENT, CLIENT, SUPPLIERS etc.).

FUNCTION :

A group of business activities that together completely support one aspect
of furthering the mission of the enterprise (MARKETING, ACCOUNTING, R&D).

FUNCTIONAL AREA:

Synonymous to function. It represents a domain of business expertise.

FUNCTION CORRESPONDENCE TABLE:

Detailed facts about a business model, documented in a tabular format.

FUNCTION DECOMPOSITION:

The breakdown of business activities into their sub-components.

INFORMATION ENGINEERING:

A set of complementary design disciplines that create an integrated
information system. It is compromised of logical and physical design
phases (i.e. the combination of business modeling, data modeling,
process modeling and enterprise modeling).

INFORMATION ENGINEERING WORKSTATION:

PC component of CASE-SW, where local project models reside.

INFORMATION GROUPS:

The data being passed between a business function and its correspondents
most often used in a business modeling context).

INTERNAL CORRESPONDENT:

A functional area within the enterprise that passes information to or receives information from a function under study (e.g. Business Modeling).

JUNCTION RECORD:

An intersection entity which resolves many-to-many relationships among entities.

KEY:

One or more attributes which uniquely identify an entity.

LOGICAL DESIGN:

The set of business, data and process models needed to support a particular area of the business (technology independent).

LOGICAL DESIGN REVIEW FORM:

A form used to officially approve logical design and endorse the initiation of the physical design process.

MAIN FUNCTION:

The business model function being studied.

MODEL MERGING:

A technique for integrating project data models into an enterprise model. Supported by CASE-SW Encyclopedia.

MODEL SUBSETTING:

A technique for re-applying data defined in the enterprise model. Supported by CASE-SW Encyclopedia.

NORMALIZATION:

Normalization is a process for simplifying complex data structures. Nominated entities are normalized to yield stable data models. Once normalized, each entity can be uniquely defined by a key.

PHYSICAL DESIGN:

The databases and programs needed to support a particular area of the business (technology dependent).

PLANNING TOOLSET:

Tools in the CASE-SW which support the information systems planning discipline of IE

PROCEDURE MODULE:

The actual ADD, DELETE, and MODIFY pseudocode for a process model (i.e. elementary process).

PROCESS:

Defined in process modeling, this is a low level activity for which an input and an output are defined (comprised of one or more procedure modules).

PROCESS ACTION DIAGRAM (PAD):

A diagram which is created with the CASE-SW during process modeling. It defines the logic to support a process.

PROCESS DEPENDENCY DIAGRAM (PDD):

A diagram which is created with CASE-SW during dependency analysis. It represents chronological steps which must be taken to perform a process.

PROCESS HIERARCHY DIAGRAM (PHD):

A diagram which is created with the CASE-SW during process modeling. It depicts a hierarchy of business activities (functions and processes).

PROCESS LOGIC ANALYSIS:

The study of the add, delete and modify rules for entities defined in data modeling. It is used to define procedure modules (elementary process).

PROCESS MODELING:

Third step in the logical design phase. It identifies how data is manipulated in the performance of business activities.

RELATIONSHIP:

An association between two entities.

RELATIONSHIP CARDINALITY:

Defines the nature of the relationships between two entities (i.e. one-to-one, one-to-many or many-to-many).

REPOSITORY:

Similar to data dictionary, a repository is a mainframe tool that stores data models, process models, enterprise models, database designs and program definitions.

REVERSE ENGINEERING:

An automated method for converting old systems into new ones using
structured techniques and relational technology.

SYSTEM LIFE CYCLE:

Time period in which a system is initiated, tested, implemented, and set
in production. It is conducted in two phases: logical design and
physical design.

X-TEST ANALYST:

The person responsible for stress testing any application requiring access
to the x-test environment.

Bibliography

Chapter 1

Peter F. Drucker, *Innovation and Entrepreneurship.* New York: Harper & Row, 1985.

James C. Emery, *Management Information Systems.* New York: Oxford University Press, 1987.

Donald A. Marchand and Forest W. Horton, Jr., *Infotrends.* New York: John Wiley & Sons, 1986.

William R. Synott and William H. Gruber, *Information Resource Management.* New York: John Wiley & Sons, 1981.

Chapter 2

Kim B. Clark, Robert H. Hayes, and Christopher Loreng, Eds., *The Uneasy Alliance.* Cambridge, MA: Harvard Business School Press, 1985.

Lawrence M. Miller, *Barbarians to Bureaucrats.* New York: Clarkson N. Porter, Inc., 1989.

Larry M. Singer, *The Data Processing Manager's Survival Manual.* New York: John Wiley & Sons, 1982.

Robert E. Umbaugh, Ed., *Handbook of MIS Management.* Boston, MA: Auerbach Publishers, 1988.

Chapter 3

Bernard H. Boar, *Application Prototyping.* New York: John Wiley & Sons, 1984.

Chris Gane, *Rapid Systems Design.* Englewood Cliffs, NJ: Prentice-Hall, 1989.

Jane Wood and Denise Silva, *Joint Application Design.* New York: John Wiley & Sons, 1989.

Chapter 4

Arnaldo C. Hax and Nicolas S. Majiuf, *Strategic Management.* Englewood Cliffs, NJ: Prentice-Hall, 1984.

Peter G. W. Keen and Michael S. Scott Morton, *Decision Support Systems: An Organizational Perspective.* Reading, MA: Addison-Wesley, 1978.

John F. Rochart and David W. Delong, *Executive Support Systems.* New York: Dow Jones-Irwin, 1988.

Chapter 5

Kenneth C. Laudon and Jane Price Laudon, *Management Information Systems.* New York: Macmillan Publishing, 1988.

Raymond R. Panko, *End User Computing: Management Application and Technology.* New York: John Wiley & Sons, 1988.

Chapter 6

Arthur Young & Co., *The Arthur Young Practical Guide to Information Engineering.* New York: John Wiley & Sons, 1987.

David M. Kroenke, *Database Processing.* Chicago: Science Research Associates, Inc., 1983.

Texas Instruments, *A Guide to Information Engineering Using the IEF.* Texas Instruments, Plano, TX: 1988.

Chapter 7

Kamran Parsaye, Mark Chignall, Setrag Khoshafian, and Harry Wong, *Intelligent Databases.* New York: John Wiley & Sons, 1989.

Sally Shlaer and Stephen J. Mellor, *Object-Oriented Systems Analysis.* Englewood Cliffs, NJ: Yourdan Press, 1988.

Chapter 8

Carma McClure, *CASE is Software Automation.* Englewood Cliffs, NJ: Prentice-Hall, 1989.

Max Schindler, *Computer-Aided Software Design.* New York: John Wiley & Sons, 1990.

Chapter 9

Jeffrey S. Keen, *Managing Systems Development.* New York: John Wiley & Sons, 1987

Chapter 10

Stuart E. Madnik, Ed., *The Strategic Use of Information Technology.* New York: Oxford University Press, 1987.

Stephanie K. Marrus, *Building the Strategic Plan.* New York: John Wiley & Sons, 1984.

James Martin and Joe Leben, *Strategic Information Planning Methodologies.* Englewood Cliffs, NJ: Prentice-Hall, 1989.

Alan J. Rowe, Richard O. Mason, and Karl E. Dickel, *Strategic Management and Business Policy.* Reading, MA: Addison-Wesley, 1985.

Chapter 11

Robert A. Buzzell, Ed., *Marketing in an Electronic Age.* Cambridge, MA: Harvard Business School Press, 1985.

Robert E. Filman and Daniel P. Friedman, *Coordinated Computing.* New York: McGraw-Hill Book Co., 1984.

Phylis K. Sokol, *EDI: The Competitive Edge.* New York: McGraw-Hill Book Co., 1989.

Chapter 12

Richard P. Brennan, *Levitating Trains and Kamikaze Genes.* New York: John Wiley & Sons, 1990.

James Martin, *Technology's Crucible.* Englewood Cliffs, NJ: Prentice-Hall, 1987.

Glossary

ACCEPTANCE TEST A process whereby the end user decides whether a new system meets requirements.

AD/CYCLE Application development cycle is an integrated set of CASE technologies sold by IBM.

AD HOC QUERY A random search for information within a database. Tools are available that help to define and execute these queries.

AJAD Automated joint application development.

APPLICATION The collection of computer programs and databases that collectively automates a particular business activity or function.

APPLICATION DEVELOPMENT PLAN The component of an information systems plan that specifies the systems that must be built in order to help the business achieve its mission.

APPLICATION LOGIC TRANSLATOR A prototyping tool that interprets program logic and translates it into English.

ARTIFICIAL INTELLIGENCE Using computer technology to solve problems that ordinarily require human intelligence.

ATTRIBUTE Pieces of information that comprise an entity.

AUTOMATED JOINT APPLICATION DEVELOPMENT A systems development technique that engages end users in the application specification process and uses CASE tools to document the requirements as they are discussed.

AUTOMATION FACTORIES A future application development environment where CASE tools are used to churn out code from quickly defined business specifications.

AWARENESS PROGRAM Any approach aimed at exposing an organization to new systems tools and methods.

BACK-END TOOLS The technologies that comprise the code and design generation capabilities of CASE software.

BRAINSTORMING A technique for gathering information whereby participants are encouraged to freely speak their minds and explore new ideas.

BUSINESS FUNCTION An organizational entity that is responsible for performing a group of activities essential to the achievement of company goals and objectives.

BUSINESS MODEL The graphical representation of the information flow within a business function.

BUSINESS MODELING A technique for defining the information that is generated and received by a business function.

BUSINESS PLANNING The process of defining the mission, goals and objectives of an enterprise.

BUSINESS PROCESS The activities that a business function is responsible for performing. Business processes are automated through applications.

CASE   Computer-aided software engineering.

CASE EVALUATION COMMITTEE A group formed within an organization that is charged with investigating and selecting CASE technology.

CASE MANAGEMENT GROUP An organizational unit within the information systems (IS) department that is responsible for supporting the implementation and use of CASE technology.

CD-ROM Compact disc, read-only memory is a data storage device that can only be read from, and not written to. Special machines are needed to both create and read CD-ROMs.

CENTRAL PROCESSING UNIT The main component of a computer. It is responsible for interpreting programs, retrieving data, and calculating results.

CHANGE AGENT A person who introduces and implements innovative tools and techniques. IS executives will be called upon to be change agents.

CHIEF INFORMATION OFFICER The executive in charge of the information systems department. CIOs set technology direction within their organizations based on the needs of the enterprise.

CIO Chief information officer.

CLASS An OOPS term for object categories. A cat is a member of the animal class, for example.

CLASS HIERARCHY An OOPS technique used to group classes of objects to facilitate inheritance.

CLIENT-SERVER APPLICATION A system that is divided into two segments—one that is centralized and made available to all users of the system, and another that is particular to the individual user. Client-server applications are becoming popular in management information centers.

CODE GENERATOR A CASE tool that converts process models into executable program logic.

COMPUTER-AIDED SOFTWARE ENGINEERING Software technology that automates the activities of systems developers. Computer-aided software engineering tools help practitioners diagrammatically represent user requirements and convert them into applications.

CONSTRUCTION A term used to define the process of transforming systems designs into working applications.

CONTRACT PROGRAMMING The process of using third-party consultants to design and implement applications.

COST/BENEFIT ANALYSIS A method for estimating and comparing the cost and benefit of an information systems proposal. Cost/Benefit analysis is performed prior to any major technology acquisition or development.

CPU Central processing unit.

DA Data Administration. An organizational unit that is charged with managing a firm's data resources. Data administration personnel are generally responsible for supporting the data dictionary and maintaining the integrity of logical data definitions within a company.

DATABASE ADMINISTRATION An organizational unit that is charged with managing the technical and operational aspects of a firm's data resources. Database administration personnel are generally responsible for designing and implementing database systems, as well as supporting the database management system technology used within a company.

DATABASE MACHINE A type of computer that has a built-in DBMS that provides a means of supporting high throughput database applications.

DATABASE MANAGEMENT SYSTEM The software used to create and manage a database.

DATABASE SIMULATOR A prototyping tool that is used to mimic a shared database environment. It is used to demonstrate how a new application will perform in the production environment.

DATA DICTIONARY OR DIRECTORY A software application used to define and manage the data used in an organization.

DATA-DRIVEN DEVELOPMENT Any systems analysis approach that defines data requirements of an application before determining how the data will be processed. Information engineering is a data-driven approach.

DATA ELEMENT See Attribute.

DATA MODEL —A graphical representation of data and its interrelationships. Data models are used to specify database requirements.

DATA MODELING A process for defining a data model.

DATA MANAGEMENT PLAN The component of an information systems plan that defines the data needed to support the business.

DATA NORMALIZATION A data modeling process used to simplify random groupings of data into entities.

DATA STRUCTURE DIAGRAM A graphical representation of a database design.

DATA-TO-SYSTEM MATRIX A chart that cross-references entities to the systems that manipulate them. It is used to determine systems integration opportunities.

DBA Database administration.

DBMS Database management system.

DECISION SUPPORT CENTER An organizational unit charged with developing and supporting decision support systems.

DECISION SUPPORT SYSTEM An application that enhances a decision-maker's ability to make accurate management decisions. Decision support systems are usually developed for mid-level management.

DESIGN GENERATOR A CASE tool that converts data models into database systems.

DEVELOPMENT CENTER An organizational unit charged with providing IS departments with guidance and support in the use of advanced systems construction tools and techniques.

DSS Decision support system.

DUAL REPOSITORY A strategy that calls for the integration of two encyclopedias. One encyclopedia will manage the data models and the other will manage the databases. It is particularly useful in situations where a firm has an existing encyclopedia and wishes to acquire a new higher powered one.

EDI Electronic data interchange.

E&DS CENTER Executive and decision support centers are organizational units charged with developing and supporting EIS and DSS applications.

E&DS SUPPORT REPRESENTATIVE Executive and decision support personnel responsible for building and supporting EIS and DSS applications.

EIS Executive information systems.

ELECTRONIC DATA INTERCHANGE Technology that facilitates electronic trade between organizations. It is comprised of telecommunication, application, and computer technology.

ENCAPSULATION A feature of OOPS that allows an object to exist and have meaning without having a relationship with any other object in an object-oriented system.

ENCYCLOPEDIA An advanced data dictionary that stores the use and significance of data along with its definition. Encyclopedias, unlike data dictionaries, have the capability of storing and managing program logic and database designs.

END USER The individuals that use an application.

END USER SUPPORT REPRESENTATIVE Management information center personnel who work with and report to business unit personnel.

ENTERPRISE MODEL A composite data model that represents all modeled data within an organization.

ENTERPRISE MODELING The process of creating and managing an enterprise model.

ENTERPRISE MODEL ADMINISTRATOR An individual charged with overseeing the use and evolution of an enterprise model. Most enterprise model administrators are data administration personnel.

ENTITY A person, place, or thing about which information is stored and managed. Data models are comprised of entities and their interrelationships.

ENTITY NOMINATION The process of defining the data that a business function cares about. Data normalization is performed on the random data groupings developed through entity nomination.

ETHICAL AUDIT A business planning practice that evaluates the moral implications of a business strategy.

EXECUTIVE INFORMATION SYSTEM An application developed to help senior managers make decisions.

EXECUTIVE INTERMEDIARY A person who represents an executive during EIS development. They are usually high-level assistants to the executive and have been empowered to make judgments regarding the content of the EIS application.

FINALIZED DESIGN A tested application that is ready to be moved into the production environment.

FINANCIAL ANALYSIS A business planning practice that examines the financial status of an organization.

FIRST-CUT DESIGN An untested application that is ready for end user review.

FOURTH-GENERATION LANGUAGE An easy-to-use programming language that provides quick ways for developing queries and reports.

FUNCTIONAL CORRESPONDENT An organizational unit that passes information to or receives information from a business function.

FUNCTION-TO-DATA MATRIX A chart that cross-references business functions to the data entities they use. It shows the information that is important to a business function.

FUNCTION UNDER STUDY The business function that is being examined during business modeling.

FUTURIST A forward-thinking individual who can anticipate the trends that will emerge and effect companies in years to come. IS executives will be called upon to be futurists.

FRONT-END The application interface that an end user must interact with in order to execute system functions.

FRONT-END TOOLS The component of CASE technology that provide ways to graphically depict user requirements.

IE Information engineering.

IE LIFE CYCLE The steps that must be taken to develop an information engineering-based application.

INDUSTRY ANALYSIS A business planning practice that evaluates the strategies of the competition within a particular industry or market segment.

INFORMATION CENTER An organizational unit responsible for providing end users with the tools they need to build their own applications. In the future most information centers will give way to management information centers.

INFORMATION ENGINEER A person that uses information engineering techniques exclusively to build applications.

INFORMATION ENGINEERING A data-driven design discipline that encompasses business, data, process, and enterprise modeling practices.

INFORMATION RESOURCE MANAGEMENT The practice of managing information as a corporate asset.

INFORMATION SYSTEMS The organizational unit responsible for building applications and managing computer technology.

INFORMATION SYSTEMS PLANNING A practice that defines the data, applications, technology, and technical personnel needed to achieve the mission of the business.

INHERITANCE An OOPS feature that facilitates the reuse of previously defined objects.

INTEGRATED SERVICES DIGITAL NETWORK Telecommunications technology that enables companies to transfer data and voice through the same phone lines.

INTEGRATOR An individual who can reconcile business requirements and technology directions into a consistent action strategy. IS executives will be called upon to become integrators.

IRM Information resource management.

IS Information systems.

ISDN Integrated services digital network.

ISP Information systems plan.

ISP STEERING COMMITTEE A group of senior executives from different areas of the business who are responsible for overseeing the creation of an information systems plan.

IS SPECIALTY SHOPS IS organizational units that are geared towards providing individualized support to different types of users. An E&DS center is an example of an IS specialty shop.

ITERATIVE INTEGRATION An enterprise modeling approach for merging multiple data models into a single concise and consistent model.

JAD Joint application development.

JAD FACILITATOR The individual charged with conducting the JAD workshop. JAD facilitators must possess exceptional communication, team building, and technical skills.

JAD SCRIBE The individual charged with documenting the JAD workshop. In an AJAD session, the JAD scribe uses CASE tools to capture user requirements.

JOINT APPLICATION DEVELOPMENT A systems development technique that harnesses end user involvement in the application specification process. It can be automated by using CASE technology.

LAN Local Area Network. An interconnection of computers in a single complex through telecommunication devices.

LOGICAL DESIGN An application specification that reflects the end user's view of the system. Logical designs are absent of any hardware or environmental constraints.

LOGICAL DESIGN PHASE The steps in a project life cycle that pertain to the creation of the logical design.

MANAGEMENT INFORMATION LIFE CYCLE The steps that must be taken to develop a management information center application.

MANAGEMENT INFORMATION CENTER An organizational unit charged with providing end users with summary information needed to make decisions. It is the next evolutionary step in information centers.

MATRIX ANALYSIS An information systems planning practice that cross-references different aspects of business and technology to identify opportunities to apply automated solutions.

MESSAGE The parameters needed to invoke methods within an OOPS application.

METHOD The logic contained in a OOPS object. Methods define how an object can be manipulated by other objects.

MIC Management information center.

MIC ANALYST Management information center personnel.

MISSION CRITICAL SYSTEMS Applications that absolutely must be built in order for a firm to survive and prosper.

MODEL MERGING Integrating data models to form an enterprise model.

MODEL SUBSETTING Extracting information from an enterprise model for reuse in current systems development efforts.

OBJECT Comprehensive modules that combine data definitions and processing logic. Objects are what OOPS manipulate.

OBJECT LIBRARY A data dictionary for OOPS applications. It is where object definitions are stored.

OBJECT-ORIENTED DBMS A database management system that can store and manage a variety of data types, including multi-faceted arrays, images, and character strings.

OBJECT-ORIENTED PROGRAMMING SYSTEMS The term used for all applications built through object-oriented application development.

OFFICE AUTOMATION Systems that automate traditional office activities, like sending and receiving mail, maintaining calendars, and writing memoranda.

ONLINE PROCESSING Processing transactions as soon as they are sent to the central processing unit.

OOPS Object-oriented programming systems.

PACKAGED SOFTWARE A set of standardized computer programs and documentation commercially marketed to serve as the basis of an application. Organizations can purchase packaged software to avoid internal application development.

PDLC Project development life cycle.

PERSONNEL PLAN An ISP component that specifies the kind of technical talent required to manage and develop company automation.

PHYSICAL DESIGN An application specification that reflects the technological constraints of the target implementation environment. Physical designs specify what will ultimately be delivered to the end user.

PHYSICAL DESIGN PHASE The steps in the PDLC that must be performed to specify a physical design.

PILOT PROJECT A scaled down development effort that tests the feasibility of new tools or techniques. Pilot projects are usually done in 3 to 6 months and do not involve mission critical systems.

POLITICIAN An individual who is sensitive to the underlying culture of the organization and can use this insight to achieve personal goals and objectives. IS executives will be asked to become better politicians.

PRE-IMPLEMENTATION AUDIT An activity that examines the current application and technology environments of EDI trading partners. Pre-implementation audits are conducted to identify the tasks that must be performed to implement an EDI application.

PROACTIVIST An individual who is ready to take action in order to accomplish goals and objectives. IS executives will be asked to be proactive.

PROBLEMS DATABASE The component of a DSS application where previously defined decision parameters are stored. A problems database is consulted to review characteristics of past decisions and determine ways to meet current decision-making needs.

PROCEDURE MODEL A collection of process modules that collectively represent the logic needed to automate a business activity.

PROCESS-DRIVEN DEVELOPMENT Any systems analysis approach that focuses on defining the program requirements before discovering the data needs of the business. Many process-driven development approaches are criticized for delivering systems that are difficult to maintain.

PROCESS MODULE Psuedocode that defines the ADD, DELETE, MODIFY, and RETRIEVAL logic of an application. Process modules are converted into program logic during physical design.

PROCESS MODELING The IE discipline that defines the ADD, DELETE, MODIFY, and RETRIEVAL logic of an application.

PROCESS-TO-FUNCTION MATRIX A chart that cross-references business processes to the business functions that perform them. It shows the activities being performed across the enterprise.

PRODUCTION ENVIRONMENT The combination of computer technology and software that comprise the place where applications are used and supported.

PROJECT DEVELOPMENT LIFE CYCLE The steps that must be performed to define and build an application.

PROTOTYPE A model of a system that demonstrates the features and functionality of a target application. Prototypes are built to gain insight into systems requirements prior to expending extensive resources on systems development.

PROTOTYPER'S LIFE CYCLE The steps that must be taken to rapidly develop applications.

PROTOTYPING The practice of developing systems models that demonstrate application functionality to end users. Software is available that supports the prototyping process.

PSEUDOCODE A method for expressing program logic through English-like expressions. Pseudocode is used extensively in information engineering and CASE technology.

RAD Rapid application development.

RAD REVIEW PANEL A group of end users responsible for reviewing RAD project progress.

RAPID APPLICATION DEVELOPMENT A systems development technique that aims to define and deliver systems under extremely tight timeframes. The process involves the use of CASE, prototyping, and AJAD.

RE-ENGINEERING The process of enhancing existing relational database applications and extending their use and functionality.

RELATIONAL DBMS A type of database management system that treats data as if it were stored in two-dimensional tables. Relational database systems are easier to build and maintain than systems built in other DBMS models.

REPOSITORY A CASE component that facilitates the storage, sharing and management of enterprise models, data models, procedure models, databases, and programs.

REUSABLE CONSTRUCTS Any previously defined component of an application that can be reapplied in a new development effort. Data models, process models, and OOPS objects are examples of reusable constructs.

REVERSE ENGINEERING The process of converting existing applications into integrated database systems. Many CASE vendors are developing tools that support the reverse engineering process.

SCREEN PAINTER A prototyping tool that facilitates the rapid creation of application screens. Screen painters are used to show end users how a proposed application will look before time is invested in actual program development.

SOLUTIONS DATABASE The component of a DSS where the results of previous decisions are stored. Solutions databases are consulted to help determine the proper course of action in a current decision-making situation.

STAFF PROFESSIONAL An individual whose work on special projects helps the organization achieve its goals and mission. IS executives will be asked to play this role by their firms.

STANDARD TRANSACTION The information that is being passed between trading partners of an EDI application. Standard transactions are transformed into a format that can used by each partner's existing systems.

STRATEGIST An individual that can define a long-term course of action for an enterprise. IS executives will be asked by their firms to play this role.

STRUCTURED ANALYSIS Any rigorous method for determining systems specifications that can be applied universally within a firm.

SUBJECT MATTER EXPERT End users that know the workings of particular business activities and have the authority to make judgments about the way these activities will be performed in the future. Subject matter experts are called upon to participate in a variety of IS activities including JAD workshops and ISP planning sessions.

SYSTEMS ANALYSTS Individuals charged with specifying and building applications for end users.

SYSTEMS GLOBALIZATION The notion that applications can span nations through the use of EDI tools and techniques.

SYSTEMS MAINTENANCE The process of repairing and enhancing existing applications to better meet end user needs.

SYSTEMS REALIGNMENT LIFE CYCLE The steps that must be taken to effectively maintain existing applications.

SYSTEMS TRANSACTION The information that is being passed to an EDI trading partner's internal application after a standard transaction has been received and converted.

SYSTEMS-TO-GOALS MATRIX A chart that cross-references applications to business goals. It shows the extent to which systems are helping firms achieve their mission.

TECHNOLOGY FORECASTING The process of evaluating and selecting the computer technology needed to support the business in years to come.

TECHNOLOGY NEEDS ASSESSMENT The ISP component that specifies the computer technology needed to help the business achieve its goals and objectives.

TECHNOLOGY TRANSFER The process of keeping IS personnel abreast of emerging industry trends.

TEST ENVIRONMENT The combination of computer technology and software that comprise the place where applications are built and examined for conformance to systems specifications.

TRADE AGREEMENT The contract between EDI trading partners. Trade agreements specify EDI technology, discount arrangements, and operating procedures that apply to the firms electronic trading.

TRADING PARTNER An organization that agrees to use EDI technology to transfer information to another organization.

TRANSACTION CONVERTER An EDI software component that creates and interprets standard transactions being passed between trading partners.

UNIT TESTING A process that examines individual application components for their conformance to systems specifications.

WHEEL OF SYSTEMS The notion that multiple life cycles can be developed and used by firms to build better end user applications.

WOTS-UP ANALYSIS A business planning practice that identifies a firm's weaknesses, opportunities, threats, and strengths.

Index